A
Birder's
West
Indies

A Birder's

NUMBER THIRTY *The Corrie Herring Hooks Series*

West Indies

AN ISLAND-BY-ISLAND TOUR

BY ROLAND H. WAUER

DRAWINGS BY MIMI HOPPE WOLF

FOREWORD BY BRADFORD C. NORTHRUP

AFTERWORD BY PAUL BUTLER

UNIVERSITY OF TEXAS PRESS ⬥ Austin

Library of Congress
Cataloging-in-Publication Data
Wauer, Roland H.
    A birder's West Indies : an island-by-
island tour / Roland H. Wauer ;
drawings by Mimi Hoppe Wolf.—1st ed.
        p.   cm. — (The Corrie Herring
Hooks series ; no. 30)
    Includes bibliographical references and
index.
    ISBN 0-292-79098-8.
    ISBN 0-292-79101-1 (pbk.)
    1. Bird watching—West Indies—
Guidebooks.   2. West Indies—
Guidebooks.   I. Title.   II. Series.
QL688.A1W38   1996
598'.07234729—dc20   95-32518

DEDICATED TO

GEORGE A. SEAMAN

AND OTHER NATURALISTS

WHO HAVE FOUGHT

FOR THE PRESERVATION

OF THE WEST INDIES'

SIGNIFICANT NATURAL

RESOURCES

CONTENTS

$\mathcal{I}$t was on Martinique, at a meeting of the Caribbean Conservation Association in 1988, that I first encountered Ro Wauer and his contagious zeal for nature. But it was another island that Ro had on his mind when he hailed me across the crowded room: St. Croix.

"Save Salt River Bay!" he said, spotting The Nature Conservancy on my name tag. He was referring to a gem of a place, one of the last intact marine estuaries in the Virgin Islands. This mosaic of mangroves, coral reefs, and freshwater wetlands on St. Croix's north coast is also of world-class historical significance: the only known site of a Columbus expedition landing in what is now U.S. territory, and an archaeological key to vanished cultures.

At the time of our meeting, Salt River Bay was threatened with massive development. A proposed resort and marina would have entailed dredging the bay, blasting the coral reef, and razing the mangroves. Because the area provides habitat for more than twenty-five species of threatened and endangered plants and animals, including the highest diversity of bird life in the Virgin Islands, the prospect was particularly devastating for conservationists like Ro. He had spent an entire year studying St. Croix's bird life, and was well aware of the consequences of such development.

The St. Croix Environmental Association had already challenged the development permits in court, and Ro was rallying reinforcements wherever he could. We at The Nature Conservancy soon got more deeply involved (we had already protected a small tract of land on Salt River Bay in the 1970s), as did several other conservation organizations.

As the National Park Service liaison for the Virgin Islands for three years, Ro became intimately familiar with the islands—a familiarity that is the basis of *A Birder's West Indies*. During that time, Ro was the principal author of the "park alternatives" document that became the cornerstone of legislation establishing the Salt River Bay National Historical Park and Ecological Preserve. Signed by President Bush in 1992, the landmark legislation was a victory for the entire region.

This coalescing of various groups, both local and international, stands as a model for the successful protection of the Caribbean's exquisite natural heritage. It illustrates not only the need for partnerships, but also the utility of conservation in the islands—for St. Croix's new park carries broad implications for increasing quality tourism while protecting key natural resources.

The West Indies give new meaning to the term diversity. Their watery isolation has given rise to an exorbitant number of unique species. Up to 40 percent of the plant life in some Caribbean forests is found nowhere else on earth. And the West Indian flyway is a critical link in the migratory routes of shorebirds and songbirds.

Tropical forests and coral reefs, which dominate the West Indies, are the earth's most biologically diverse types of ecosystems. In the islands, these ecosystems are inextricably linked. In a climate of heavy tropical rainfall, forests prevent soil erosion that would damage the productive reefs. Together with seagrass beds and mangrove forests, the reefs protect the islands from the battering sea, especially during hurricanes.

This chain of emerald islands, legendary for their beauty, lends new meaning to diversity in other, even more complex ways. The region is awash in a sea of varied cultures, languages, political institutions, and economical structures. The gulf between two neighboring islands' histories, societies, and landscapes can be wide and deep. Thus it can be difficult to get a handle on the Caribbean as a region, to grasp its strengths and problems as a whole.

One unifying factor is limited space, a reality shared by islands everywhere. In the Caribbean, the problem of finite land is compounded by dense human populations. The concept of wilderness is a foreign one there. Inhabited for more than 4,500 years, the West Indies' capacity to sustain life has been pushed to the limits in many cases, and their natural resources have been used intensively. The islands have the highest proportion of deforested land in the Western Hemisphere, warning of a vicious cycle of overuse and destruction of natural resources, not to mention ensuing economic woes.

The islands of the Caribbean thus share a common need for sustainable practices and ways of life compatible with their insular environments. Population growth, spiraling rates of development, and destructive agricultural practices are insidious threats to natural and human communities alike. As the integrity of the natural resource base is threatened, so is the economic health of the region.

One bright economic spot is the tourist industry, the most important source of revenue for the Caribbean. Although many of the islands have chosen to build opulent resorts and golf courses to attract tourists, others have chosen to capitalize on their natural resources and scenic beauty to attract escalating numbers of tourists seeking nature-based holidays. Island nations such as Jamaica, the Dominican Republic, Puerto Rico, Dominica,

St. Lucia, and St. Vincent are beginning to realize that protection of their forests and reefs pays important dividends. Their long-term stability—not to mention prosperity—will undoubtedly stem from their ability to live compatibly with their natural environments.

A group like The Nature Conservancy must carefully consider how best to bring its resources to bear in the Caribbean, a region of such biological richness and faced with such basic yet contentious questions as how to sustain nature and people. Addressing the region's long-term environmental and economic health is no inconsiderable task.

The Conservancy's mission is to preserve plants, animals, and natural communities that represent the full array of life on earth by protecting the lands and waters they need to survive. Through the Caribbean Areas Program, which we established in 1989, we work closely with in-country partners to make local conservation a priority by building independent, self-sustaining conservation organizations.

The centerpiece of our strategy is the protection of areas that have been designated as protected, but are still threatened; often, they are referred to as "paper parks." First, we work to strengthen both nongovernmental and governmental conservation organizations. The rise in local conservation groups, such as the Jamaican Conservation and Development Trust and Grupo Jaragua in the Dominican Republic, reflects increased interest in conservation locally. The Conservancy wants to see these groups flourish, to give conservation steady footing in the Caribbean.

Second, we work with our partner organizations to provide basic park resources: posting the boundary at Jaragua National Park in the Dominican Republic, building a visitors center at Morne Trois Pitons National Park in Dominica, or improving a trail at Blue Mountains/John Crow National Park in Jamaica. Throughout the Caribbean, we are helping recruit and train park managers, provide basic equipment, and initiate community outreach and education efforts in protected areas.

Finally, to help bring the all-important financial resources to bear at these sites, we are establishing continuous funding mechanisms to support conservation over the long term. For example, we have developed trust funds for parks in Jamaica and the Dominican Republic using innovative debt-for-nature swaps. These trust funds become dedicated sources of funds for protected areas and vehicles for other revenues, such as user or concession fees charged to those of us fortunate enough to walk or swim in these tropical parks.

I cannot emphasize enough the clear connection between economic development and conservation in the Caribbean, a connection that is perhaps stronger here than in any other region I know. Economies based on tourism need to protect their natural assets. Tourists are becoming more and more sophisticated in their search for pristine and biologically diverse places—many of which are found in the parks of the Caribbean. With this insightful guide in hand, I urge you to seek out these magnificent places and support their protection.

Parks and reserves will become institutions as valued as schools, libraries, and hospitals only when governments of the Caribbean are convinced of the economic benefit of conservation. Meanwhile, there is a growing cadre of dedicated Caribbean conservationists, many of whom I have the privilege to work with, who already know that there is a much deeper reason to save their natural heritage. This is our ethical imperative for future generations. This is the force that moves people like Ro Wauer and will eventually move the politicians of the region. This is the case made so forcefully and clearly by Edward O. Wilson, Harvard biologist and Pulitzer Prize winner, when he says, "We should judge every scrap of biodiversity as priceless while we learn to use it and come to understand what it means to humanity."

Bradford C. Northrup
Vice President and Director
of Caribbean Region
The Nature Conservancy

ACKNOWLEDGMENTS

*D*ozens of friends and associates provided companionship and assistance prior to and during my many visits to the islands. A few additional individuals reviewed chapters or helped in numerous other ways. Without them such a book would have been impossible; I thank them one and all. Any errors that might still exist are my fault.

I want to acknowledge the following individuals, alphabetically, for their kind assistance: Paul Butler for help in finding Dominica's endemic parrots and advice about other Lesser Antilles; Virgin Islands Representative to Congress Ron DeLugo for his many efforts that led to the establishment of St. Croix's Salt River Bay National Historical Park and Ecological Preserve, and also for assistance in obtaining permission to visit Cuba; Audrey Downer for her help on-island and reviewing the Jamaica chapter; Craig Faanes for numerous reports on his adventures in the West Indies; Tighe Geoghegan for assistance in obtaining pertinent references; Ann Haynes-Sutton for advice about travel and birds on Jamaica; Beth Hillis for her kind assistance during my 1990 visit to St. Croix; Houston Holder for being an enjoyable traveling companion at Dominican Republic; Jay and Sandy Isherwood for their assistance with trips to Dominica; Arturo Kirkconell for much help on Cuba and reviewing that chapter; Walter Knausenberger for his kindness and general assistance during my three-year residence on St. Croix and providing pertinent reference materials; Doug McCrea for being an excellent tour leader on Cuba; Chino Martínez for his attentiveness to Cuba's Zapata Swamp and locating the Zapata Wren for our group of birders; Bruce Moorhead for the long-term loan of David Lack's book, *Island Biology*, and for being an enjoyable traveling companion on Puerto Rico; Brad Northrup for writing the foreword to this book and his concern about St. Croix's Salt River Bay; Rob Norton for his friendship, insight into Caribbean bird life, putting me up at his home on St. John, and being a good birding companion on Martinique; Allan Putney for assistance with obtaining pertinent references and his concern about the natural resources of the eastern Caribbean; Earl Roebuck for his friendship and being an enjoyable birding companion on St. Croix; Bill Robertson for his friendship and assistance in obtaining pertinent references; Anton Teytaud for his companionship on Dominica; George Seaman for his friendship, unique perspective on the Virgin Islands, reviewing the chapter on Saba, and continual support for this and other projects; Fred Sladen for his friendship, much assistance on St. Croix, being a great traveling companion on trips to St. Lucia, St. Vincent, Grenada, and Jamaica, and review of the St. Croix chapter; Robert Sutton for his advice about Jamaica's Cockpit Country; Jessie Thomson for her attention to St. Croix's Salt River Bay National Historical Park and Ecological Preserve; Tito Vilella for his assistance in finding the Puerto Rican Nightjar and review of the Puerto Rico chapter; Mike Walsh for his friendship and companionship on Dominica; Liz Wilson for her friendship and constant attention to St. Croix's Salt River Bay; and Ed and Nina York for their kind assistance during my 1990 visit to St. Croix.

Last and certainly not least, I thank Betty Wauer, my wife, for her longtime support, her companionship on several island trips, being my first-line editor, and putting up with the times that I was away from home exploring many wonderful, out-of-the-way places in the West Indies.

R.W.

A
Birder's
West
Indies

INTRODUCTION

*W*est Indies! Those two words usually conjure up an image of an idyllic Caribbean setting: sun, sand, and sea; calypso music; colorful bird life; gorgeous sunsets. The West Indies are all that, and much more. For the birder, someone with love and enthusiasm for the outdoors and the desire to find birds in their native habitats, the West Indies provide a wealth of unique opportunities practically at our doorstep.

Until recently, travelers to the Caribbean were limited to tours that featured a variety of stops at exotic ports but few opportunities to truly see the countryside. Emphasis was placed on shopping and sunbathing, with little time left for exploring the natural world of the islands. But today, several nature tours are available that introduce the participant to the real West Indies or look at one or several choice islands in greater depth. In addition, many travelers are discovering that they can visit the various islands on their own, with their own itineraries, and with little more concern than is necessary when traveling in North America.

Although there already exists a wide range of literature about West Indian travel, accommodations, and restaurants, little information is available for the nature lover. This book intends to partially fill that vacuum.

THE SETTING

The West Indies form a sweeping, 2,500-mile-long arc of islands that run east and south from Cuba to Grenada (Map 1). Cuba lies only 90 miles south of Key West, Florida, and 125 miles due east of Mexico's Yucatan Peninsula, while Grenada is located 85 miles off the eastern tip of Venezuela. The majority of the islands abut the Caribbean Sea on the south and west and the Atlantic Ocean on the north and east. They include a total land area of about 90,000 square miles. The islands range in size from Cuba, the largest of the West Indies, with a land surface of 42,827 square miles, to tiny Saba, with only 5 square miles. Elevations vary from the low coral islands, barely above sea level, to mountainous Hispaniola, which rises to 10,417 feet at the summit of Dominican Republic's Pico Duarte.

Geologists believe that none of the West Indies were ever connected to the mainland of North or South America. They are true "oceanic" islands,

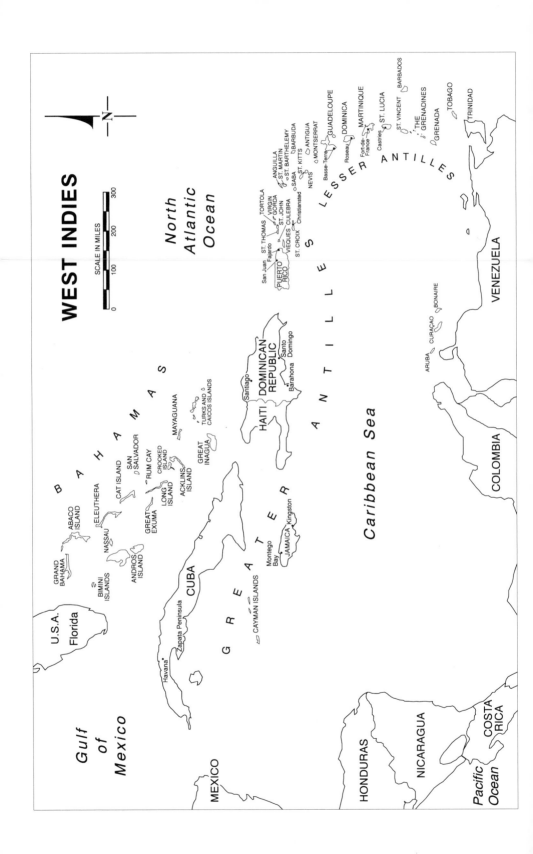

having risen from beneath the ocean's surface. A few of the islands, however, may have been interconnected during the Ice Age, when the oceans were somewhat lower, since much of their water was frozen on continental ice sheets. Relatively shallow banks occur between Jamaica and Hispaniola, Puerto Rico and the northern Virgin Islands, and St. Vincent and Grenada. Most of the West Indies, however, are surrounded by extreme ocean depths. The Puerto Rico Trench, lying north of Dominican Republic, Puerto Rico, the northern Virgin Islands, and Anguilla, is the greatest depth in the entire Atlantic, 28,374 feet.

The origin of the Caribbean Basin is fairly recent, geologically speaking, and is still evolving via emerging volcanic and coral reef islands. The volcanic islands owe their origin to plate tectonics. The Lesser Antilles mark the edge of the great Atlantic plate that is slowly being driven westerly under the Caribbean plate. The great heat from the friction of the moving plates, 30 to 100 miles below the surface, creates overheated magma that eventually escapes at weaker places in the earth's crust as volcanic activity. The most notable volcanic peaks of the Lesser Antilles include (north to south) Saba, Guadeloupe's La Soufrière, Morne Trois Pitons on Dominica, Pelée on Martinique, and the other Soufrière on St. Vincent.

The topography of the Greater Antilles owes its origin to the same tectonic activities that were responsible for the mountains and valleys of eastern North America. Taking into account the great depths of the underwater trenches, the overall relief of the West Indies is most impressive. For example, the topographic relief between the Puerto Rico Trench and the summit of Dominican Republic's Pico Duarte is 38,791 feet.

Coral islands form along shallow banks that may be only a few feet in depth and are washed by the warm Gulf Stream waters throughout the year. Water surface temperatures vary only from about 82 degrees Fahrenheit in summer to 77 degrees Fahrenheit in winter. Although many of the West Indies are fringed with "barrier" reefs, coral islands usually originate from "bank" reefs that form on shallow banks just below the surface. The bank reefs gradually build a platform and eventually rise above the surface. Barrier reefs then begin to fringe the island.

The majority of the West Indies possess sandy beaches of varying lengths and colors. White-sand beaches, famous throughout the Caribbean, generally are derived from broken-down coral, while beaches with black sand reflect the island's volcanic past.

The West Indies are normally divided into the Greater and Lesser Antilles; the Lesser Antilles can be further divided into the northern Leeward Islands and the southern Windward Islands. The several Caribbean islands along South America—Trinidad and Tobago, Aruba, Curaçao, and Bonaire—are part of that continent and are not members of the West Indies.

There is some confusion about where to separate the Greater from the Lesser Antilles. All the large islands in the west—Cuba, Jamaica, Hispaniola, and Puerto Rico—are readily recognized as the Greater Antilles. But the Virgin Islands have been listed as both Greater and Lesser Antilles, depending, it seems, upon political whims. Geologically, the division must lie between the Virgin Islands and the Leeward Islands. The northern Virgins are part of the Puerto Rico Bank and so are most appropriately part of the Greater Antilles. The southern Virgin Island of St. Croix, however, could fit in either. All of the easternmost islands, from Anguilla to Grenada, lie along a shallow north-south plateau. The word "Antilles" was derived from the legendary island of Antilia that, until 1492, was thought to lie somewhere between Europe and Asia.

FLORA AND FAUNA

The ecological principle of "the larger the island and the nearer the continent, the greater the diversity of flora and fauna" generally holds true for the West Indies. Since all of the islands arose from the sea, all life forms originally arrived by air or water, carried either by the wind, on rafts of plant debris, or by people from the continents who brought plants and animals with them. Birds and bats flew to the islands from the mainland. This explains the presence of several large mammals and also, perhaps, the large green or tree iguana. But, in general, oceanic islands never support the number of plants and animals that occur in a similar space at similar latitudes on the continents.

James Bond included about 400 bird species in the 1985 edition of his classic book, *The Birds of the West Indies*. More than one-quarter of those 400 species were Neotropical migrants that occurred only as transients or winter residents, nesting only in North America. Of the remaining 300 species that nest on the West Indies, 138 possess widespread distribution, and 161 species are West Indian endemics (Table 1). These are highlighted in boldface type when they are discussed in the text. Of those 161 endemics, 95 are single-island endemics, 32 are multi-island (two or three islands only) endemics, and 34 species are more widespread within the greater Caribbean Basin (a few may extend peripherally to south Florida or the Yucatan or may winter south of their breeding range). An earlier list was published in a double-issue article I wrote on this subject for the February and August 1990 issues of *Birding*, a magazine of the American Birding Association.

The high degree of endemism in the West Indies is typical for islands. Simplified ecosystems, such as those that exist on islands, stimulate evolution that results in higher percentages of endemic organisms. However, endemics rarely possess large populations and therefore are more susceptible to extirpation. Miklos Udvardy wrote in his book, *Dynamic Zoogeography*, that "the larger the fauna of an island, the more species that belong to

Table 1. West Indian Endemic Birds

Species	JA	CA	CU	HS	PR	VI	AA	SA	MT	GU	DO	MQ	SL	SV	GR
1. West Indian Whistling-Duck	X	X	X	X	X		X								
2. Gundlach's Hawk			o												
3. Ridgway's Hawk				o											
4. Zapata Rail			o												
5. Caribbean Coot	X	X	X	X	X	X	X	X	X	X	X	X	X	X	X
6. Scaly-naped Pigeon	X		X	X	X	X	X	X	X	X	X	X	X	X	X
7. White-crowned Pigeon	X	X	X	X	X	X	X	X	X	X	X	X	X		
8. Plain Pigeon	X		X	X	X										
9. Ring-tailed Pigeon	o														
10. Zenaida Dove	X	X	X	X	X	X	X	X	X	X	X	X	X	X	X
11. Grenada Dove [1]															o
12. Caribbean Dove	M	M													
13. Key West Quail-Dove			X	X	X										
14. Bridled Quail-Dove					X	X	X	X	X	X	X	X	X		
15. Gray-headed Quail-Dove			M	M											
16. Crested Quail-Dove	o														
17. Blue-headed Quail-Dove			o												
18. Hispaniolan Parakeet				o											
19. Cuban Parakeet			o												
20. Cuban Parrot		M	M												
21. Yellow-billed Parrot	o														
22. Hispaniolan Parrot				o											
23. Puerto Rican Parrot					o										
24. Black-billed Parrot	o														
25. Red-necked Parrot											o				
26. St. Lucia Parrot													o		
27. St. Vincent Parrot														o	
28. Imperial Parrot											o				
29. Great Lizard-Cuckoo			M												
30. Puerto Rican Lizard-Cuckoo					o										
31. Hispaniolan Lizard-Cuckoo				o											
32. Jamaican Lizard-Cuckoo	o														
33. Chestnut-bellied Cuckoo	o														
34. Bay-breasted Cuckoo				o											

Table 1. (continued)

Species	JA	CA	CU	HS	PR	VI	AA	SA	MT	GU	DO	MQ	SL	SV	GR
35. Ashy-faced Owl				o											
36. Puerto Rican Screech-Owl					M	M									
37. Bare-legged Owl			o												
38. Cuban Pygmy-Owl			o												
39. Jamaican Owl	o														
40. Antillean Nighthawk	x	x	x	x	x	x									
41. Least Poorwill			o												
42. St. Lucia Nightjar													o		
43. Greater Antillean Nightjar			M	M											
44. Puerto Rican Nightjar					o										
45. Lesser Antillean Swift										x	x	x	x	x	
46. Antillean Palm Swift	M		M	M											
47. Jamaican Mango	o														
48. Antillean Mango				M	M										
49. Green Mango					o										
50. Purple-throated Carib							x	x	x	x	x	x	x	x	x
51. Green-throated Carib					x	x	x	x	x	x	x	x	x	x	x
52. Antillean Crested Hummingbird					x	x	x	x	x	x	x	x	x	x	x
53. Cuban Emerald			M												
54. Hispaniolan Emerald				o											
55. Puerto Rican Emerald					o										
56. Blue-headed Hummingbird											M	M			
57. Streamertail	o														
58. Vervain Hummingbird	M			M											
59. Bee Hummingbird			o												
60. Cuban Trogon			o												
61. Hispaniolan Trogon				o											
62. Cuban Tody			o												
63. Broad-billed Tody				o											
64. Narrow-billed Tody				o											
65. Jamaican Tody	o														

Table 1. (continued)

Species	JA	CA	CU	HS	PR	VI	AA	SA	MT	GU	DO	MQ	SL	SV	GR
66. Puerto Rican Tody					o										
67. Antillean Piculet			o												
68. Guadeloupe Woodpecker										o					
69. Puerto Rican Woodpecker					o										
70. Hispaniolan Woodpecker				o											
71. Jamaican Woodpecker	o														
72. West Indian Woodpecker		M	M												
73. Cuban Green Woodpecker			o												
74. Fernandina's Flicker			o												
75. Jamaican Elaenia	o														
76. Caribbean Elaenia		X			X	X	X	X	X	X	X	X	X	X	X
77. Greater Antillean Elaenia	M			M											
78. Greater Antillean Pewee	X		X	X											
79. Lesser Antillean Pewee					X					X	X	X	X		
80. Sad Flycatcher	o														
81. Grenada Flycatcher														M	M
82. Rufous-tailed Flycatcher	o														
83. La Sagra's Flycatcher		M	M												
84. Stolid Flycatcher	M			M											
85. Puerto Rican Flycatcher					M	M									
86. Lesser Antillean Flycatcher							X	X		X	X	X	X		
87. Gray Kingbird	X	X	X	X	X	X	X	X	X	X	X	X	X	X	X
88. Loggerhead Kingbird	X	X	X	X	X										
89. Giant Kingbird			o												
90. Jamaican Becard	o														
91. Cuban Martin			o												
92. Caribbean Martin	X				X	X	X	X	X	X	X	X	X	X	X
93. Golden Swallow	M			M											

Table 1. (continued)

Species	JA	CA	CU	HS	PR	VI	AA	SA	MT	GU	DO	MQ	SL	SV	GR
94. Palm Crow			M	M											
95. Cuban Crow			M												
96. White-necked Crow				o											
97. Jamaican Crow	o														
98. Zapata Wren			o												
99. Cuban Gnatcatcher			o												
100. Cuban Solitaire			o												
101. Rufous-throated Solitaire	X			X							X	X	X	X	
102. White-eyed Thrush	o														
103. La Selle Thrush				o											
104. White-chinned Thrush	o														
105. Red-legged Thrush		X	X	X	X						X				
106. Forest Thrush									X	X	X		X		
107. Bahama Mockingbird²	M		M												
108. White-breasted Thrasher												M	M		
109. Scaly-breasted Thrasher							X	X	X	X	X	X	X	X	X
110. Pearly-eyed Thrasher				X	X	X	X	X	X	X	X	X	X	X	
111. Brown Trembler								X	X	X	X			X	
112. Gray Trembler												M	M		
113. Palmchat				o											
114. Black-whiskered Vireo	X	X	X	X	X	X	X	X	X	X	X	X	X	X	X
115. Thick-billed Vireo		M		M											
116. Jamaican Vireo	o														
117. Cuban Vireo			o												
118. Puerto Rican Vireo					o										
119. Flat-billed Vireo				o											
120. Blue Mountain Vireo	o														
121. Black-whiskered Vireo	X	X	X	X	X	X	X	X	X	X	X	X	X	X	X
122. Adelaide's Warbler					M		M						M		
123. Olive-capped Warbler			M												

Table 1. (continued)

Species	JA	CA	CU	HS	PR	VI	AA	SA	MT	GU	DO	MQ	SL	SV	GR
124. Vitelline Warbler		o													
125. Plumbeous Warbler										M	M				
126. Arrow-headed Warbler	o														
127. Elfin Woods Warbler					o										
128. Whistling Warbler														o	
129. Green-tailed Ground Warbler				o											
130. Yellow-headed Warbler			o												
131. Oriente Warbler			o												
132. Semper's Warbler													o		
133. White-winged Warbler				o											
134. Lesser Antillean Tanager														M	M
135. Jamaican Euphonia	o														
136. Antillean Euphonia				X	X		X	X	X	X	X	X	X	X	
137. Stripe-headed Tanager	X	X	X	X	X										
138. Black-crowned Palm-Tanager				o											
139. Gray-crowned Palm-tanager				o											
140. Chat Tanager				o											
141. Puerto Rican Tanager					o										
142. Cuban Bullfinch		M	M												
143. Cuban Grassquit			M												
144. Black-faced Grassquit	X			X	X	X	X	X	X	X	X	X	X	X	X
145. Yellow-shouldered Grassquit	o														
146. Puerto Rican Bullfinch					o										
147. Greater Antillean Bullfinch	M			M											
148. Lesser Antillean Bullfinch						X	X	X	X	X	X	X	X	X	X
149. Orangequit	o														
150. St. Lucia Black Finch												o			

Table 1. (continued)

Species	JA	CA	CU	HS	PR	VI	AA	SA	MT	GU	DO	MQ	SL	SV	GR
151. Zapata Sparrow			o												
152. Tawny-shouldered Blackbird			M	M											
153. Yellow-shouldered Blackbird					o										
154. Jamaican Blackbird	o														
155. Cuban Blackbird			o												
156. Greater Antillean Grackle	X	X	X	X	X										
157. St. Lucia Oriole													o		
158. Montserrat Oriole									o						
159. Martinique Oriole												o			
160. Jamaican Oriole	o														
161. Antillean Siskin				o											
Totals	51	20	52	56	40	18	21	20	21	25	29	26	31	23	19
Single-island Endemics	26	1	21	22	12	0	0	0	1	1	2	1	5	2	1

JA = Jamaica; CA = Caymans; CU = Cuba; HS = Hispaniola; PR = Puerto Rico; VI = Virgin Islands; AA = Anguila & Antigua/Barbuda; SA = Saba, St. Eustatius, St. Christopher & Nevis; MT = Montserrat; GU = Guadeloupe; DO = Dominica; MQ = Martinique; SL = St. Lucia; SV = St. Vincent & Grenadines; GR = Grenada.

o = single-island endemic; M = multi-island endemic (two to three islands only); x = widespread West Indies endemic.

1 = Gray-fronted Dove by AOU; 2 = also occurs in Bahamas.

the rare category and the larger the rate of extinction among them." Island populations, in comparison with larger mainland populations, are extremely susceptible to catastrophes such as hurricanes, habitat destruction, and overhunting that can wipe out entire species. N. J. Collar and P. Andrew, in the ICBP (International Council for Bird Protection) 1988 book, *Birds to Watch*, pointed out that 46 percent of all birds at risk of extinction are island species. Ninety-three percent of all bird species and subspecies that are known to have become extinct since 1600 are island species.

Further, an assessment of West Indian bird life reveals that it includes two endemic families (Todidae includes five Todies and Dulidae includes the Palmchat) and a host of additional endemic genera: *Cyanolimnas*, Zapata Rail; *Starnoenas*, Blue-headed Quail-Dove; *Hyetornis*, Bay-breasted and Chestnut-bellied Cuckoos; *Saurothera*, Great, Jamaican, Hispaniolan, and Puerto Rican Lizard-Cuckoos; *Pseudoscops*, Jamaican Owl; *Eulampis*, Purple-throated and Green-throated Caribs; *Orthorhynchus*, Antillean Crested Hummingbird; *Cyanophaia*, Blue-headed Hummingbird; *Trochilus*, Streamertail; *Mellisuga*, Bee and Vervain Hummingbirds; *Priotelus*, Cuban and Hispaniolan Trogons; *Nesoctites*, Antillean Piculet; *Xiphidiopicus*, Cuban Green Woodpecker; *Ferminia*, Zapata Wren; *Cinclocerthia*, Brown and Gray Tremblers; *Ramphocinclus*, White-breasted Thrasher; *Margarops*, Scaly-breasted and Pearly-eyed Thrashers; *Cichlherminia*, Forest Thrush; *Catharopeza*, Whistling Warbler; *Microligea*, Green-tailed Ground Warbler; *Terestistris*, Yellow-headed and Oriente Warblers; *Leucopeza*, Semper's Warbler; *Xenoligea*, White-winged Warbler; *Torreornis*, Zapata Sparrow; *Nesospingus*, Puerto Rican Tanager; *Phaenicophilus*, Gray-crowned and Black-crowned Palm-Tanagers; *Calyptophilus*, Chat Tanager; *Euneornis*, Orangequit; *Melanospiza*, St. Lucia Black Finch; *Loxipasser*, Yellow-shouldered Grassquit; *Loxigilla*, Puerto Rican, Greater Antillean, and Lesser Antillean Bullfinches; and *Nesopsar*, Jamaican Blackbird.

It is obvious that the West Indies contain much to whet the birder's appetite. The islands possess an exciting world very different from the one that exists on the continents.

WHEN TO GO

Although any time of year is good in the Caribbean, the principal tourist season runs from December through April. That is the winter dry season in the West Indies, the time of year when North Americans most appreciate warmer climates. Hurricanes can be extremely disruptive in late summer, the summer rainy season runs from May to November, and midsummer can be hot and humid. Year-round temperature extremes range from 70 to 90 degrees Fahrenheit in the lowlands and 60 to 85 degrees Fahrenheit in the mountains.

For the naturalist, March through May produces the greatest array of flowering plants, although many species bloom and produce fruit year-round. Birds are most active in the spring.

ENTRY

Getting to the West Indies is not quite as easy as simply driving across the border into Mexico or Canada. Most travel agents can provide travelers with a range of airline and cruise options, and if arrangements are made far enough in advance they usually include excellent cost-saving fares. BWIA and Liat Airlines offer special fares for twenty- and thirty-day unlimited travel from a West Indian entry point such as Puerto Rico or Jamaica. Also, occasional intra-island travel by boat is possible, such as between St. Thomas and Tortola, but longer trips rarely are worth the extra time required.

Always obtain advance room reservations, especially for your first night on each island. Arriving at an unfamiliar destination after dark without knowing where you are bound can be not only confusing but an awful introduction to a new island. Remember that few airlines arrive on schedule. In the Caribbean, expect delays and you will have a more relaxing trip.

Getting through customs is rarely a hassle, although each island has its own unique system, and you must follow directions. Waiting for baggage seems to take the greatest amount of time. Proof of citizenship is an absolute necessity. The best proof is a passport, but a copy (preferable) of your birth certificate or voter's registration card will also suffice.

If you are not on a tour and plan to travel on your own, you will need to rent a vehicle. Be sure to reserve a vehicle well in advance. If you arrive late and the rental office is closed, go on to your hotel and either return the next morning or ask the people at the hotel to obtain a vehicle for you. Also, the free road maps available at the rental car agencies are seldom adequate for negotiating more than the principal highways. If you plan on driving any of the out-of-the-way routes you should purchase a map at home prior to your trip or spend time the first day finding a map store; some hotel gift shops carry adequate maps, but most do not.

Pre-entry inoculations are not required. Take insect repellent with you. Although insects are rarely a bother, mosquitoes and no-see-ums, locally called "mompies," can be a nuisance; ticks and chiggers are uncommon. Be on the watch for bees and wasps in the brush; tiny "Jack-Spaniards" and larger wasps can pack a wallop. Also take sun-block. Visitors from North America tend to suffer more from sunburn and dehydration than from insects and diseases. The Caribbean weather is usually warm and humid, and visitors can easily forget to drink enough water. Take a canteen or bottle of water with you every time you go outdoors.

What to wear? Because of the usually pleasant temperatures, lightweight clothing is essential. The mountains, however, can be much cooler. A cap or wide-brim hat is also essential, and so is light rainwear or an umbrella for sudden showers. Although daytime dress runs from bathing suits and shorts at the beach areas to more modest attire in the towns and shopping areas, long pants and shirts for men and skirts and blouses or dresses for women are expected for dining or entertainment in the evening.

Although most of the Lesser Antilles share a common currency, called "EC" for Eastern Caribbean dollar, most of the Greater Antillean countries have their own money; Puerto Rico and the U.S. Virgin Islands use U.S. dollars. Although the U.S. dollar is generally in demand, don't depend upon being able to use it away from the cities. Country businesses usually require common currency. Jamaica, for example, accepts only Jamaican currency. Credit cards are accepted throughout the islands, although some businesses take only currency.

I usually obtain the appropriate currency from the money changers at the Miami, Atlanta, or New York airports prior to flight time so that I am prepared when I arrive. Although money exchange is possible at most of the island terminals, they often close early or at odd times of the day, so it is easy to miss those opportunities. Many island banks also provide an exchange service, but they too may be closed or out-of-the-way. Exchange rates vary from year to year and even from one day to the next.

Travel costs of accommodations, food, rental vehicles, and fuel are comparable with those in the United States, but they are considerably higher than those in Mexico.

ROAD CONDITIONS AND FUEL

Road conditions vary from island to island and season to season. On most of the islands an automobile will suffice, but a jeep is recommended for St. Lucia.

Gas stations are available in most towns, and only rarely will you be driving any great distance. Exceptions are Jamaica, Cuba, Dominican Republic, and Puerto Rico. In those countries take extra care to fill your gas tank before you take off on an extended trip.

THE LANGUAGE

Four principal languages are spoken in the West Indies, although you will hear numerous dialects as well. English is the principal language on Jamaica, Cayman Islands, Virgin Islands, Anguilla, Barbuda, Antigua, St. Barts, Nevis, Saba, Montserrat, Dominica, St. Lucia, St. Vincent and the Grenadines, and Grenada. Spanish is the principal language on Cuba, Dominican Republic, and Puerto Rico. French is the principal language on Haiti, French St. Martin, Guadeloupe, and Martinique. Dutch is the principal language on Dutch St. Martin. But in spite of speaking only English with a smattering of Spanish, I have never had a problem obtaining accommodations, food, rental cars, fuel, and other necessities.

FOOD AND DRINK

Most people who travel in Third World countries have learned to be extra careful about what they eat and drink. In the West Indies there is little to worry about in the cities and towns. All have safe drinking water, and food served in restaurants can usually pass the same test for cleanliness that exists in the States. Away from the principal towns, however, you should be more careful about drinking water. Whenever you are going into the country, be sure to carry your own supply. Although most of the small towns and villages possess safe drinking water, a few do not. It also is wise to carry some snacks such as granola bars and nuts for the times when a lunch place is not available.

Food and drinks often are made from crops that are grown or raised locally. Favorite dishes are made from fish, shrimp, chicken, goat, beef, and pork. Beans and rice are important staples. Common vegetables include plantain (cooking bananas), cassava, pumpkin, taro, breadfruit, okra, and cabbage. Common fruits include banana, pineapple, coconut, mango (in season), and citrus. Spices are often unique and require some adjustment; caper, coriander, curry, ginger, nutmeg, and pepper are most popular.

Drinks include orange and grapefruit juices, coffee and tea, imported mineral waters, soft drinks, imported and local beers, and various liquors. Drinking coffee on the Spanish islands can be a shock to your system unless you add milk or cream to dilute the coffee syrup. Tea is common on all the British islands. Many islands produce their own brand of soft drinks, some of which are quite good, and Coca-Cola is available everywhere. Many islands also produce rum, a sugarcane product. Some of the brands, such as Puerto Rico's Bacardi, St. Croix's Cruzan, Martinique's J. Bally, and Cuba's Bucanero, are imported around the world. Rum drinks are favored within the islands because that liquor is often cheaper than soft drinks. During the years I lived on St. Croix (1986–1989), I could purchase a bottle of Cruzan rum for only $2.50. A shot of rum in the juice of a squeezed fresh lime (grown everywhere), a shot of liquid sweetener, and water produced a wonderfully refreshing and inexpensive drink.

Food quality varies from island to island. I have eaten some of the finest meals imaginable in the islands. Some of the best ones have been on the

French islands, at French restaurants on British islands, or at the abundant seafood restaurants.

Whatever your taste in food, drink, entertainment, and scenery, you will find much to enjoy in the West Indies. A wonderful new world awaits naturalists wanting to see the islands' unique flora and fauna. To the birder wanting to find new and unique species, the West Indies offer a special treat.

PERSONAL CONCERNS

Any time we visit a place that is different from one with which we are familiar, we feel apprehensive. But a visit to any of the West Indies is usually as safe as visiting unfamiliar places in North America. International travel does possess hazards, but the vast majority of them can be alleviated by using old-fashioned horse sense about what you do. Most concerns are no different from the ones you would consider when you travel in the States. For instance, it would be foolish to wander alone around the cities of Kingston, San Juan, or Santo Domingo after dark, just as it would be foolish to walk alone after dark in downtown Toronto, New York, Dallas, or San Francisco.

It also would be foolish to leave personal effects unguarded on a beach or park bench. For that matter, leaving money and expensive equipment in a hotel room is just as foolish. Every island possesses individuals who will take advantage of your carelessness; petty thieves and robbers are as much a reality in the West Indies as they are in the States. However, the vast majority of people you will meet in the West Indies are as honest and dependable as most people elsewhere. Nevertheless, get in the habit of always carrying your money, passport, camera, and other choice items with you at all times, either in a fanny pack or backpack.

JAMAICA: *The Blue Mountains at mid-elevation*

PHOTOGRAPHS BY ROLAND H. WAUER

CUBA: *Sunset at Los Canales*

DOMINICAN REPUBLIC: *Greater Flamingos at Lago Enriquillo*

opposite

PUERTO RICO: *Elfin woodland in El Yunque, the Caribbean National Forest*

above

BRITISH VIRGIN ISLANDS: *The Baths at Virgin Gorda*

ST. JOHN: *Cruz Bay*

ST. CROIX: *above, Christopher Columbus landing site; below, hibiscus*

SABA: *The town of Windwardside from the Mount Scenery trail*

ANGUILLA:

above, Rendezvous Bay with St. Martin in the background; below, porcupine fish

above

ANTIGUA: *Nelson's Dockyard*

opposite

MONTSERRAT: *Great Alps Falls*

opposite

GUADELOUPE: *Deep fumarole near the summit of La Soufrière*

above

DOMINICA: *Imperial Red-necked Parrot habitat, Picard River gorge*

MARTINIQUE: *Ferret Point, La Caravelle Peninsula*

ST. LUCIA: *above, Grande Anse Beach; below, pitons*

GRENADA: *Grenada Dove habitat*

Jamaica THE MOST ENDEMICS

Crested Quail-Dove

The deep-throated "whoo-woo" call of a **Crested Quail-Dove** was very close now, just ahead of us, around the bend. Probably along the roadside still in deep shadows. Dawn had not yet reached that canopied roadway. We moved ever so slowly so that we would not frighten this elusive bird. We already had missed this endemic species on at least four earlier occasions during our six days in Jamaica. Each time it had managed to elude us, to slip back into the shadows of the forest.

We literally crept around the bend, ever so slowly, almost without breathing. Inch by inch we moved along the shadows, searching the roadside ahead. Suddenly, there it was! Right where I had expected it to be, at the right side of the roadbed in the deep shadows. It was next to impossible to see it well with only enough light to be sure of its general size and shape and its somewhat flattened topnotch.

"There it is!" we whispered to one another, as if on cue. Fred and I froze to the spot, trying to make ourselves smaller and less obtrusive. The bird had seen us, too, we were certain, because it too seemed to freeze in place. But then it moved out of the shadows into the center of the roadbed. It was in better light there, and we watched it bob down the road like a strange pull-toy. It actually tipped its body, head to tail, up and down, with each step. One end was up when the other was down.

My first impression was that it wasn't as colorful as I had expected. It was mostly two-toned, silver-gray in front and greenish-black on the back. But on more careful inspection in better light I found it to be a truly beautiful creature. Once it came out of the deep shadows I could better see its short but obvious crest. Its cheeks were a reddish-buff color, and rufous color was evident on its primaries. Its legs were red. It possessed a collar of gold, while the majority of its back was an iridescent purple. It was a gorgeous bird!

It continued down the roadway to where a second bird joined it for a second or two before flying into the adjacent vegetation. The first bird continued on for several more minutes, bobbing along like nothing I had ever seen before, and then it too disappeared into the forest.

It wasn't until then that Fred and I looked at one another. We shook hands to congratulate each other on another successful "lifer." But this one was extra special. It had come on our last try, only hours before we were to leave Jamaica for home. It was our 103rd Jamaican bird of the trip and a perfect ending to our six-day visit to that incredible country.

We had found all but one of Jamaica's twenty-five endemic bird species. Our one miss was the **Jamaican Owl,** and this was in spite of searching an area near Mandeville where it was known to have nested a few weeks earlier. But all in all our Jamaican trip had been extremely successful. We had explored the Blue Mountains and Cockpit Country, Jamaica's two best birding regions. We had driven for miles along the coastlines, and we had visited several significant wetlands. When we left Jamaica, it was with true appreciation of its magnificent natural resources and with the realization that, of all the West Indies, Jamaica is the easiest of all for finding unique birds.

THE BLUE MOUNTAINS

A visit to Jamaica's Blue Mountains is an absolute necessity for anyone who appreciates the combination of beautiful mountain scenery and

Caribbean bird life. From the highlands, Kingston Harbor glimmers like a hazy sapphire. The sprawling capital city of Kingston seems unreal from a Blue Mountains perspective. To the north and west, the abundant mountain ridges seem to gradually dissipate into the depths of the blue Caribbean. The pervasive haze gives the scene a surrealistic character. I couldn't help but think how reminiscent the northern slopes of Jamaica's Blue Mountains are of the Great Smoky Mountains of Tennessee and North Carolina.

The Blue Mountains run east to west for about 25 miles and dominate the entire eastern third of the island. The highest point is Blue Mountain Peak at 7,402 feet above sea level, also the highest point on the island. The cross-mountain road passes through Hardwar Gap, a natural pass at 4,000 feet elevation. It was named for Captain Hardwar, who directed the construction of the road that crosses the mountains between Kingston on the south coast and Buff Bay on the north coast. Overnight camping and picnicking sites are available at Hollywell National Recreation Park just above the pass. Several trails emanate from Hollywell, although the more popular Blue Mountain trailheads are at Newcastle and Mavis Banks. The Jamaican Office of Tourism has published a useful little book, *A Hiker's Guide to the Blue Mountains*, written by Bill Wilcox, a Peace Corps volunteer.

Newcastle, at about 3,500 feet elevation and only 2 miles below Hardwar Gap, is a picturesque little village and army camp of red-roofed buildings perched high on an open ridge. Newcastle has a fascinating history. It was founded in 1841 by the British government as an alternate training site for troops. Lowland training sites were overrun with yellow fever, a disease believed at the time to be caused by "buttercups" growing nearby. Newcastle provided a site which not only lacked buttercups but also provided cooler mountain temperatures.

The cross-mountain road passes right through the Newcastle parade grounds, where the regimental Badge of the North Staffordshire Regiment, imbedded there in 1886, still exists. After Jamaica was granted independence in 1962 (it remains a member of the British Commonwealth of Nations), Newcastle continued to serve as a training post for the Jamaica Defence Force.

The best examples of Jamaica's mountain vegetation begin about halfway up the mountain from Kingston, above mile marker 16. Below are only remnants of the forest that once existed there. The open landscape seems European in nature due to the neat fencerows and rock walls around the various properties. Native vegetation still exists along the streambeds, where it often forms a lush canopy. But the more extensive montane forest, sometimes improperly called "rain forest" by the locals, doesn't begin until near Newcastle. David Lack, who did a thorough study of Jamaica's bird life and wrote a fascinating book on his findings (*Island Biology Illustrated by the Land Birds of Jamaica*), provides the best description of the upland vegetation:

> Montane forest grows on the steep slopes on either side of the Blue Mountains, and its form varies greatly with the condition. Typical montane forest occurs . . . in sheltered stream gullies where the trees form a closed canopy at 30 m [98 ft.], have moderately broad leaves and carry a small number of bromeliads and other epiphytes, and it is dark on the ground. But on the exposed flanks of the hills, at times only a few meters away, there is more open sclerophyll forest, with narrow-leaved trees only 6 to 7 m [20–23 ft.] high, and grey *Usnea* lichens are the only prominent epiphytes. Higher up, again, a little below the Gap itself, which allows clouds to come through earlier in the day than elsewhere, there is a cloud forest of trees 12 m [39 ft.] high with thick dark leaves, numerous ephiphytic bromeliads and many tree ferns. There are similar contrasts on the subsidiary ridge above Hardwar Gap, but the trees are in general rather lower here. In this area, parts of forest were felled in the distant past, but have re-grown with native forest trees, and but for the presence of old stone walls inside, it would be hard to tell this secondary from primary montane forest. . . . Finally, on the top of the main ridge, notably between Blue Mountain Peak and East Peak, there is a narrow belt of elfin forest, a thicket with closely growing trees 4 to 5 m [13–16 ft.] high, with narrow twisted trunks covered with moss, but with hardly any side branches and without large epiphytes such as bromeliads.

BLUE MOUNTAIN BIRD LIFE

Fred Sladen (a friend from St. Croix) and I arrived in Jamaica on June 6, 1989, via a BWIA flight from San Juan, Puerto Rico. Kingston's Norman Manley International Airport was bustling with people. We quickly cleared customs, exchanged U.S. for Jamaican dollars, and obtained what appeared to be the last rental car available. Although I had made reservations for a Budget rental car through my travel agent, the Budget agent in Kingston informed us that they were fresh out of cars. Fortunately, Hertz had a car that had just been returned. A passerby informed us that most visitors to Jamaica enter at Montego Bay, on the northwestern coast; more rental cars are available there. We later found that indeed the northern coastal communities were much more oriented toward tourism. On the down side, friends Craig Faanes and Jon Andrews, on a May 1990 Jamaican visit that originated in Montego Bay, were called names on a couple of occasions and a stick was thrown at their rental vehicle in Kinloss.

In planning our Jamaican trip, I had written to Audrey Downer of Kingston about the best places to find certain birds as well as adequate accommodations. She had kindly made reservations for us at the Mayfair Hotel in the northeastern portion of the city. Its location provided fairly easy access to the Blue Mountains. She also offered to spend the first morning with us to help us find some of the Blue Mountain specialties. We had jumped at the opportunity to bird with such a knowledgeable lady; she and Robert Sutton are the authors of a 1990 book, *Birds of Jamaica — A Photographic Guide.*

Mrs. Downer met us at the Mayfair Hotel lobby at 4:00 A.M. on June 7, and by dawn's first light we were high above Kingston, just below the little village of Newcastle. Our early start was designed to help us find **Crested Quail-Doves** along the roadway before any traffic frightened them. We discovered instead that the roadway was being used by Jamaican soldiers in training; we found a jogging troop along the roadway at dawn.

In spite of missing the quail-dove, that first morning with Mrs. Downer was an unqualified success. She knew the best places to stop for birds, and in less than half a day we found and observed fifteen of the island's twenty-five endemics. Jamaica is fortunate to have people such as Audrey Downer involved with the long-term study of birds and their habitats. Her book features the excellent bird photography of Yves-Jacque Rey-Millet of the Cayman Islands. Rey-Millet also took the photographs for Patricia Bradley's book, *Birds of the Cayman Islands.* Many of the Jamaican bird photographs represent the first time some species have been adequately photographed.

Looking back at that first morning, the **Jamaican Blackbird** was undoubtedly the most important bird recorded; we did not find it anywhere else. As the name suggests, it is an Icterid (endemic genus *Nesopsar*) that is listed in the AOU 1983 *Check-list of North American Birds* bètween the blackbird genus *Agelaius* and meadowlark genus *Sturnella.* However, unlike most blackbirds and meadowlarks, it utilizes a very limited habitat within the highlands, where it feeds principally among bromeliads. In Jamaica bromeliads are known as wild pines, thus the local name for this bird is wild pine sergeant.

We stopped just beyond Hardwar Gap at a little drainage containing several bromeliad-clad trees to find our first wild pine sergeant. And sure enough, a pair of these birds suddenly appeared among the mass of bromeliads as if by magic. We watched for several minutes as they chased one another up and down the trunk and from one tree to another. I had never before seen blackbirds climb up vertical trunks or squeeze between clumps of bromeliads. Their very different behavior certainly helped explain their unique classification.

I was initially attracted to the Jamaican Blackbird, even before it first appeared, by its very different call, a strange rattle. James Bond, in *The Birds of the West Indies*, described its voice as "a rather loud note, followed by a rattling sound (kep-chur-r-r-r)." At least one of the birds, probably the male, uttered rattle calls a good part of the time we were watching them, even during their short flights, which I assumed were part of courtship behavior.

Jamaican Blackbirds are overall black color but can appear glossy in good light. They possess a rather sharp, pointed bill, typical of Icterids. They are slightly smaller than the brighter-plumaged **Jamaican Oriole,** a bird that was fairly common that day in the Blue Mountains.

I did not know at the time about the endemic bromeliad crab that lives among Jamaican bromeliads. I later learned about its existence from Timothy Johnson's book, *Biodiversity and Conservation in the Caribbean: Profiles of Selected Islands,* an ICBP (International Council for Bird Preservation) publication. The fact that a crab evolved with bromeliads suggests rather extensive areas of this epiphyte on Jamaica. I wonder about its continued survival with the obvious decline of Jamaica's forests.

At another stop, at a place where the road skirts a section of reasonably intact montane forest, we discovered several more endemic birds. I was most impressed by the **Blue Mountain Vireo,** a rather large vireo that is far more beautiful than Bond's illustration suggests. Its plumage had a subtle bluish color that in the right light was exquisite. Its large bill gave it a shrikelike appearance. Lack pointed out that at one time this bird was placed in a separate genus, *Laletes,* but it is now known as *Vireo osburni* and listed by the AOU between Gray and Solitary Vireos.

A second endemic vireo, **Jamaican Vireo,** also occurs in the Blue Mountains, as well as in lowland areas throughout the island. Its song is a little like that of North America's White-eyed Vireo but more varied. We detected it almost everywhere we went. The larger **Black-whiskered Vireo,** which occurs throughout the West Indies, was also present in substantial numbers. From March through September it can be one of Jamaica's most common land birds.

In addition, we found several endemic **Arrow-headed Warblers** in the forest. At first glance they looked like dark Black-and-white Warblers, because they are so heavily streaked with black and white. Their name was derived from the heavy markings on their breasts that are "more or less triangular or arrow-head in shape," according to Bond. Lack stated that their closest relative is probably Puerto Rico's endemic Elfin Woods Warbler.

During the very early hours of the morning, as we drove into the uplands, we found two thrushes on the road: the common **White-chinned Thrush** and the less numerous **White-eyed Thrush.** Both are Jamaican endemics. The White-chin is the larger of the two by as much as an inch. It is a dark gray bird with a deep orange-red bill and feet; a bold white wingpatch is another good characteristic because it shows up so well in early morning light. The smaller White-eyed Thrush is distinctly brown on the head with a white neck (actually streaked with brown) and upper breast. Its local name is glass-eye, while the local name for the White-chinned Thrush is hopping Dick, due to its hopping behavior and tail that is often held erect.

The morning songs of these two thrushes provide long-lasting memories for me of the Jamaican highlands. The most impressive of the two songs was that of the White-eyed Thrush, which sounded a little like that of the Northern Mockingbird. The song of the White-chinned Thrush was similar to the American Robin's song. But of all the bird songs that first morning, the most outstanding voice heard was that of a third thrush, the Rufous-throated Solitaire.

Although it is not a single-island endemic, Jamaica's **Rufous-throated Solitaire** is a unique subspecies which some ornithologists believe should be a separate species. Its song is different from Rufous-sided Solitaire songs that I have heard in Dominica, Martinique, St. Lucia, and St. Vincent. The Jamaican solitaire song ends in a rattle, which I have not heard in the Windward Island solitaires. Other people have been impressed with this songster as well. Lack wrote:

> Ian Fleming, creator of the other James Bond, was so moved by the songs of the Jamaican solitaire that he wrote a special article on it. This almost unbelievable strange and beautiful noise, unique except for the songs of other solitaires, is the characteristic sound of the mountains of Jamaica in summer. It consists of sustained clear liquid notes, some with the character of musical glasses, others trilled, uttered over a very wide range of frequencies, often at harmonic intervals of several tones, and sometimes the bird even appears to sing two sustained notes simultaneously.

Probably no other birds in Jamaica receive so much local attention as do the hummingbirds, especially the endemic **Streamertail,** considered Jamaica's national bird. It appears on Jamaican currency and a wide range of publications, and for a very good reason. Male Streamertails exhibit a pair of very long and fashionable black tail feathers. These exquisite feathers

Streamertail

usually are longer than the length of the bird's body, and they emit a whirring noise in flight. Streamertails are fairly common throughout the island, but birds from the eastern end, where they possess a completely black bill, rather than the normal red and black-tipped bill, may be a separate species. Males of both forms possess bright green throats and bellies, black crests and tails, and the incredibly long streamertails.

If Jamaica's Streamertails do not provide a world-class hummingbird show, a second endemic hummer, the larger-bodied **Jamaican Mango,** is also present. But the Jamaican Mango is not a mountain species; it prefers more arid regions in the lowlands. Bond described it as "a sturdy hummingbird, dark greenish bronze above, black below; outer tail feathers purple, edged with black and sides of head and neck glossy purple." Both sexes are alike.

We found two other nectar-feeders that first morning in the Blue Mountains, the widespread Bananaquit and the endemic **Orangequit.** The Bananaquit's black throat, unlike Bananaquits found elsewhere in the West Indies, helps explain its unique subspecific status on Jamaica. This bird was placed between warblers and tanagers by the AOU, while the similar Orangequit was listed between bullfinches of the genus *Loxigilla* and the St. Lucia Black Finch (genus *Melanospiza*). The two "quits" were once lumped together in the genus *Coereba*, but the Orangequit is now known to scientists as *Euneornis campestris*. Mrs. Downer told me that the orange in its name comes from the bird's fondness for fruit. This beautiful little bird is grayish to bright blue color. In the right light one can see a bright chestnut throat-patch on the male. Females and young are brown.

Another of Jamaica's specialty birds is the **Jamaican Tody,** a member of the Todidae family, which occurs only in the West Indies. Jamaica's representative is a tiny ball of bright green, crimson, and yellow. From the back view, perched among the bright green foliage, it is next to impossible to find. From the front view, however, its bright red bill and throat, surrounded by white, and its yellow belly are much easier to locate. I watched birds fly-catching on several occasions. They would perch on a branch among the shrubbery or upper canopy with their bills pointed upward. Suddenly they would dart out and capture a reasonably large insect either from a leaf or in midair and then fly to a new perch. On most occasions I detected it first by its short "cherek" calls.

Then there are several Tyrant flycatchers. These include three *Myiarchus*, two elaenias, two kingbirds, and a pewee. Two of the three *Myiarchus* are endemics, the Sad and Rufous-tailed Flycatchers. The little **Sad Flycatcher,** which is reasonably common along the Blue Mountain highway, is pretty well restricted to the highlands. The much larger **Rufous-tailed Flycatcher** prefers middle elevations. The third *Myiarchus*, the **Stolid Flycatcher,** occurs in the lowlands; it is widespread throughout much of the Greater Antilles.

The most elusive Jamaican flycatcher is the **Jamaican Elaenia,** considered widespread but scarce. We found it in the forest in association with Jamaican and Blue Mountain Vireos, Arrow-headed Warblers, and Orangequits. Mrs. Downer pointed out its high-pitched "tse-tse-tse-u" (from Bond) calls on a couple of occasions, but we saw only one that morning. The larger **Greater Antillean Elaenia** was fairly common.

Both the Gray and Loggerhead Kingbirds, as well as the **Greater Antillean Pewee,** occur elsewhere in the Greater Antilles. Although the **Loggerhead Kingbird** can be fairly common on Puerto Rico, I had never seen it as numerous as it was in the Blue Mountains. A few days later, at Robert Sutton's Marshall Pen Estate near Mandeville, we found adults feeding youngsters not yet fledged.

We found five other Jamaican endemics in the Blue Mountain highlands that morning or the next: we saw several **Ring-tailed Pigeons** flying overhead; the common **Jamaican Woodpecker;** a nesting pair of **Jamaican Becards;** the little **Jamaican Euphonia,** which is a rather drab version of the brightly colored Antillean Euphonia that occurs in the West Indies from Hispaniola east; and the remarkable **Yellow-shouldered Grassquit,** which sang a song that reminded me of Golden-winged Warbler songs in Tennessee.

By midmorning the sky was filled with aerial acrobats. Our best sightings were from Hardwar Gap, where dozens of vultures, hawks, swifts, and swallows were evident. We recorded many Turkey Vultures; several American Kestrels; a lone Red-tailed Hawk; several Black, White-collared, and **Antillean Palm Swifts;** and a handful of swallows. The majority of the swallows were Cave Swallows, but at least a few were the endangered **Golden Swallow.** These lovely birds possessed bright white underparts and shiny bluish backs.

Driving back to Kingston in the afternoon, at a somewhat lower elevation we encountered one of Jamaica's two endemic cuckoos, the **Chestnut-bellied Cuckoo.** This sighting was one of those fortunate incidents when you see movement out of the corner of your eye, and intuition, more than anything else, forces you to stop and find whatever it is. In a matter of seconds we had located this large, long-tailed bird, which possessed a deep chestnut belly and contrasting silver-gray chest and throat. Due to its gray "beard" and bass voice it is locally called old man bird. The smaller

Jamaican Lizard-Cuckoo, which we encountered later on, is locally known as old woman bird. Lack explained that this name comes from the fact that it possesses a "much longer dagger-shaped beak and a higher and more prolonged cackle."

Throughout the Blue Mountain highlands we found evidence of Hurricane Gilbert, which had caused such widespread damage to Jamaica in September 1988. At one location only the walls of a previously attractive home remained. Mrs. Downer told us that the bare hillside behind the house had been covered with mature pines before the storm. We found several pine trunks snapped in two like matchsticks, grim reminders of the force of Mother Nature. Certain other parts of the forest showed evidence of damage as well, but it was difficult to judge the extent of that damage because so much of the area was already covered with secondary vegetation. All of the bird species we were seeking were still present. The wildlife of these islands has evolved with occasional storms such as Gilbert, and each time the plants, animals, and birds somehow have been able to survive and repopulate their essential niches.

THE COCKPIT COUNTRY

The wildest part of Jamaica lies in the west-central portion of the island, an area known as the "Cockpit Country." The name was derived from the very rugged landscape that features great depressions surrounded by high walls, like cock-fighting pits. The depth of these "pits" may be several hundred feet. Actually, they are solution holes in the limestone plateau. The result is a very inaccessible and uninviting landscape. Apparently, runaway slaves thought so, too. During Jamaica's Spanish and British colonial periods, these "Maroons" actually established independent villages within the region. They were so entrenched and able to harass the local settlements and plantations to such an extent that treaties of independence were granted to them for self-government.

Most of the Cockpit Country is dominated by a wet limestone forest. In describing the vegetation of this area, Lack wrote that "the trees form a more or less closed canopy at about 20 m [66 ft.], with emergent *Terminalia latifolia* [tropical almond] and *Cedrela odorate* [bitter cedar] rising to 30 m [98 ft.], and they support lianas and many large bromeliads, especially *Hohenbergia* species. On the steep slopes, the closely growing trees with thin trunks reach only 10 to 12 m [32–39 ft.], but they are rather taller again on top."

Fred and I approached the area from the south, via Mandeville, Christiana, and Albert Town, then across the Barbecue Bottom road to Clark's

Town and Duncans. We had spent a good part of a day with Robert Sutton at his 300-acre ranch and bird preserve (Marshall's Pen) and had taken his advice on the birdiest route across the Cockpit Country uplands. It was advice well taken, because we were impressed with the wild beauty of our route, in spite of the fact that we did not reach the more remote portion until midday. The next morning we drove back to that same area to sample its bird life at dawn.

There were several species of Jamaican birds that we had not found in the Blue Mountains and that were known to be more numerous in the Cockpit Country. We wanted to find the additional Jamaican endemics as well as experience the fabled "Cockpit" environment at a better time of day. Our bird want-list at this point on our trip still included the Jamaican races of Plain Pigeon and Olive-throated Parakeet and the endemic Yellow-billed and Black-billed Parrots, Jamaican Lizard-Cuckoo, and Jamaican Crow.

The **Jamaican Crow** was almost everywhere once we started into the more rugged karst uplands beyond Albert Town. The local name of this Corvid is jabbering crow, due to its habit of jabbering continually to its neighbors. Lack wrote that its voice is like "a wavering semi-musical jabbering, described by Goose (1847) as 'like half a dozen Welshmen quarrelling.'" I was impressed by this bird's similarity to the American Crow of North America, but it is somewhat smaller.

The **Jamaican Lizard-Cuckoo,** on the other hand, looks like nothing ever found in the United States, although it is almost as large as the Squirrel Cuckoo of Mexico and Central America. From the front it looks much like its larger cousin, the Chestnut-bellied Cuckoo. But the resemblance stops there. There are several very distinct differences: its buff belly, compared with the deep chestnut belly of the Chestnut-belly; the deep cinnamon primaries of the Lizard-Cuckoo, compared with the plain pattern of the Chestnut-belly; the bright red eye-ring of the Lizard-Cuckoo, compared to the plain eye-ring of the Chestnut-belly; and the longer and straighter bill of the Lizard-Cuckoo. We found a pair of Lizard-Cuckoos on the upper slope at midday and another individual farther down the north slope the next morning. We did not encounter this unique species anywhere else during our six-day excursion.

We also found that the Cockpit Country was a parrot haven. Jamaica's two *Amazona* parrots, especially the **Yellow-billed Parrots,** were abundant. They clearly preferred middle elevation habitats over the montane forests in the Blue Mountains. Yellow-bills also occur in the wet limestone forests of the John Crow Mountains, east of the Blue Mountains. The rugged and pitted limestone formations apparently provide nesting sites not available in the higher, volcanic mountains. In the Cockpit Country we found hundreds of parrots in flocks of four to forty-five individuals throughout the day. The greatest numbers were recorded soon after sunup; these gregarious and vocal birds fly from their roosting sites to choice feeding areas at that time of day.

The **Black-billed Parrots** were less numerous than the slightly larger Yellow-bills and fairly common during the early morning hours. Lack points out that their natural foods "are almost unknown," although Gosse reported them "eating bananas and pimento seeds." Black-bills possess a much thinner beak than Yellow-bills, suggesting that the two species occupy slightly different niches. But the fact that Jamaica is one of only three West Indian islands to support two species of *Amazona* parrots is of special interest.

Both of Jamaica's endemic parrots are reasonably small in stature. In flight they can best be identified by the red wing speculum of adult Black-bills. Yellow-bills lack the red wing-markings, although immature Black-bills also lack the red speculum.

We found a few of the smaller Olive-throated Parakeets along the northern edge of the Cockpit Country uplands, but they were more numerous in the lowlands closer to the coast. This is another of Jamaica's endemic races; the species is common throughout eastern Mexico and south into central Mexico. However, several ornithologists believe that the Jamaican birds should be a full species.

We also found a lone **Plain Pigeon.** Sutton had told us to watch for this bird because it may have arrived with Hurricane Gilbert and may not be the "native" form (*Columba inornata exigua*), which had not been reported for several years; it was considered extinct. The bird's appearance after Hurricane Gilbert suggests that it may be one of the Hispaniolan or Puerto Rican birds. However, Mrs. Downer thought that recent sightings may be the result of the more open vegetation resulting from the storm.

During our two short surveys of the Cockpit Country, we recorded ten species of Columbids: White-crowned, Plain, and Ring-tailed Pigeons; White-winged, Zenaida, Mourning, and Caribbean Doves; Common Ground-Dove; and Ruddy and Crested Quail-Doves. That is an extremely large number of closely related birds (which assumedly possess similar requirements) to occur together in the same general environment.

SUMMARY

Why does an island the size of Jamaica, only 146 miles long and 22 to 51 miles wide, possess more endemic birds (twenty-five species and eighteen subspecies) than any of the other islands of the West Indies? Also endemic, according to Ann Haynes-Sutton, are "at least 912 plant species, 197 invertebrates, 27 reptiles, 4 mammals and 2 fish. A total of at least 1,167 species are peculiar to Jamaica."

The answer is not an easy one to discover, but the high ratio of endemism can partly be explained by two facts. First, Jamaica initially possessed an extremely wide range of habitats, each in reasonable abundance. More than half of the island's 4,500 square miles is over 1,000 feet elevation. Five distinct forest types have been identified, although only three still exist: montane forest occurs on the shales in the Blue Mountains; wet limestone forest occurs in the Cockpit Country and John Crow Mountains; and lowland arid limestone forest occurs in parts of the southern lowlands.

Second, although Jamaica was never connected to the Central American mainland, three large "land-bridge" islands were exposed along the Honduras-Nicaraguan Bank, the closest within 250 miles of the island, during the last Ice Age. Honduras lies 380 miles to the southwest. That and Jamaica's close proximity to the huge island of Cuba (only 90 miles to the north) provide good biogeographic logic for having a higher rate of endemic bird life than anywhere else in the West Indies.

The longer an island has been isolated from the mainland, the greater the likelihood for endemic flora and fauna, as long as the island's natural environment supports the varied forms. It appears that the combination of time and conditions is more propitious on Jamaica than elsewhere.

"Jamaica is more than a part of the Caribbean, it is the heart of the Caribbean," according to the slick pamphlet I received from the Jamaica Tourist Board. It goes on to describe everything else Jamaica has to offer, from great hotels, exquisite dining, and historic hideaways to off-the-beaten-path values where "anything more than a bikini can be considered overdressed." Such descriptions have a way of catching the imagination of almost anyone.

For the true naturalist and an increasing number of ecotourists, such brochures contain little of interest, beyond some of the illustrations of the countryside. Jamaica's principal attraction can rarely be found in the slick tourist publications. For naturalists, the thrill of new places and wildlife and the experience of watching a Jamaican Blackbird among the Blue Mountain bromeliads or the bobbing gait of the Crested Quail-Dove far exceed the more commercial opportunities Jamaica has to offer.

CHAPTER TWO

Cuba ISLAND OF CONTRADICTIONS

The mist was all around us that early morning at the outskirts of Santo Tomás. We stood at the edge of a dwarf woodland and ate bread and cheese with strong Cuban coffee. Bird song filled the air, interrupted now and again by sounds from the village. A house was under construction down the street; the town's sawmill had begun to process its valuable resource; and several workers at a new charcoal plant were carrying small offerings of the adjacent forest to a growing pyramid. I already had seen samples of recently cut forests. The long Cuban embargo by the United States had created serious shortages of cooking oils; many people could no longer afford kerosene and had begun to use charcoal instead.

Chino Martínez arrived as we finished our breakfast. A resident of Santo Tomás, Chino had been studying a nearby swamp community for many years. He had monitored the steady decline of the Zapata Wren and had agreed to guide our little party of naturalists into the swamp to find this rare and elusive bird.

Our route began in the woods and followed a long ditch that had been cut years earlier in an attempt to drain the area. The unsuccessful attempt had only created a "moat" filled with black muck that looked like something out of a horror movie; I wondered if I would disappear if I fell in. All around us was a moist woodland of short trees, each festooned with mosses and bromeliads. As we walked through the woodland, I recognized the songs of several Cuban birds singing among the vegetation: Cuban Tody, Cuban Trogon, Greater Antillean Pewee, Cuban and Black-whiskered Vireos, and Cuban Bullfinch. We had a brief but good view of a Gray-headed Quail-Dove at one point. A Louisiana Waterthrush, a winter visitor from North America, kept ahead of us as we progressed along the edge of the long ditch.

Finally, we came to a place where small logs had been placed across the ditch, so we were able to cross. From there it was only another couple of hundred yards to a place where we suddenly emerged into an open tall grass prairie. This was the swampy area, our destination, where Chino had last seen Zapata Wrens.

Sawgrass dominated the wet prairie; clumps were often 5 to 6 feet in height. Two taller shrubs were also present but widely scattered: buttonwood, with its rounded, single white flower heads, and a slightly larger woody shrub that Chino called *arrayán*. Each step we took was like walking on a wet sponge, and at one place my foot disappeared below the surface. When I retrieved my leg it made a sucking sound, so I was thankful the swamp had temporarily claimed only one part of my anatomy. A rather sweet but jerky bird song sounded a hundred feet or so ahead of us, then two towhee-size birds flew from one shrub to another. One of the two perched in good view and sang again. Chino called out, "Zapata Sparrow!"—one of Cuba's endemics. We studied the bird thoroughly through our binoculars. It stayed still for three or four minutes, singing several more times, before flying off to another singing post. It was a most welcome lifer!

Although I had studied the **Zapata Sparrow** illustrations in James Bond's *Birds of the West Indies*, I had not expected this sparrow to be so bright and colorful. In the sunlight that morning its rufous cap and yellow belly were gleaming bright. Its facial markings of white, grays, and black, behind a rather heavy bill, were obvious. It was an altogether dynamic bird.

We continued onward through the sawgrass, pausing now and then to listen for the song of a Zapata Wren. It was amazing how quiet a group of fourteen people could be when they were trying to find one of the world's rarest birds. Common Yellowthroats called from the grasslands all around us. Three to four flocks of White-crowned Pigeons, eight to twelve individuals in each flock, passed swiftly overhead. An occasional Turkey Vulture wheeled by.

Chino decided he would climb up into one of the woody *arrayán* shrubs so he could hear better. I was surprised that the thin branches of the shrub were able to bear his weight. He apparently had used this listening technique before. For another four or five minutes we were perfectly quiet.

Suddenly, he pointed toward the right and began to descend from his perch. Chino grabbed his "boom box," which I had been holding during his ascent, and off he went in the direction he had pointed. He had heard a wren some distance away; I had not. We stopped in about 50 yards. He held the tape player over his head, aimed ahead of us, and played a tape of the Zapata Wren song. The tape player was turned up extremely loud, and just when I began to protest this obnoxious pollution of the swamp, he just as suddenly turned it off and pointed to the lower portion of a shrub just ahead of us. A moment later I could see the movement of a dark bird almost at ground level. We all froze, binoculars focused on the place where we could see movement. A second later a **Zapata Wren** came into view, working upward into a more open position. There it was! I had an excellent view for several seconds, then it dropped down into the brushy ground cover, which apparently had hidden its approach.

A second bird appeared briefly in an adjacent shrub. It scolded us for a few seconds but was then silent. Very briefly I had both birds in view at once. After that it was difficult to see either bird clearly, although both remained in the protective branches at the base of the shrubs for another four or five minutes. I wrote field notes as follows: "buffy back, barred tail, flanks and crissum. Buff-gray chest. Heavy, long bill, whitish line behind eye, not superciliary; eye ring elliptical."

We soon departed because we did not want to disturb these birds any further. Although we had been careful not to damage the habitat, our presence there could only create additional impact on a species that should be considered endangered. No one knows for sure how rare the species truly is because of its disjunct populations within Cuba's isolated Zapata Peninsula. However, Guy Mountfort, in *Rare Birds of the World*, wrote: "It is thought to be at risk because of the ease with which its habitat could be destroyed by large scale drainage, and it is listed as rare. Although no drainage scheme has taken place, the species declined to near extinction in the 1960s and 1970s owing possibly to burning of the habitat by local people, but some records in the 1980s offer some hope that it may be recovering."

ACCESS AND LOGISTICS

The old adage of "you can't get there from here" fits Cuba better than anywhere else I know. U.S. citizens must go somewhere else first to get to Cuba. Cubana Airline is not allowed to fly out of the United States, nor is the Cuban airline allowed airspace over the United States, except for a narrow corridor along the St. Lawrence Waterway. Cubana does fly out of Canada, however, a country that has not participated in the Cuban embargo. Canada and Cuba have good relations, and Canada has provided considerable technical assistance to Cuba over the years. In fact, Cuba's Varadero Airport was constructed with Canadian assistance, and Canadian and Cuban scientists have developed a significant bird-banding program in Cuba. Over the years this program has obtained valuable information on North American songbird migration and winter requirements.

The Canadian-Cuban bird-banding program is coordinated by the Long Point Bird Observatory of Ontario, Canada, and much of the Cuban support costs are raised by conducting birding tours to Cuba. These tours provide rare opportunities for U.S. citizens to visit Cuba with the minimum of trouble. Exceptions include departure from Toronto instead of more southerly terminals in the United States and the difficulty of obtaining legal travel authorization. Since the onset of the 1963 embargo, all travel to Cuba by U.S. citizens must be approved by the Office of Foreign Assets Control, Department of the Treasury. Permission is limited to individuals going for a family visit, on official government business, or for professional reasons, such as journalists, scientists, and writers. My authorization was approved because of my desire to include Cuba in this book. My approval was obtained with the kind assistance of Ron DeLugo, U.S. Virgin Islands' representative to Congress.

Our tour group departed Toronto's Pearson Airport at about 3:30 P.M. (EST) and arrived at Cuba's Varadero Airport less than four hours later. Doug McCrea, tour coordinator with Long Point Bird Observatory, had met us at the Toronto Airport and remained with us throughout our seven-day trip. It took us about one hour to get through Cuban customs and out of the terminal, where we were met by two of our Cuban guides with a Cubatour bus and driver. Biologist Arturo Kirkconnell and Ricardo Quintata (who handled logistics) were to be our Cuban guides throughout our stay. Later that night we added two additional guides who lived in the Zapata region, Rogelio García and his son Nelson.

We left Varadero by bus and drove south about 110 kilometers (68 miles) to Playa Larga Resort, where we were to spend the next five nights. Playa Larga is located on the southwestern corner of the Zapata Peninsula, at the head of Bahía de Cochinos (better known to Americans as the Bay of Pigs), where Cuban exiles were defeated in their attempt to capture Cuba in April 1961. The final battle took place at Playa Larga. Tad Szulc's book *Fidel: A Critical Portrait* provides a good overview of the invasion and CIA participation. There is little remaining evidence of the invasion at Playa Larga. The series of concrete bunkers, mostly filled with sand, that exist along the beach every few hundred yards were constructed after the invasion.

Playa Larga is now a popular beach resort. My cabana, one of about sixty units, was less than 100 feet from the beach. It was clean and adequate for my purpose; I spent very little time indoors. All of our meals were eaten in the central dining room; they were plain but good and consisted primarily of fish, chicken, or (once) steak with rice, yuca (cassava), or potatoes, and cabbage and tomato salad.

Each day we ate breakfast at 7:00 A.M., then went out to explore various preselected locations. We returned at midday for lunch, after which we had an hour or two to either rest, swim, or explore the immediate area. We visited one or two other locations during the late afternoon and returned to Playa Larga at dusk for dinner.

The Zapata Peninsula (shaped like a huge shoe, hence the name "Zapata," which is Spanish for shoe) is almost 80 miles long and contains a broad mix of natural habitats: bay, beach, tidal flat, mangrove woodland, littoral woodland, thorn woodland, deciduous forest, semi-evergreen forest, savanna, swamp forest, herbaceous swamp, and freshwater ponds and lakes. These names, derived from J. S. Beard's classic paper in *Ecology* titled "Climax Vegetation in Tropical America," seemed most appropriate for this area.

The majority of the peninsula is included within Zapata National Park, large portions of which are accessible only with special authorization. We could reach the swamp and tidal flats by passing through a checkpoint where a rope blocked our progress. The guard on duty checked our identity and lowered the rope so that we could continue. All of our entries had been prearranged, so our access was without incident.

I awoke before dawn, probably in anticipation of my first day in Cuba. All was quiet except for the waves slapping the nearby beach. I lay there briefly thinking about how many years I had wanted to visit Cuba, and at last I was there, actually at the ignominious Bay of Pigs. A few minutes later I was standing under the stars, surprisingly bright and clear, listening for sounds I might investigate. Roosters were crowing in the distance, country sounds anywhere on earth. A dog barked farther away. Then the repetitious "too too too" call of a **Cuban Pygmy-Owl** sounded from the trees just behind the next row of cabanas. Within a few minutes I was standing directly under the tree where the owl was continuing to call, "Too too too." I used my strong flashlight to search for the bird that I knew was only 6 to 7 inches tall. But in spite of examining every visible branch, I couldn't locate the bird; it apparently was hidden from my view. I moved to a different position, and the next time I flashed my light into the branches I must have startled it. It suddenly shot down over my head, only a few feet above me, and flew off into the dawn.

I followed it as best I could for several hundred feet. Then I stood still again, quietly listening for more telltale calls. By now other birds were starting to greet the dawn. Gray Kingbirds were the first of the daytime songsters. A pair of West Indian Woodpeckers called from the same tree in which the Pygmy-Owl had been calling. The tree's large, flat, tan-colored seedpods and new green leaves identified it as a tibet. Cuban Crows were calling from the trees along the beach.

Suddenly, almost directly in front of me was the "too too too" call again. I froze in place, searching the branches of a stunted flamboyant tree. This tree was without the bright red flowers that would appear in a few weeks. Then I saw it! The Pygmy-Owl was at the very summit. It continued calling, "Too too too," as I watched it through my binoculars. It was light enough now, and I could clearly see its buff-colored head and neck, speckled with white. Its tail was barred, and it kept it cocked up as if to show off its white, fluffy crissum. What a bird! It was slightly larger than the Ferruginous Pygmy-Owl, its closest relative in North America. It was my first Cuban endemic, one of twenty Cuban bird species that occur nowhere else.

I walked back to my cabana to drop off the flashlight before breakfast. A brightly colored male **West Indian Woodpecker** was excavating a cavity in the tibet tree when I passed. It reminded me of the closely related Red-bellied Woodpecker, but the Cuban bird had a black eyepatch that extended behind the eye and a white area behind the bill.

Several blackbirds flew into an adjacent tree. I knew immediately they were **Cuban Blackbirds,** in spite of sounding and acting very much like Brewer's Blackbirds of western North America. I wondered why this bird was classified in the genus *Dives* with the larger Melodious Blackbird of Mexico and Central America, rather than *Euphagus*, with Brewer's and Rusty Blackbirds. Still later, after watching the species for a longer time, its behavior of creeping around palm fronds reminded me of the Jamaican Blackbird.

As I neared my cabana I discovered the flock of **Cuban Crows** in the adjacent coconut palms. They looked all the world like ordinary American Crows of the United States, but their calls were very different. Their vocal repertoire included every squawk imaginable as well as lengthy jabberings that could more likely be expected from cartoon caricatures than real-life Cuban birds.

Breakfast was a necessity that took time from the more meaningful part of the day. But the large glass of freshly squeezed orange juice became the highlight of breakfast for me. The Cuban coffee was barely drinkable from my perspective. It was much too strong. But when the syrupy coffee was mixed with hot milk, in the proper Cuban style, it was palatable.

The Playa Larga road continued south along the western shore of Bahía de Cochinos to Playa Girón, another beach resort which seemed to cater to younger, bikini-clad sun-lovers. North of Playa Girón is the village of Vermajas, where dirt tracks enter a deciduous forest that provides habitat especially suited to Cuba's **Fernandina's Flicker.**

We walked one of the tracks past stacked logs into the remaining forest. Almost immediately Rogelio spotted a pair of flickers. One of the birds was a Fernandina's Flicker, but the other was a yellow-shafted Northern Flicker, a resident subspecies to the common North American flicker. Neither bird stayed long enough for a good look, so we continued down the track. Soon we reached a place where Rogelio pointed to a hole in a rather skinny tree. A few scratches on the tree trunk produced another Fernandina's Flicker. It came out of the hole, where it apparently was nesting, and perched at the entrance in full view with little concern for its admirers.

The Fernandina's Flicker is restricted to Cuba's dry forest and palm groves in the lowlands and to deciduous forests of the mountains. Our guides expressed concern about the newly cut forest and said that this flicker was becoming increasingly difficult to locate. It should be given special protection before it declines further. Kai Curry-Lindahl, in his 1972 book, *Let Them Live*, listed it as one of Cuba's most threatened birds.

It was while we were admiring the flicker that one of our guides detected the soft calls of quail-doves. We shifted our attention immediately, and I

Cuban Trogon

began to scan the forest floor ahead of us for quail-doves, birds that for me had long been the essence of tropical forests. Cuba has four of the six West Indian quail-doves, and all four were possible in those woods.

I could hear the deep, double notes of a quail-dove very close, but we couldn't locate it. Nelson decided to walk into the woods and make a circular swing to drive the bird out into the open track ahead of us. We stood still, gazing down the opening. We had only seconds to wait before out into the open track walked a quail-dove with an incredibly blue head. Its cap can only be described as bright blue-blue. A **Blue-headed Quail-Dove!** Just below the cap were black-and-white lines that crossed its cheeks. Below that was a velvety blue throat and bib. The rest of the bird was a buff color. During the next few days everyone in our party got several good looks at this unique species.

All the while we were observing the flicker and quail-dove we had been hearing the incessant and rather monotonous calls of **Cuban Trogons.** They were all around us. But when one suddenly flew into the open branches of a nearby tree, our attention riveted on that bird. The Cuban Trogon is considered Cuba's national bird, and it well deserves this status. It is a gorgeous creature with a purple-blue cap, snow-white throat and chest, orange-red belly, and black-and-white barred tail with peculiar bluish fringes. Doug called it "a real stunner!" It certainly was that. We found it in all the forested areas we visited, from the seashore to the mountains.

Another Cuban endemic we saw that first morning was the **Cuban Tody,** representative of a family which is found only in the Greater Antilles. It has blue color, too, but it is less obvious than on the trogon and quail-dove, occurring only on its cheeks, which are highlighted by an emerald head and carmine-red throat. These little birds were not so easily observed, although their sharp "terk terk terk" calls, usually repeated twelve to fifteen times, were common in all of the forested areas we visited. Doug had an appropriate pet name for this bird as well: "psychedelic kingfisher." See the chapter on Dominican Republic for additional information about todies.

I found Cuba's deciduous forest habitat drier than I had expected, probably due to the long-standing drought as well as the time of year. Many of the trees had not yet fully leafed out, so it was fairly easy to see some distance into the forest. The smooth, red-barked gumbo limbo trees stood out among the more abundant grayer trunks. Eugenia, a small tree with mottled bark and small opposite, short, pointed leaves, was also common. There were few really large trees in the forest, and none were buttressed. Cuba's deciduous forest is essentially a two-storied habitat with little ground cover, few mosses and ferns, and even fewer epiphytes. The lower stratum consisted of small and immature trees that possessed foliage between 10 and 30 feet high and a second stratum that formed a canopy at about 65 feet.

We visited two additional deciduous forest areas in the afternoon, Los Cenotes and El Roble. Los Cenotes was a fascinating place. Water had carved a deep sinkhole in the limestone terrain with an underground connection to the sea. Divers often explore the underground passageway. Saltwater fishes occur there in numbers; I identified several species by standing at the edge of the cenote: immature schoolmasters, a grunt, a damselfish, sergeant majors, either a clown or yellowhead wrasse, and striped parrotfish. There were several smaller species, too; I identified a blenny and a goby.

It was there at the cenote where we got our first good look at a pair of **Cuban Bullfinches.** Both birds were in the process of constructing a nest on the outer branches of a little tree hanging out over the water. The nest was surprisingly large, like a Cactus Wren nest made of grasses. I watched these birds for several minutes, and I was amazed at their uninterrupted efforts at nest building with more than a dozen people standing so close. I also better understood the reason this bird was classified with grassquits and seedeaters rather than with other bullfinches. It is much smaller and very different from other bullfinches. Its scientific name is *Melopyrrha nigra*, "little black finch." David Lack, in his book *Island Biology Illustrated by the Land Birds of Jamaica*, suggested that *Melopyrrha* "is probably derived from the mainland *Sporophila* [seedeaters], though it is of similar size and has a similar shaped beak to *Loxigilla* [bullfinches] and is probably an ecological equivalent."

We also got good looks at several lizards at Los Cenotes. They seemed especially numerous that afternoon. They were later identified from my descriptions by Alberto Esbrada, a Cuban herpetologist whom I visited one evening at Playa Larga. The largest of the lizards was a 12- to 14-inch giant anole (genus *Luteolous*) that someone found 10 feet high in the crotch of a tree. Another was a rather plain lizard, about 8 inches in length, but with a tail that curved up over its back. Alberto told me the genus of this species was *Leicephalus*. Finally, I saw a ground-lizard that I was able to identify as *Amevia*. When I asked Alberto about this lizard he told me that all Cuba's ground-lizards are the same species (*auberi*) but that he and a colleague had recently presented a paper in which they described more than forty subspecies of *Amevia auberi* for Cuba.

We completed our first day in a way that only true naturalists can fully appreciate. After dinner we retired to Doug's cabana to go over the day's activities and discuss plans for the following day; this lasted about an hour. It was then time for night birds, to attempt to locate any nightjars and owls that might be in the area. There was one species I was especially interested in finding; I had missed seeing the Stygian Owl on several earlier trips to Mexico and Dominican Republic, yet this same species is sometimes found within the Playa Larga compound. We began to wander around the area, listening for its song.

The Stygian Owl's call is little more than a deep "whoo," but it was enough to create considerable excitement. We had been searching for less than fifteen minutes when the clear, unmistakable call of a Stygian Owl sounded from near the center of the compound. Arturo and I heard its call simultaneously and in unison proclaimed its presence. Within minutes we had gathered under the tree where the owl was singing. It took us only a few more seconds to locate this nocturnal raptor. It was perched on a horizontal branch about 30 feet above the ground in the open. In spite of being highlighted by three bright flashlights it remained still for as long as we wished to study it. We all had wonderful looks at this incredible bird.

It is well named. Stygian refers to its dark color; "gloomy and dark," according to my dictionary. It reminded me of the closely related Long-eared Owl because of its long ear-tufts and size. Its eyeshine was a deep orange color.

DAY TWO: MARCH 25

Dawn found me on the beach at the far side of Playa Larga. I heard at least three Pygmy-Owls as I made my way up the beach. As the eastern sky brightened, a flock of Cuban Parrots formed part of the mosaic of trees and birds. I expected to find shorebirds on the beach, but except for a lone Spotted Sandpiper and four Ruddy Turnstones it was deserted. A couple of Brown Pelicans, four Laughing Gulls, and a lone Tricolored Heron flew by, heading no doubt to feeding grounds elsewhere.

The water of the Bay of Pigs is much like many other warm tropical waters, beautiful but not very productive. Colder, more northern waters produce greater quantities of plankton, which attract significant fisheries, which in turn attract greater numbers of fish-eating birds and mammals. Cold versus warm water productivity is a fact I must realize time and time again. It seems to me that beautiful tropical waters should be alive with fish and wildlife, but sadly they are not.

Our morning trip was to Los Sábalos, farther inland than Los Cenotes but still within the deciduous forest habitat. Most of the birds encountered there were the same as those we had found the previous day; a total of sixty-four on our first day, of which fourteen were Cuban endemics. Day two, like all of the following, was designed to see new habitats and find the remaining Cuban specialties.

Los Sábalos, however, is a good place to find the **Bee Hummingbird,** and Nelson had also located a Bare-legged Owl there. Cuba's Bee Hummingbird is renowned as the smallest of all birds. Bond wrote that one is "more apt to mistake it for a bee than a bird." Like many hummingbirds, females are nondescript. But the male Bee Hummingbird possesses a bright red head and gorget that flares out on both sides of its head like elongated plumes. Its back and flanks are emerald-green, and its rump and tail are a sparkling blue color. However, because it likes to sit at the very top of the tallest trees and shrubs, it can be difficult to spot. But on occasions one will sit at a lower level long enough to reveal its finery. Then it is truly unmistakable. Unlike most hummingbirds, Bee Hummingbirds often sing a surprisingly loud but squeaky song.

Cuba's other hummingbird, the **Cuban Emerald,** is common almost everywhere in the country, and so it is often taken for granted. However, it too is a beautiful bird. It is almost twice the size of the Bee Hummingbird and possesses a forked tail that is readily evident when it is sitting. It is an impressive bird in spite of coming in second place because of its tiny cousin's notoriety.

We followed a dirt track through the forest for about a mile beyond the roadway. The forest was dry, and last season's leaves crunched under our feet. A **Great Lizard-Cuckoo** sailed across the track ahead of us and perched in the upper branches of a small tree. We stopped to admire this West Indian relative of the Roadrunner. It was almost 2 feet in length, including a long, narrow, black-and-white banded tail that seemed to be more of an annoyance than a benefit. As we got closer we could see the bare skin surrounding its bright red eyes. I was amazed that we were able to get so close; it apparently thought it was hidden from our view.

The Great Lizard-Cuckoo occurs only on Cuba and in the Bahamas and is one of only four species of lizard-cuckoos in the world. All are classified in the genus *Saurothera* and confined to the Greater Antilles, one each on Jamaica, Cuba, Hispaniola, and Puerto Rico. The Cuban species is the largest of the four.

The bird of the morning, however, was the **Bare-legged Owl.** Nelson located it first in a thicket of vegetation not too far off the track, perched about 12 feet above the ground. It was about halfway in size between Flammulated and Spotted Owls; all three possess all-brown eyes. It is not, however, related to those North American birds, according to the AOU check-list, which lists it next to the Puerto Rican Screech-Owl. It does not possess ear-tufts, and to me it looks a little like a Burrowing Owl. I was able to move into a close enough position to obtain several photographs. It remained frozen in place all the while.

The other bird of note that morning was the endemic **Cuban Grassquit**, *Tiaris canora*. Although it is most clearly related to the Black-faced Grassquit, a species common on the nearby islands of Jamaica and Hispaniola, it is very different in appearance. The Cuban Grassquit is another real "stunner," to quote Doug. The illustration in Bond does not do it justice. The male's yellow-and-black head can be a bright contrast in sunlight. We found only one individual throughout our stay, and I could not help but wonder if this unique species is at risk.

We spent the late afternoon at Los Chuzos, a seasonally flooded savanna habitat northeast of Playa Larga. We added several waders and a few shorebirds to our growing bird list. Local resident water birds found at Los Chuzos included Pied-billed Grebe, Neotropic Cormorant, Great and Snow Egrets, Little Blue and Green Herons, Roseate Spoonbill, Purple Gallinule, Common Moorhen, Killdeer, Northern Jacana, and, most important, West Indian Whistling-Duck.

We found six **West Indian Whistling-Ducks** on the far bank of a little pond, and we all got excellent looks at these birds with spotting scopes. Although this duck was once reasonably common throughout the Greater and northern Lesser Antilles, it is now very difficult to find anywhere but in Cuba and on the tiny island of Barbuda. Cuba undoubtedly has the greatest population. Mountfort listed it as "vulnerable" in 1988 and stated: "It disappeared from Jamaica in 1960. Cuba and Hispaniola apparently have most of its small surviving population, but hunting is likely to exterminate it on both islands. Hunting is prohibited in Cuba but not enforced, and the ducks are not protected on Hispaniola. Barbuda holds a reasonable population and there may still be small numbers in the Bahamas and Cayman Islands."

The other avian endemic found that afternoon was the **Cuban Parakeet.** Flocks of six to twelve individuals careened through the forest as we made our way to and from the wet savanna. One group of six landed in the treetops ahead of us, and we were able to get reasonably good looks with the aid of our scopes. They were all green with a scattering of red feathers on their bodies and heads. Large patches of red and yellow under their wings were only evident in flight. They were extremely noisy birds, giving continuous, shrill screeches in flight. Once they landed they remained silent. Arturo mentioned that this bird nests in holes excavated in royal palms by West Indian Woodpeckers.

DAY THREE: MARCH 26

The entire southern end of the Zapata Peninsula consists of tidal flats with scattered mangroves. Beyond the guardhouse, we proceeded south toward Las Salinas on a shell road that soon became little more than a slightly elevated track through the flooded salt flats.

Our first stop that morning was to look at a Common Black-Hawk that was perched on top of a dead snag less than 200 feet from the track. This raptor has created considerable interest in the bird world because it is so different from Common Black-Hawks elsewhere. It was my first experience with the Cuban bird and I was curious about its appearance and behavior. I had seen black-hawks many times in the southwestern United States and in Mexico and also had observed it in St. Vincent's Vermont Forest.

The Common Black-Hawk stayed in place long enough for us all to get excellent looks. However, there was little about the bird's appearance when perched that seemed odd. It was not until it took flight that I realized a difference in both its wing pattern and the flight itself. The underside of its wings had large, noticeable white windows just inside the outer tips, much larger than the tiny whitish patches hardly visible on North American birds. When it took off it ascended like most raptors. North American black-hawks, perhaps because they usually are found in riparian or forest habitats, flap harder and ascend in tighter circles.

One of the earliest descriptions of Cuba's Common Black-Hawk appeared in Herbert Friedmann's 1950 book, *The Birds of North and Middle America, Part XI*. He considered it to be a totally separate species and called it "Cuban Crab Hawk *Buteogallus gundlachii*." I cannot help but agree.

All the time we were studying the black-hawk, swarms of martins and barn swallows were flying overhead. Arturo announced that we probably were seeing the endemic **Cuban Martin** and that the birds were nesting in the slender snags sticking out of the flooded salt flats. Sure enough, with the aid of a spotting scope we could clearly see martin heads poking out of various holes in the snags. When asked about the difference between the local martins and those passing through as migrating Purple Martins, our Cuban hosts admitted that they could only be sure if the birds were in hand. They are very, very similar. Arturo said that Cuban Martin males possess slightly streaked (with white) crissums compared with the fully dark crissums of Purple Martins.

The farther we progressed toward the tip of the peninsula the more our surroundings looked like so many other coastal flatlands in the tropics. We added twenty species of birds to the trip list during the morning, including a Double-crested Cormorant; a lone adult male Magnificent Frigatebird; a Great Blue Heron; a surprisingly large number of Reddish Egrets (both reddish and white phases); a number of Greater Flamingos, far off across the flats; a great look at a Clapper Rail that ran across the track; lone Black-bellied and Wilson's Plovers, Lesser Yellowlegs, and a Whimbrel; several Least Sandpipers and Short-billed Dowitchers; a number of Caspian and Royal Terns; three Black Skimmers; and several singing Yellow Warblers. Repeat bird species included Great Egret, Tricolored Heron, Roseate Spoonbill, White Ibis, Osprey, Killdeer, Greater Yellowlegs, and Laughing Gull.

The shell track ended at a ranger station alongside an old and unused salt works. Salt was once gathered from the drying flats, which were now left to the sandpipers and plovers and to the occasional visitor who might wish to visit that portion of the national park.

We left Playa Larga that afternoon for the region of the peninsula locally called the rice fields, or Los Canales. The area contained a series of canals that drained freshwater Laguna de Tesoro near Guamá and flowed southward into the Bay of Pigs. Arturo told me that the state had developed the rice fields many years earlier but had let the entire area fall into disrepair. The rice fields and canals were being refurbished to restore Cuba's rice production; we found considerable activity under way.

We followed a series of dikes along the canals and pastures and added a number of birds to our list. A few were lingering wintertime visitors, such as Blue-winged Teal, Ring-necked Duck, Northern Harrier, Merlin, Sora, Tree Swallow, and Indigo Bunting. I discovered a lone Yellow-breasted Chat, undoubtedly a migrant and, according to Arturo, only the third record for Cuba. But the most interesting birds seen were some of the full-time residents: Anhinga, Glossy Ibis, Snail Kite, the endemic Gundlach's Hawk, King Rail, Eastern Meadowlark, Red-winged Blackbird, and Savannah Sparrow.

We watched the Snail Kites for the longest time. They were hunting over the wet pastures and every now and again would swoop down and alight on the ground. They would soon fly up to a low perch with their prey, an apple snail, and delicately extract the snail body from its shell. I found dozens of empty shells at the various perches along the edge of the pastures; one can only imagine how a bird's bill could evolve in such a manner to allow an entire species to depend upon such prey.

The bird of the day was the endemic **Gundlach's Hawk,** which suddenly appeared over a pasture, flying near enough for an excellent view; it disappeared into a palm grove. This raptor is an accipiter that looks very much like a large, heavy-bodied Sharp-shinned Hawk. It is another of Cuba's species at risk; Mountfort reported that "a maximum of about 200 are left."

DAY FOUR: MARCH 27

Morning was spent in the Zapata Swamp near Santo Tomás, and we revisited Los Chuzos during the afternoon. It was an eventful day, and my Cuban bird list amounted to 134 species when we returned to Playa Larga at dusk.

DAY FIVE: MARCH 28

We again started early and ate our bread and cheese breakfast at La Boca, the Guamá boat dock. We soon boarded a ferry and were en route up the canal and across Laguna de Tesoro to the Guamá Indian Village. Anhingas and Limpkins posed for us along the edge of the canal. Suddenly, the throbbing of the ferry boat motor stopped. We were dead in the water. Doug explained jokingly that it was because the Long Point Bird Observatory tour was aboard. He informed us that on the last tour the ferry had not only broken down so that another ferry was required, but that the entire group had been drenched by a heavy rainstorm.

Arturo pointed into one of the Australian pines along the edge of the canal. There was one of the strangest mammals I had ever seen; it seemed to be a mixture of opossum, raccoon, and marmot. It was sitting near the top of the tree with its prehensile tail hooked over one of the branches. I estimated its length at about 24 inches. "It is a hutia," said Arturo, "a mammal native to Cuba." We all gawked at this strange creature. I couldn't help but be glad that the ferry had taken that moment to stop.

Later, after returning home, I did a little research on Arturo's hutia and discovered that it indeed is a stranger-than-fiction creature. E. Raymond Hall (1981) includes hutias in the family Capromyidae, which includes seven genera. Arturo's hutia is known to science as the prehensile-tailed hutia (*Capromys prehensitis*). Hall describes it as a heavy, thickset rodent almost 2 feet in length, with a tail one-third of its length. It possesses wide feet and is able to climb. Although it dens underground or among rocks, it spends much of its waking hours in trees, where it feeds on new leaves. It occurs throughout Cuba.

I was enjoying a look at this new mammal so much that I hardly noticed that the motor had restarted until we again began to move up the canal and out onto the lake. Nearly 1 mile across, the lake covers an area of about 6 square miles and is Cuba's largest natural lake. The "reconstructed" Taino Indian village and tourist center is situated on a small island near the far shore and contains cabanas, a restaurant, and other tourist facilities. It appears to be a wonderful retreat, but I was told that the facilities are inadequate and the cost of staying overnight is exorbitant.

We spent about two hours on the island, walking along the grassy shore and the many paths. We added no new birds to our list, but I found the largest concentration (fifty or more) of Purple Gallinules in one place that I had ever seen.

When we again disembarked from the returning ferry we spent another couple of hours walking through Cuba's largest crocodile breeding farm. I was amazed at the number and size of many of the crocs. The Cuban crocodile (*Crocodylus rhombifer*) is one more of Cuba's endangered species. The purpose of the farm is to ensure the continued survival of this unique reptile, as well as to maintain a source of skins for purses and boots.

We departed Playa Larga after lunch en route northeast to Havana. We checked into the Havana Libre Hotel, once the Havana Hilton, by midafternoon and the rest of the day were free to roam. I immediately set out to find some bookstores and to acquire my own impression of Cuba's capital city of over two million people (20 percent of Cuba's total population). It was a fascinating experience.

I followed the Malecón (the grand boulevard between the city and the Strait of Florida) west to Cathedral Square, then back through Old Town and past Havana University to the hotel. I was totally ignored during my three-hour stroll. I felt safe and unconstrained, but as I mingled with the huge swarms of people I began to realize that many of them were waiting in lines to enter grocery and clothing stores. I found out later that they were waiting to use their monthly coupons for food and clothing. All goods in Cuba are rationed, including fuels. The average citizen is allotted only 40 liters (about 10.5 gallons) of gasoline monthly. Taxi and bus drivers are given additional coupons based upon assigned tours. All tours like ours are state-controlled by Cubatours.

In spite of the large numbers of people on the Havana streets, I did not see anyone who looked hungry. No one asked for a handout. I was told that everyone had work. I also learned that health care as well as education through college are free. Cuba boasts the lowest stillbirth rate and the highest literacy rate in the West Indies.

Vehicle traffic was light, both in the city and on the highways. There were very few new automobiles, but there were lots of the old classics still running and in what seemed to be near mint condition. Most of these were Chevrolets, Chryslers, Dodges, and Oldsmobiles; they would be collectible in the United States.

I was also surprised to see so few smokers. I guess I expected to find everyone smoking cigars, but happily this was not the case. Although I found that a lot of Cuban youths smoked cigarettes, except for some of the old men of Havana and a few businessmen and military officers I encountered, hardly anyone still smokes the once famous Havana cigars.

I found two bookstores during my walk. Neither one was crowded, and I could immediately see why. The largest bookstore had fewer than three hundred titles, of which at least half were on social issues, many with a photograph of Castro on the cover, and the rest covered an assortment of other topics. Neither bookstore stocked any books about Cuba's natural history. The embargo has created serious shortages of almost every product imaginable. Arturo told me that his scientific society could no longer acquire paper to publish papers.

DAY SIX: MARCH 29

The destination for our last full day in Cuba was La Guira National Park in the Sierra de Guaniguanico, approximately two hours east of Havana. We turned off the expressway at the La Guira junction and proceeded through town to where we turned right again at the park entrance. We passed through huge stone gates, once the entrance to an estate visible to the left, and climbed into the foothills. The highest point in the park is only 2,300 feet elevation, but the relief seems much more, and the vegetation changes from a semi-evergreen to a pine forest. The road dead-ends at a rustic resort at the base of bold, rocky cliffs.

The plant life along the base of the cliffs is a two-tiered formation with a closed canopy. The mature trees averaged about 18 inches in diameter and possessed umbrella crowns. Lianas were abundant, but epiphytes, ferns, and mosses were scarce. There was an obvious shrub layer, but the ground vegetation was scanty.

Royal palms were fairly common, and many poked their heads above the surrounding canopy. Cecropia trees were common as well, especially at disturbed areas. Several large figs were present, including a species with numerous half-inch fruits. Mangos were intermixed with the native trees. Wild coffee and several malestoma shrubs seemed to dominate the lower tier.

This was the habitat of the endemic **Cuban Solitaire,** one of the finest songsters of the bird world. Almost immediately we heard its unmistakable songs emanating from the forest, but it took us almost an hour to locate a bird. The day was rather windy and so the solitaires were perched in the canopy, rather than at the treetops, as they normally would be. But when we finally discovered one, we all had excellent looks at it from a distance of 30 to 40 feet. We watched this plain-colored thrush sing a song of the most beautiful notes imaginable. Strangely, its most colorful feature was its orange-yellow mouthparts, visible only when it was feeding. We watched it consume several small figs.

We then began our search for our last expected Cuban specialty, the **Olive-capped Warbler.** This is a bird of the pine forests and is closely related to North America's Pine Warbler. We walked along the roadway, which was lined with Caribbean pines, and it wasn't long before we located warblers. Almost immediately we discovered an Olive-cap among the lower foliage and were able to study it for some time. We found it to be quite different from Bond's illustration; it had no black border below the bright yellow throat, and the yellow seemed to fade into the white belly. Also, the yellow color extended onto the neck and cheeks, which were capped by a rich olive color. We watched several Olive-caps among the pines, singing and chasing each other here and there. Their behavior reminded me very much of Pine Warblers.

We spent the rest of the morning exploring the park area, walking the roads and a few trails into the forest. Then we boarded our bus for our return trip to Havana. As the bus sped along the almost deserted highway, I could not help but compare Cuba with other West Indian countries I had visited.

Cuba is first and foremost a land of contradictions, from both a biological and sociological point of view. The fact that at least twenty species of birds have evolved on the island, even though it is so close to the North American continent, attests to its truly unique character. Are additional species, such as the Black-Hawk and Stygian Owl, soon to follow?

Although all the Cuban people I met were friendly and kind, like country people anywhere, there was an underlying uneasiness everywhere. Here is a country that boasts the highest literacy rate and lowest stillbirth rate in the West Indies, but yet its inhabitants must line up to buy everything from bread to shoes. When the people must begin to destroy their natural resources in order to cook and stay alive, especially when they have protected those areas until now, there is something dreadfully wrong.

There is a huge mural on the mezzanine wall of the Havana Libre Hotel. The mural was completed in 1979 to honor the twentieth anniversary of the

Cuban Revolution. It depicts an oxcart stacked with hay and various foods (fish and pineapples are most obvious) with revolutionaries hiding in the hay. Only their guns, poking out of the stack in all directions, are visible. The mural, it seems to me, is a fascinating symbol of Cuba's past glory. Although the mural is still bright and shiny (it is obviously well cared for), the hotel, like the Cuban infrastructure itself, was in disrepair. My room in the faded Havana Libre had no hot water, only miniature light bulbs (made in the USSR) in broken lamps, and a Cuban television set that provided only three channels.

There is much in Cuba for a naturalist to appreciate: its natural setting, its diverse wildlife, the kindness of its people. One can only hope that the creeping cancer that is starting to eat away at Cuba's natural resources can be stopped before it destroys them.

CHAPTER THREE

Dominican Republic

LAND OF CONTRASTS

Dominican Republic, more than any of the other Caribbean countries, is a land of contrasts. It contains the highest peak (Pico Duarte is 10,417 feet elevation) as well as the lowest elevation (Lago Enriquillo is 150 feet below sea level). Fourteen distinct natural environments occur within the country: marine estuaries and bays, beaches, marshes, freshwater streams and ponds, mangrove woodlands, littoral woodlands, savannas, deserts, cactus scrub, thorn forests, deciduous forests, semi-evergreen forests, montane rain forests, and pine forests. The island of Hispaniola, of which Dominican Republic is the major portion, possesses the greatest number of amphibians and reptiles in the West Indies and a grand total of twenty-three endemic bird species, second only to Jamaica.

Dominican Republic shares the island of Hispaniola (29,537 square miles) with Haiti, the impoverished nation that claims the western one-third of the island. Dominican Republic covers an area of 18,816 square miles, about the size of Vermont and New Hampshire combined, second in size in the West Indies only to Cuba at 44,218 square miles.

The eastern end of Dominican Republic is situated only 70 miles across Mona Passage from Puerto Rico. The island's northern shores are bounded by the Atlantic Ocean, and the southern shores are washed by the milder Caribbean Sea. The combined influence of the northern ocean and southern sea and the great contrast of topographic relief also create an extremely diverse climate. Conditions range from hot and arid to cold and wet. Desert landscapes prevail over much of the western lowlands, and rain forest exists in the southeast. The mountain highlands possess habitats that are similar to the uplands of the southern Appalachians in North America. Winters usually are dry, but two rainy periods occur: April to June and August to November. Annual rainfall varies from a low of 12 inches in the Enriquillo Valley to up to 75 inches in the central mountains.

The great physical and biological diversity of Dominican Republic makes it one of the most interesting islands, if not the most interesting island, of all the West Indies. For naturalists, it is a biological paradise.

WHERE TO BEGIN

The greatest assemblage of Dominican Republic's natural environments occurs within the southern Caribbean half of the island, and the highest diversity of habitats is concentrated within the southwest. Santo Domingo, therefore, is the most appropriate entry site for a visit to southwestern Dominican Republic. Las Americas International Airport, east of the city, provides daily air service from all the key North American cities, as well as San Juan, Puerto Rico. The city of Santo Domingo has many hotels, so finding accommodations there is never a problem. I have stayed at the Hotel Hispaniola and found it to be first-rate. It is located on Avenue Independencia, close to the sea and along the east-west highway. Old Town, the oldest colonial city in the New World (founded in 1498), is reasonably accessible as well. Actually, the original city was mostly destroyed in a 1930 hurricane, so "old" is somewhat of a misnomer. The Botanical Garden and Zoological Park, both worth visits, are located on the north side of the city. An additional incentive for staying at the Hotel Hispaniola is the nearby

Vescuvio Restaurant, which serves superb seafood and is within walking distance.

The highway west of Santo Domingo passes through a countryside that changes rapidly from rural to agricultural to a lush thorn forest, near Baní, that is dominated by acacia, mimosa, yucca, and cactus, including prickly-pear and pipe-organ cactus. Beyond Baní the landscape changes more gradually, but by Azua it has become true desert. The woody plants are shorter and more widely spaced, so there is less competition for available rainfall.

The only town with adequate accommodations within the entire southwest is Barahona. Located on the Bahía de Neiba, Barahona provides access to the coastal beaches and lush foothills, as well as the arid Enriquillo Valley and adjacent mountains. I have stayed at Barahona's Hotel Guarocuya on two different occasions. Food at the Guarocuya is fair to good; the La Rocca Restaurant, directly across the street, is good also. But the El Rancho Restaurant along the beach road at the opposite end of town is best.

DESERT LOWLANDS

Dawn in the desert, whether it is in southern Arizona, southwest Texas, northern Mexico, or southwest Dominican Republic, can be an exhilarating experience. Daylight comes suddenly with a burst of bird song. Once you experience the dawn chorus on the desert, you will want to enjoy it time and time again.

Houston Holder, a friend from the Virgin Islands, and I left the Guarocuya in the dark. We drove northwest for about an hour before we turned onto a little desert road, just west of Mella, that ended on a little hill overlooking the surrounding desert. A rosy glow was just beginning in the east as we climbed out of our rental car and breathed in the dry, cool atmosphere.

Almost immediately the mournful song of a Mourning Dove broke the silence. It was soon followed by other Mourning Doves, responding to their territorial urge. I also detected the "who-cooks-for-you" song of a lone White-winged Dove. Then Northern Mockingbirds began to sing. Their spirited songs vibrated across the landscape from every direction.

I suddenly realized that I was also listening to a *Myiarchus* flycatcher song that blended with the mockingbird's varied refrains. It took me a few more minutes to find the lone **Stolid Flycatcher** perched on a nearby acacia. This species of *Myiarchus* flycatcher was widespread in the Greater and Lesser Antilles until it was split into four separate species by the AOU: Stolid in

Jamaica and Hispaniola; La Sagra's in the Bahamas and Cuba; Puerto Rican in Puerto Rico and St. John; and Lesser Antillean in the Lesser Antilles.

The most common flycatcher that morning, however, was the **Gray Kingbird,** which also was contributing to the dawn chorus. In fact, Gray Kingbirds and Bananaquits were the most numerous of all the birds present. The loud "chichery" songs of Gray Kingbirds and the wheezy-trill songs of Bananaquits were all around us as the sun poked its red head above the horizon.

A hummingbird was feeding at a flowering vine next to a Bananaquit. Through binoculars I could see that it was a reasonably large hummer with a deep green back and throat and a bluish-black front and wings; a male **Antillean Mango.** I followed it from flower to flower until I could see the chestnut color on its tail that is described in James Bond's *Birds of the West Indies.* This same species frequents similar habitats in Puerto Rico.

Two larger birds suddenly appeared out of the same vine-covered shrub. They paused in the open, and I could clearly see their contrasting olive backs, gray collars, and black-and-white heads; a pair of **Black-crowned Palm-Tanagers,** one of Hispaniola's most common endemics. It is locally known as *cuatro ojos,* or four-eyes, referring to the white spots on both sides of its forehead that give it the appearance of possessing an extra pair of eyes.

Alexander Wetmore and Bradshaw Swales, in their 1931 Smithsonian Institution Bulletin, *The Birds of Haiti and the Dominican Republic,* summarized Hispaniolan bird life and described the Black-crowned Palm-Tanager thus:

> This palm-tanager inhabits thickets of growth of forest in both humid and arid sections. It is found usually in fairly heavy cover where it moves about in a slow and leisurely manner, occasionally twitching its tail, hopping over the trunks and larger limbs of the trees where it clings to the rough bark as easily as a pine warbler or black and white warbler, holding with strong feet and occasionally fluttering the wings slightly to help it over some difficult spots.

The most fascinating bird that morning on the desert was the tiny **Broadbilled Tody.** We found a pair of these endemics fly-catching among the shrubs at the base of our little desert hill. I was first attracted to them by their very distinct calls, a rather plaintive "terp-terp-terp." Their "terp" notes are similar to all the other todies, although "all the other" may be a little strong; there are only five tody species in the entire world. But all are restricted to

Broad-billed Tody

the Greater Antilles. What is most interesting, and an excellent indication of Hispaniola's biological diversity, is that two of the five species occur only on Hispaniola. Jamaica, Cuba, and Puerto Rico have one species each.

Todies are some of the most appealing of all birds. First, they are tiny; some tropical hummingbirds are larger. Second, they possess a really unique shape: a plump body with a long bill and a short tail; the bill and tail are about equal in length. Third, they all possess an emerald-green back and bright red throat and lower mandibles. Fourth, todies dig nest holes in dirt banks like kingfishers and motmots. Finally, their feeding behavior is fascinating to watch.

Feeding todies utilize open perches in dense vegetation that can range from near ground-level to the highest branches in the canopy. Their emerald-green back makes them almost impossible to detect among the green foliage. They perch with their tail pointed down and their large bill pointed upward at a 45-degree angle. They usually sit perfectly still except for some side-to-side head movement while searching for prey. They will suddenly fly out or straight upward to take an insect on the wing or off the underside of a leaf. There is an audible snap of their bill as they capture their prey. They then perch and consume their catch. Soon their bill is back at a 45-degree angle; they are watching for their next snack.

That desert morning in Dominican Republic was reminiscent of many other mornings I had spent in the Sonoran and Chihuahuan Deserts of the American Southwest and Mexico. Mourning and White-winged Doves, Common Ground-Doves, American Kestrels, and Northern Mockingbirds are common to all three deserts. But there are some fascinating analogs. In Dominican Republic, Gray Kingbirds replace Cassin's Kingbirds of the southwestern United States; Stolid Flycatchers replace Ash-throated and Brown-crested Flycatchers; Hispaniolan Woodpeckers replace Ladder-backed and Gila Woodpeckers; and Antillean Mangos replace Costa's and Black-chinned Hummingbirds. Biological analogs like these are commonplace in nature, but they are not always so obvious. It makes one appreciate the fascinating complexity of our natural world.

LAGO ENRIQUILLO

Lago Enriquillo is one of the great natural wonders of the West Indies. The lake lies within a long "trench" that stretches from Haiti's Cul-de-Cas Plain eastward to Bahía de Neiba at Barahona, a total distance of about 120 miles. This deep valley is an ancient sea channel that once separated southwestern Hispaniola from the "main" island. Evidence of its long submergence can be found throughout the region in its ancient coral- and shell-strewn sands. Two huge lakes still exist, Haiti's Etang Saumâtre and Dominican Republic's Lago Enriquillo. Lago Enriquillo is the largest lake in all the West Indies. More than twice the size of Etang Saumâtre, it is approximately 55 miles long and up to 8 miles wide. It is totally below sea level and is often the consistency of concentrated brine, varying from 40 to 90 parts salt per million. The lake is fed by seasonal streams, and the shoreline includes numerous wetlands.

One of the most outstanding features of Lago Enriquillo is its population of Greater Flamingos. One to six dozen of these long-legged waders frequent the south shore, often feeding near a little side road that skirts the lake for a couple of miles. The flamingos' salmon-red color, long legs and neck, and heavy, curved bill make them easy to identify even at a considerable distance. In flight, their neck and legs are fully extended, giving them an obviously long and lean appearance.

The feeding behavior of flamingos is unique. They actually forage with their bill inverted so that the hinged upper mandible is on the bottom. The birds swing their bill in a complete circle. Water and food are taken in by a pumping action of the throat that also forces water out through the filtering mechanism of the bill. Tiny brine shrimp and other crustaceans, mollusks, insects, fish, and even tiny aquatic plants are consumed.

Lago Enriquillo provides the perfect habitat for these huge creatures. Ralph Palmer, in *Handbook of North American Birds Volume 1*, described the flamingos' preferred habitat as "isolated, remote, desert-like. . . . Typical setting is a shallow lake of high salinity, in a desolate region, the area virtually uninhabited except by Greater Flamingos and a few small creatures capable of dwelling where extremes in salinity and temperature are the rule."

The vicinity of Lago Enriquillo is just that, a place where salinity and high temperatures are the rule. However, at least during the wintertime, there often are more than a "few small creatures" present along the shoreline. In November we found several Killdeer, Semipalmated Sandpipers, Willets, and Lesser Yellowlegs and a few wading birds, including Great Blue and Tricolored Herons and Snowy Egrets. We saw both Royal and Caspian Terns flying over the lake, and a family of Black-cowled Orioles were chasing each other around the shrubbery along the shore.

The main highway, little more than a dirt track between Duverge and Jimaní, completely circles the lake, a total of about 115 miles. The town of Jimaní lies at the westernmost end of the lake and serves as the principal port of entry from Haiti. Houston and I stayed one night at the Jimaní Hotel and left early the next morning after a long, bug-infested night that ranks as one of my worst experiences ever.

Farther on is the village of La Descubierta, a significant date-growing area. The rare **Ridgway's Hawk** had been reported in the area a few weeks earlier, so we spent several hours searching the area beyond La Descubierta for this small *Buteo*, but to no avail. We later found one of these endemic and declining hawks near Parque Nacional de Este on the southeastern corner of the island.

We did find several other birds of interest near La Descubierta. The abundant date and coconut palms along the lakeshore provide a green oasis that attracts a lot of wildlife. Most obvious were the hundreds of **Antillean Palm Swifts**. These little black-and-white birds nest on the palms, and their soft "chippering" calls literally filled the air. Bond explains that the species nests in colonies in the palms: "Nest composed of soft materials cemented together with saliva, situated in a hollow palm spathe or attached to the underside of a drooping frond; globular in shape with entrance near the bottom." Although we had seen this bird throughout the trip, it was nowhere as abundant as it was about the palm groves at La Descubierta.

Another widespread Hispaniolan species that we found there was the endemic **Palmchat**. This bird is truly unique; it is the world's only representative of the family Dulidae. It is most closely related to waxwings and silky-flycatchers, according to its placement in the AOU *Check-list of North American Birds*. Bond described the Palmchat as "gregarious and feeds on berries and on blossoms of various flowering plants." It possesses gray-olive to olive-brown upperparts and buff-white underparts with bold, dusky streaks.

I was greatly impressed with the Palmchat's nest. It is a bushel basket–size pile of sticks built near the top of a tall palm tree. The stick nest forms an apartment that is shared by three or more pairs of Palmchats, each pair with its own separate compartment. Wetmore and Swales examined several nests and provided the following description:

> In each unit a tunnel led to a central chamber 100 to 125 mm [4–5 in.] across with the bottom well filled with fine shreds of bark and other soft materials to form a distinct cup. Though each nest was a separate unit with its own portal to the exterior there were roughly defined channels or passages running through the interlacing twigs at the top of the nests that could permit the birds to creep about under cover. The separate nests were very compact so that it was necessary to cut and break away the twigs to get at the interior. Subsequent examination of a number of other completed nests indicated that this was the normal type of construction, each communal structure consisting of several compartments opening separately to the outside. The twigs used in construction were usually slightly smaller in diameter than a lead pencil and were dead twigs of light wood, coffee and orange twigs being usual in the lowlands.

Palmchats are most abundant in the lowlands, but they also range into the mountains to the lower edge of the pines. On one late March trip into the Sierra de Baoruco, my wife, Betty, and I discovered a Palmchat nest in a palm tree just below El Aguacate (3,600 feet elevation). At least twenty Palmchats were present at the "apartment," as well as a pair of **Greater Antillean Grackles.** The larger grackles seemed to be equally at home there and were undisturbed by the active nest builders. The grackles' use of Palmchat nests was also observed by Wetmore and Swales, who pointed out that Abbot (an early-day ornithologist) had also found the nest of a grackle tacked onto the side of a Palmchat nest.

Lago Enriquillo is impressive for several reasons. It not only is outstanding biologically, but its physical position within a deep basin bordered by two high mountain ranges is equally impressive. To the north is the Sierra de Neiba, a mountain range that is mostly Haitian but extends east at least to the Río Yaque del Sur in Dominican Republic. According to Annabelle Dod, a naturalist who wrote the most recent book on Dominican Republic birds, "the Sierra de Neiba habitat is practically destroyed due to bad agricultural practices." Houston and I drove 24 miles into these mountains searching for natural habitats but found only pastures and remnants of burned-over forests.

To the south of Lago Enriquillo is the Sierra de Baoruco, another range shared with Haiti. The high point of the Sierra de Baoruco is Morne La Selle, which rises to 8,793 feet above sea level. The Dominican Republic portion of the range still retains considerable montane forest habitat. This area contains the greatest avian diversity still remaining in the country. It is reasonably accessible.

THE SIERRA DE BAORUCO

The town of Duverge, located on the main roadway about 40 miles west of Barahona, has no public overnight accommodations, but it does possess a gas station. It also contains the junction of the side road into the Sierra de Baoruco. At the edge of town, just before the road begins a steep climb onto the first plateau, is a small hydroelectric power plant at a lovely stream that is worth a short stop. We found a Burrowing Owl, Loggerhead Kingbirds, Black-crowned Palm-Tanagers, and Bananaquits there in November.

The gravel road runs through a rather extensive thorn forest for approximately 5 miles before arriving at the farming village of Puerto Escondido. The forest contains acacias, mimosas, agaves, cactuses, the red-barked gumbo limbo, and a little palm with a bulbous lower trunk.

Puerto Escondido Valley is an agricultural center with extensive flatlands that usually are bright green with vegetables and fruits. Rows of tall, stately royal palms line the irrigation ditches. Above the valley are the high ridges of the Sierra de Baoruco, an outstanding backdrop to the lush cultivated fields.

Approximately 5 miles beyond Puerto Escondido, beyond the irrigated fields, the road begins a steady climb into a long canyon. In late March I spent a full morning exploring the thorn forest along the lower canyon. Birds were singing vigorously; courting behavior was robust. Doves and pigeons were especially active. From one stop I recorded several Scaly-naped and Plain Pigeons, White-winged and Mourning Doves, and Common Ground-Doves. A lone Ruddy Quail-Dove sang a mournful "cooooo," descending slightly in pitch, that resounded from the wooded slope.

The songs of **Antillean Euphonias** were common, as well. Close up, their dark violet chin and throat, a special feature of the Hispaniolan race, were obvious. Wetmore and Swales provides us with the following description of the species: "A tiny bird being only 120 to 125 mm [4.5–5 in.] long. The male is deep steel blue on wings, tail, back, and throat, and sides of head, light blue on crown and hindneck, and orange yellow on rump, forehead, and underparts." The female is overall greenish to yellow color. This species was split by the AOU from the Blue-hooded Euphonia, the brighter, more boldly marked Mexican form. However, like their Mexican cousins, the Antillean birds feed almost exclusively on mistletoe berries.

Two even smaller birds were also present that morning: the Hispaniolan Emerald and the **Vervain Hummingbird.** The Vervain Hummingbird is the second smallest bird in all the West Indies (Cuba's Bee Hummingbird is the smallest). A lone male Vervain (its name was derived from its use of vervain plants) was perched on the very top of an acacia and singing a squeaky song that was surprisingly loud for such a tiny songster.

The bird of the morning, however, was a **Bay-breasted Cuckoo,** one of three cuckoo species present in the thorn forest habitat. The more common Mangrove Cuckoo and Hispaniolan Lizard-Cuckoo were also present, but I had somehow missed finding the more colorful Bay-breasted Cuckoo on my previous trip. But there it was, with its deep reddish-brown throat, breast, and belly, russet wing-patches, and long, barred tail. It was never in the open very long, but I watched it creep around the branches and foliage as if it were attempting to stay out of view. Nor did I detect any song or call. Its call reportedly sounds like the hoarse croaking of a frog.

Other specialty birds found in the thorn forest that day included Hispaniolan Parrot and Parakeet, Hispaniolan Trogon, Narrow-billed Tody, Hispaniolan Woodpecker, Greater Antillean Pewee, Red-legged Thrush,

Palmchat, Flat-billed and Black-whiskered Vireos, Black-crowned Palm-Tanager, and Greater Antillean Bullfinch.

The endemic **Flat-billed Vireo** was the most interesting of the group. It is one of the White-eyed Vireo look-alikes but with a very different song, more of a clear "wit wit wit wit" whistle, like a North American titmouse. Its bill is wide at the base, like Mexico's Eye-ringed Flatbill. It did, however, possess the vireo behavior of being rather slow and methodical.

Beyond the thorn forest is Aguacate, situated at the head of a long canyon that, near the top, is crowded with deciduous forest vegetation, forming a canopy over the rocky roadway. Aguacate is an army camp that consists of a single headquarters building and a dozen or so small barracks. The Haitian border is nearby, and the camp serves as a control point for emigration into Dominican Republic. We stopped there briefly to inform the commanding officer of our intentions. The army officers were always cordial and understanding when told about our plans to visit the highlands to find some of the region's unique wildlife.

Beyond Aguacate the roadway continues to climb higher into the mountains, skirting the upper edges of steep barrancas. Only a short distance above Aguacate we found ourselves in a pine forest. These were West Indian pines, a species that occurs only on Hispaniola and Cuba. They are tall, stately trees, growing in stands amidst clumps of long-stemmed Stipa grasses or scattered along the edge of the montane rain forest, a distinct wet forest habitat filling the protected barrancas.

Houston and I walked along the roadway admiring the vegetation and searching for wildlife. Almost immediately we heard Pine Warblers singing in the pines. A flock of Antillean Siskins were evident, as well. High overhead were two **Golden Swallows,** a West Indian species that has declined dramatically in recent years. Then directly ahead of us, fly-catching over the pine needle–clad roadway, was a lone **Greater Antillean Pewee.** We watched it only briefly before it flew up the slope out of sight.

The **Antillean Siskin,** locally known as *canario* or *siguita amarilla*, is endemic to the island of Hispaniola. The male is a lovely little bird with an all-black head and a yellow chest, rump, and bill. It is most often located in mountain pine forests by its soft "chut-chut" or "e-see-ip" calls. During the breeding season the males also have a "low chattering trill," according to James Bond.

We continued up the roadway to where we were skirting the upper edge of the deep barranca; the entire western slope was a lush forest, while the drier south slope was dominated by pines. It was there that we first heard the flutelike songs of **Rufous-throated Solitaires.** We eventually saw several of these gray birds with reddish-brown throats. The locals call this bird *jilguero*, Spanish for "musician," because of its wonderfully varied but ventriloquistic songs.

In November North American warblers were also present in small numbers scattered throughout the forest. Black-throated Blues were most numerous, but we also found a few Prairie, Black-and-white, and Cape May Warblers, as well as a lone male Wilson's Warbler. The most numerous resident bird of this area was the endemic **Green-tailed Ground Warbler.** Although it is not an outstandingly colorful species, it is nevertheless a gorgeous bird. It is mostly gray to slate-greenish color on top and whitish underneath, but it has a bright red eye surrounded by a broken white eye-ring. It is one of the most personable creatures in the bird world. Wetmore and Swales described its mannerisms very well:

> These birds creep and clamber about in the dripping foliage of moss grown thickets or dense clumps of ferns, moving rather slowly, usually near the ground, but at times coming to feed among the branches above the denser growth. Their call is a low complaining "chewp, chewp" heard only when within a short distance. At times they show some curiosity and come near at hand to look at a human intruder. The long tail gives them a tilting flight in the short distances that they cover on the wing.

Another Hispaniolan specialty found there was the **White-winged Warbler.** It is another attractive bird, much more so than depicted in Bond. Its back and wings are greenish color, except for the prominent white wing-markings. Its head is gray except for black lores and a distinct white spot on either side of the forehead. The underparts are snowy white.

A **Chat Tanager** suddenly flew across the roadway from one clump of dense vegetation to another. I knew it immediately even though I had never seen one before; it is a distinctly marked bird. I tried to locate it in the heavy shrubbery with no success and finally made a low spishing sound, trying to attract it into the open. It immediately responded, coming into full view, allowing me to see it very clearly. For almost five minutes, every time it seemed ready to leave, I was able to keep it nearby with low spishing sounds. I was surprised that it maintained an interest for so long; it generally is considered to be a shy and elusive bird.

The one big miss on my November trip into the Sierra de Baoruca was the La Selle Thrush, a resident only of the "high ridge of Morne La Selle, chiefly above 4,500 feet," according to Bond. It necessitated a return visit there the following March.

La Selle Thrush

The upper Sierra de Baoruca in March was even more alive with birds. While the November birds were scattered, many of the March birds roamed together in parties through the forest. Once a party was found, it was then a matter of picking out those species of special interest. My March trip report stated:

> Three very distinct bird parties were detected during an extensive search at 5,000 to 6,000 feet elevation. In each case, the parties were dominated by White-winged Warblers and Green-tailed Ground Warblers. Other party members included Hispaniolan Emeralds, Black-throated Blue and Black-and-white Warblers, Antillean Euphonias, Stripe-headed Tanagers, Chat Tanagers, and Greater Antillean Bullfinches. Hispaniolan Trogons, Narrow-billed Todies, and Hispaniolan Woodpeckers were seen nearby, but I am not sure if they were integral members of the parties.

It wasn't until we were well past Aguacate by about 4 miles that I detected my first **La Selle Thrush.** Its song was coming from the forested slope above the roadway, a hundred feet or so beyond where I had stopped to listen. It was a beautiful melody, obviously a thrush but very deliberate in its delivery. Then it was silent. I waited for it to start singing again, but it remained silent. Farther away I could hear a solitaire, and other bird songs were audible below the roadway. But I was intent on finding the one songbird that had so far eluded me.

I walked very slowly up the roadway to about where I thought the first thrush had been singing. I stopped and waited, hoping that it would sing again or give itself away by a chip. But nothing happened. Finally, I made a soft but rather loud Hermit Thrush–like chip-whistle. Once again. There was movement in the adjacent shrubbery; something had been attracted by my whistle. I tried it again. Suddenly, less than 50 feet away, in full view, was a La Selle Thrush. What a gorgeous bird! It sat there, very still and cautious, and allowed me to observe it through my binoculars. It remained motionless for twenty to thirty seconds, and then it flew across the road, about 30 feet from me, and disappeared into the tangle of vegetation.

It undoubtedly was the most beautiful thrush I had ever seen. Maybe it was because it had been so hard to find, but nevertheless, it was a startling bird. The sunlight was perfect to highlight its orange-red breast and sides, which contrasted with its snow-white belly and crissum. Its wings, back, and head were coal-black, and the white streaks on its throat were obvious. Its eye-ring was a light orange color, and its bill was reddish-orange.

I couldn't locate it again, although I heard it singing off and on throughout the day. But somehow that one very good observation of the La Selle Thrush was enough. It seemed to fully satisfy my need to observe this unique bird and experience Dominican Republic's extraordinary highlands. For me, the La Selle Thrush exemplified the richness and diversity of the entire country.

CHAPTER FOUR

Puerto Rico

NORTH AMERICA'S ONLY TROPICAL FOREST

Hurricane Hugo swept across the Caribbean and smashed into Puerto Rico on the morning of September 19, 1989. The 100-plus-mile-per-hour winds destroyed thousands of homes and other structures, affecting every living thing on that island of 3,435 square miles. An anemometer reading of a wind gust to 110 knots (126.5 miles per hour) was reported from the ship *Night Cap* located in Culebra Harbor just before the storm hit land. There were no data available for wind gusts in the interior. Some estimates claim winds in excess of 200 miles per hour in the Luquillo Mountains, home of the Caribbean National Forest. Fifteen percent of the forest trees there were felled or damaged. Much of the forest canopy was eliminated, exposing some of the forest floor to sunlight for the first time in decades.

As a direct result of Hugo, "seeds of plants and trees that need the sun have germinated and are growing," according to Ariel Lugo, director of the U.S. Forest Service's Institute of Tropical Forestry. "Thanks to the hurricane, we are seeing a far richer diversity of [plant] species." Ten species of trees had disappeared during the last forty years. "The hurricane that caused an estimated $5.2 million damage to the forest has also rejuvenated the forest. It's nature's way," he added.

The forest's wildlife, on the other hand, at least in the short term, did not fare as well. The principal concern was for the rare and endangered birds, especially the **Puerto Rican Parrot.** Prior to the storm, there were ninety-seven remaining individuals, forty-six in the wild and fifty-one in a captive breeding program housed in a World War II bunker. Although none of the captive birds were killed, twenty-three of the forty-six wild birds disappeared and were considered lost to the storm.

The Puerto Rican Parrot population was at about 1,000,000 when the first Europeans arrived on the island in the fifteenth century. Since then, deforestation for agriculture, grazing, and developments, capturing of birds for the pet trade, and increased predation have severely reduced the parrot population. Devastating hurricanes in 1928, 1932, and 1972 undoubtedly added to their decline. The parrot population was at an all-time low of thirteen birds in the mid-1970s. Greater protection and a captive breeding program, begun in 1968, literally saved the birds from extinction. Fourteen chicks were fostered into wild bird nests between 1979 and 1984. Now, Hurricane Hugo has created yet another crisis for the Puerto Rican Parrot. It is too soon to predict its future. However, breeding activity in 1992, 1993, and 1994 produced forty-seven fledglings from wild nests and the Luquillo Aviary. An excellent summary of the parrot's history, causes of its decline, and the conservation program developed to save it from extinction is discussed by James Wiley in his 1985 chapter, "Bird Conservation in the Caribbean," in *Bird Conservation*.

THE LUQUILLO FOREST

The winding roadway (Highway 191) above the little town of Palmer into the Luquillo highlands provides a remarkable display of biological diversity. It undoubtedly is one of the most beautiful drives in all the West Indies. It is like driving through a huge tropical greenhouse. Scattered stands of tall bamboo shade the roadway, which passes through a gallery rain forest. Impatiens, with their beautiful pink and red blossoms, dominate the roadsides. Highway 191 passes through four distinct habitat types (lower montane rain forest, upper montane rain forest, palm forest, and elfin woodland), each providing its own special variety of flora and fauna and generally divided by altitude and exposure.

Starting at Palmer and extending upward to about 2,000 feet elevation, which is the upper edge of the cloud condensation level, is a lower montane rain forest. This forest is locally called tabonuco type, due to the dominant tree species—tabonuco—found there. Tabonuco is a tall forest tree that may reach 100 feet in height; its white trunk is very straight and without branches for the lower half of its height. Tabonucos once dominated the lowlands. However, due to their value as timber trees, combined with clearing for agricultural lands, they have been much reduced. The remaining individuals, however, still attest to the tree's earlier importance. Frank Wadsworth (1951), in describing forest management in the Luquillo Forest, stated that of the 168 tree species he found in that zone, tabonucos were most important and "often comprised as much as 35 percent of the forest canopy." Ewel and Whitmore (1973) also pointed out that this forest forms "a dark, complete canopy at about 20 m [66 ft.]" height.

Other dominant trees of the lower montane rain forest are cacao-motillo and bulletwood. Cacao-motillo possesses the typical characteristics of rain forest species, especially the great spreading buttress roots useful for supporting large trees in wet soils. The sierra palm and trumpet-tree also are abundant, and numerous epiphytes, vines, and arborescent ferns abound.

Luquillo's upper montane rain forest starts just above the lower forest and runs up the slopes to about 3,000 feet elevation. It too is dominated by a single tree, the palo colorado, a red-barked canopy tree. However, within its broader range its characteristics vary considerably. In the swamps of the southeastern United States, for instance, it is a short tree or shrub. But in the Luquillo Mountains it grows to 100 feet, can have a circumference of 20 feet, and can possess a great crown. Palo colorado is vitally important to the Luquillo ecosystem because it often has a hollow trunk, providing principal nesting sites for Puerto Rican Parrots.

Other common tree species in the upper montane rain forest include sierra palm, lechecillo (it provides fruit in March and April that is important for breeding parrots), caimitollo, husillo, and nemoca. This zone is dominated by open-crowned trees that resemble flattened bouquets. Their "leaves tend to be coriaceous [leathery] and dark, giving the canopy a brownish or even reddish cast," according to Wadsworth, who found only fifty-three tree species in this forest type. Similarities to the tabonuco forest were further discussed by Brown and colleagues in a 1983 Institute of Tropical Forestry publication: "Stem density is smaller, thicker and more coriaceous. Buttress roots are less common, but vines and epiphytic growth more so. Soils are covered by thick surface networks of roots and herbaceous; groundcover may be greater than in the tabonuco forest." On steep slopes with wet soils, the sierra palm often becomes so numerous that it forms a distinct palm forest or palm-brake habitat. Herbs, vines, and epiphytes are relatively scarce in this community.

Above approximately 3,000 feet elevation, especially along the ridges and summits, is an elfin woodland, characterized by dense stands of stunted and contorted small trees and shrubs. This habitat is often bathed in clouds, resulting in a cloud forest–like environment complete with an abundance of mosses and bryophytes and many bromeliads that grow on the ground as well as on the woody vegetation. Brown and colleagues reported that on Pico del Oeste the three most common elfin woodland plants "were an herb (*Pilea krugii*), followed by a semi-woody plant (*Wallenia yunquensis*), and a woody canopy plant called hurillo." Tree ferns are also common.

To me the elfin woodland community is the most fascinating part of the Luquillo Mountains. A walk into this misty green environment can be a surrealistic experience; it is like visiting some distant and imaginary planet. The El Toro Trail, which starts at km 13.3 on Highway 191, provides access to the upper ridges en route to El Toro Peak, where there is a superb view in every direction.

A total of 28,000 acres of the Luquillo Mountains were placed under U.S. Forest Service management as the Caribbean National Forest in 1917. Prior to that time, portions of the forest were protected under the Spanish Crown from as early as 1860. It became the first forest reserve in the New World in 1837. When Puerto Rico became part of the United States in 1898, it was again proclaimed a forest reserve. Today it represents the only tropical forest in the U.S. Forest System. The national forest is usually called El Yunque, after the highest peak in the Luquillo Mountains, but most Puerto Ricans refer to the area simply as "the rain forest."

LUQUILLO FOREST BIRD LIFE

Puerto Rico's elfin woodlands are home to one of the rarest of all West Indian birds, the **Elfin Woods Warbler.** It is locally known as *reinita de bosque enano,* or "little dwarf queen of the forest," and its scientific name is *Dendroica angelae.*

The Elfin Woods Warbler has the distinction of being the last bird species to be discovered in all the West Indies. Herbert Raffaele discussed this finding in his book, *A Guide to the Birds of Puerto Rico and the Virgin Islands*, thus:

> It is no doubt a combination of this bird's great activity, well concealed habitat, restricted range, and similarity to the common Black-and-white Warbler that allowed it to go undiscovered by science a full 45 years longer than any other bird species in the West Indies. In fact, Drs. Cameron and Kay Kepler, who discovered the bird in 1971, had resided and worked extensively in the Luquillo Mountains for over two years before they were certain that they had encountered a new species.

The elusiveness of the Elfin Woods Warbler is indeed one of the reasons it was not identified for so many years. Although the birds often join bird parties that move slowly through the canopy, Elfin Woods Warblers are rarely still. They move at breakneck speeds from one branch to another, seldom visible for long enough to allow a good sighting. They are smaller than the look-alike Black-and-white Warbler and possess a completely black crown, thin white stripes above the eyes, and an incomplete eye-ring. Rather than searching for insects by creeping over the tree trunks and branches like the Black-and-white, they glean for insects at the end of smaller branches and on leaves.

Other bird species within the elfin woodland bird parties usually include Bananaquits, Puerto Rican and Stripe-headed Tanagers, Puerto Rican Bullfinches, Puerto Rican Todies, and Puerto Rican Woodpeckers. In winter, Black-and-white and Black-throated Blue Warblers and American Redstarts are almost always present, as well.

Greater numbers of Luquillo Forest birds can be found at somewhat lower elevations, especially within the palo colorado forest. I have had the most success in finding birds in the vicinity of the El Yunque picnic area. Arriving there at dawn, before clean-up crews and tourists arrive, is a must for finding the **Puerto Rican Screech-Owl.** Listen for its tremulous trills. It also has a wide variety of other songs and calls, ranging from loud screeches to whinnies and sighs. However, the owls must be reasonably close by to hear them well, because the other night sounds, especially the incessant songs of the Coqui frogs, can be overwhelming. The tiny Coqui frog (*Eleutherodactylus coqui*) is endemic to Puerto Rico and the Virgin Islands. On Puerto Rico it is common everywhere except in the most arid parts of the island.

The dawn bird chorus from midelevation roadsides can include several of Puerto Rico's twelve single-island endemics. The loud cardinal-like whistling notes of the **Puerto Rican Bullfinch** usually are heard first. The rather sharp and vigorous "chewp" calls, repeated over and over, come from the **Puerto Rican Tanager**. I have also heard it sing a beautiful warbling song during the breeding season. The rolling "wek-wek-wek-wek" call is the **Puerto Rican Woodpecker.** It often can be found at dawn, perched in the open on the upper trunk of an adjacent trumpet-tree. From the nearby brushy edge of the forest, you can hear the harsh "cherek" call of the **Puerto Rican Tody.** It may be hard to find at first, but it is well worth the search. Puerto Rico's tody is one of only five members of the unique West Indian family Todidae. (See Chapter 3 on the Dominican Republic for a discussion of these fascinating birds.)

Two endemic hummingbirds are usually part of the early morning action at flowering roadside plants. The **Puerto Rican Emerald** is the most common of the two, and it is often detected first by a series of "tic" calls and a rapid trill that it emits in flight. The second hummer—the larger **Green Mango**—is less common in the mountains, but I have seen it several times at the picnic parking lot. Besides these endemics, the Puerto Rican form of Broad-winged Hawk can usually be found there, as well. **Scaly-naped Pigeons** are common as they streak from one site to another along the upper ridges. Once the day warms and thermals rise above the slopes, Puerto Rico's Sharp-shinned Hawk (another unique subspecies), Black Swifts, and Caribbean Martins are likely to put in an appearance.

I also have seen the endemic **Puerto Rican Lizard-Cuckoo** near the parking lot, but it is more common at lower elevations, such as at the Yokahu Tower and Catalina Field Office area. It is one of Puerto Rico's most remarkable birds. Somehow the lizard-cuckoo, a member of the unique West Indian genus *Saurothera*, epitomizes West Indian birds better than any other. David Lack, in discussing Caribbean cuckoos in *Island Biology Illustrated by the Land Birds of Jamaica*, pointed out that "this endemic Antillean genus is closest in appearance to *Coccyzus* [Yellow-billed and Mangrove Cuckoos], less close to *Hyetornis* [Chestnut-bellied and Bay-breasted Cuckoos] or *Piaya* [Squirrel and Little Cuckoos], and the beak is longer than in any of the others." As its name implies, it preys on lizards. Its behavior is slow and methodical and so it is easily overlooked.

The local name for the Puerto Rican Lizard-Cuckoo is *pájaro bobo mayor*, or "greater dunce bird." Raffaele provides us with the best description of its strange voice: "An emphatic 'ka-ka-ka-ka,' etc., of long duration gradually accelerating and becoming louder, sometimes with altered syllables at the end. It also gives soft 'caws' and other call notes." A birding

Puerto Rican Lizard-Cuckoo

trip to Puerto Rico would not be successful without experiencing this fascinating species.

GUÁNICA FOREST RESERVE

Southwestern Puerto Rico is much drier than the eastern portion of the island. The southwestern corner lies in the rain shadow of Puerto Rico's Cordillera Central. Therefore, a visit to that portion of the island is an absolute necessity for naturalists. The best place to experience the more arid habitats is at Guánica Forest Reserve. The flora and fauna there are not only different from those in the eastern highlands, but according to a comparative study by Cameron and Kay Kepler, bird diversity and populations are more than three times greater than in the Luquillo Forest. The Keplers reported that twenty-two Guánica Forest birds do not occur in Luquillo, while only six Luquillo birds were not found at Guánica.

The Guánica Forest contains three distinct vegetation types, according to Ariel Lugo and his coauthors of a 1978 paper on Puerto Rico's subtropical dry forests: upland deciduous forest, semi-evergreen forest, and scrub forest. Some of the characteristics of this area include the fact that the entire southwestern portion of the reserve is underlaid with limestone soils, there is no standing or running fresh water, and the forest canopy rarely exceeds 20 feet; sunlight is able to penetrate to the ground in most areas. Cactuses, especially pricklypear, cholla, and pipe-organ, are present and most abundant along south-facing slopes.

Access into the Guánica Preserve is limited to two dead-end driving routes. The lowland route (Highway 333) follows the coastline beyond the town of Guánica, providing access to the scrub forest. The northern access route (Highway 334) transects the semi-evergreen and upland deciduous forests. Both of these areas are usually hot and dry during midday, so exploration should be undertaken during the cooler morning hours. The upland area possesses several good trails that can be taken as loop routes.

The Guánica Forest habitats must be perfect for Puerto Rican Lizard-Cuckoos. When this species cannot be located anywhere else, the area around the preserve headquarters has always produced good observations of this amazing creature. This area also is the best bet for another single-island endemic, one that was thought to be extinct for more than seventy years, the **Puerto Rican Nightjar.** This Caprimulgid was rediscovered in the Guánica Forest by George Reynard and Ricardo Cotte in 1961. Reynard's 1962 paper in *Living Bird*, "The Rediscovery of the Puerto Rican Whip-poor-will," is well worth reading. A follow-up study in the Guánica

Forest by the Keplers revealed that the population consisted of four to five hundred pairs in an area they estimated as only 3 percent of the bird's original range. In 1988 Francisco Vilella, while a graduate student at Louisiana State University, found that the species was reasonably secure, with an estimated population of about two hundred birds. However, this remnant population continues to be threatened. The proposed development of petrochemical refineries at nearby Guayanilla and major resorts at Guánica would undoubtedly affect the species.

Reynard was curious why the bird had survived at all. He wrote:

> It is only conjecture at this point, but two reasons may be considered: First, the character of the habitat, so uninviting with its tangled, thorny undergrowth and small trees, its limited rain, and its few roads, added to the fact that it was in a forest preserve, definitely resulted in a minimum of human disturbance. Second, the thin cover of only dry leaves and practically no refuse may have limited such possible predators as mongoose and rats.

The dry forests of Guánica are a favorite habitat for yet another of Puerto Rico's endemic birds, the **Puerto Rican Vireo.** This species is not unlike the White-eyed Vireo of the eastern United States; its song is very similar and it also has the same pugnacious character. Its song has provided it with the local Puerto Rican name, Julian Chi-vi. Like most vireos, it is reasonably easy to attract for a close look with low spishing or squeaking sounds. On one occasion, a bird that I had attracted to within a few feet scolded me in a wrenlike chatter for several minutes. Its appearance, however, except for its similar size, is quite different from the White-eyed Vireo. It lacks the white eye, yellow spectacle, and wing bars; instead it is rather drab, grayish brown above and lighter gray below with a yellowish wash on its belly.

Southwestern Puerto Rico has several other bird species of interest to naturalists because of their existence on only a few West Indian islands. These include Antillean Mango, Loggerhead Kingbird, Puerto Rican Flycatcher, Lesser Antillean Pewee, Red-legged Thrush, Adelaide's Warbler, Troupial, Antillean Euphonia, and Greater Antillean Grackle. All of these birds occur in the Guánica Preserve, but a few are more abundant within the scrub forest of the lowlands.

Highway 333 extends beyond Guánica (the town) for approximately 10 miles, following the shore of the bay and seacoast to a large parking area. A trail continues north along the coast for several more miles. I walked about 5 miles on this trail one early morning in April. It reminded me of similar places I have trekked along the Sonoran coastline of Mexico. The plant life had many of the same characteristics: short, thorny, and sometimes impenetrable. Most of the birds I found at Guánica had similar Mexican analogs.

The abundant and distinct "pity-pit-pit" calls of **Antillean Nighthawks** replaced the rasping sounds of the Common Nighthawks. The songs of Troupials cannot be mistaken for any other family, and the black-and-orange pattern of this large oriole, perched atop a distant acacia, was reminiscent of Scott's Orioles. The songs and calls of **Puerto Rican Flycatchers** are also obvious and similar to the Ash-throated and Brown-crested Flycatchers of North America.

Two warblers occur in the Guánica lowlands: Yellow and Adelaide's. Yellow Warblers prefer the mangroves and other wet areas close to the coast, but **Adelaide's Warbler** was found in the driest and hottest parts of the scrub forest. The North American analog is the Lucy's Warbler of the desert riparian zones. Adelaide's physical appearance, however, is more like that of the Grace's Warblers of the middle elevation forests of western North America. I watched a number of Adelaide's Warblers that April morning and found the bird to be a truly beautiful species. It is a medium-size warbler with a bright yellow throat and breast and yellow above and below the eyes. The black-and-yellow face pattern is very distinct and is offset by a black eyeline stripe. Its back is grayish, its belly is white, it possesses two white wing-patches, and, on close examination, whitish can be seen in the tail as well.

The birds I followed through the dry scrub that morning were singing vigorously. I couldn't help but think how similar their songs were to their relatives in North America, the Lucy-Virginia-Colima warbler complex. Adelaide's Warblers were feeding on low shrubs as well as on the ground, and on a couple of occasions I watched them capture small caterpillars. Their behavior was perky and deliberate, and they also fanned their tail while feeding, much like Hooded and Fan-tailed Warblers.

There are numerous places along the trail where one can gaze out to sea in hopes of catching a glimpse of one of Puerto Rico's many seabirds. Magnificent Frigatebirds and terns are sure bets. I found Common and Sandwich Terns flying by reasonably close to shore. During the late winter and spring, White-tailed Tropicbirds often patrol the breakers, as well.

Not far from Guánica is a place where one can watch endangered **Yellow-shouldered Blackbirds** as they return to their roosting sites in the coastal mangroves. They fly overhead singly or in small groups of four to eight after a day feeding in the agricultural fields. The 1990 postbreeding population yielded 347 individuals between La Paraguera and Cabo Rojo, a significant decline from 1975, when as many as 500 birds could be seen returning to their roosts every evening. Their decline has largely contributed to increased populations of Shiny Cowbirds, which parasitize blackbird nests.

The Shiny Cowbird is native to South America and Trinidad but island-hopped its way into the West Indies, reaching Puerto Rico in the late 1940s or early 1950s. By the early 1990s it had also been reported in Florida and elsewhere in North America. Like its smaller cousin, the Brown-headed Cowbird, it is an obligate brood parasite, laying its eggs in the nests of smaller birds who tend the larger youngsters that outcompete the smaller nestlings. Because Puerto Rico's native species have never before experienced such parasitism, they are not able to cope with the gregarious Shiny Cowbirds. The Yellow-shouldered Blackbird was placed on the endangered species list in 1976.

The bay at night is also worthy of attention. It is called Phosphorescent Bay because of the presence of luminescent dinoflagellates (tiny free-swimming organisms) which live in the bay waters. These microscopic organisms can put on a great show when disturbed, especially on a moonlit night. Local fishermen from La Paraguera take people out into the bay at night so they can experience the glowing dinoflagellates for themselves. The best moonlit nights occur during the first week of October.

MARICAO

Maricao's Hacienda Juanita provides comfortable accommodations, good food, and accessible wildlife. It is an excellent place to stay in the western mountains. Yard birds include Ruddy Quail-Dove, Puerto Rican Screech-Owl, Puerto Rican Emerald, Puerto Rican Woodpecker, Loggerhead Kingbird, Red-legged Thrush, Bananaquit, Antillean Euphonia, Puerto Rican and Stripe-headed Tanagers, and Black-cowled Oriole. Nearby is Maricao National Resource Area, a Commonwealth nature preserve. The rain forest habitat at this site provides an easily accessible place for finding several of the same bird species that occur in the Luquillo Mountains. Most important, the Elfin Woods Warbler is far easier to find here than it is in the elfin woodlands of the Luquillo Mountains.

Also, nearby Maricao Fish Hatchery, situated within a narrow valley beyond the village of Maricao, is an excellent birding location. Follow the trail that goes beyond the hatchery into the valley, where the riparian forest contains a rich diversity of flora and fauna. The tall clumps of bamboo are similar to those on the much higher slopes of the Luquillo Mountains.

The Panoramic Road that passes by Maricao extends along the Cordillera Central for 165 miles, from Yabucoa in the southeast to Mayagüez on the west coast. This scenic roadway can be extremely slow driving because of the abundant turns and grades, but it provides the traveler a much better understanding of Puerto Rico than can be acquired at San Juan or by traveling the coastal highways. The Panoramic Road passes through the "real" Puerto Rico, where the rural lifestyle and landscapes have not kept pace with Puerto Rico's urban development. One gets a much truer perspective of this lovely island that is only 110 miles long and 35 miles wide.

Most of the valleys visible from the overlooks are filled with tiny villages and farms, usually well laid out and cultivated. Pastures fill many of the lower slopes, where cattle peacefully graze the bright green landscapes. On the steeper slopes and in reclaimed fields, where forest vegetation is dominant, bright reds and pinks are often evident amid the varied greens. African tulip trees produce bright red flowers throughout the year, but in spring the showy orange-red and delicate pink colors are provided by mountain immortelle and white cedar (locally called *roble blanco*), respectively.

Also in spring, the sweet fragrance of Puerto Rico's coffee shrubs can often be detected at a considerable distance. Coffee has been planted on many of the hillsides in western Puerto Rico, usually as undergrowth to the taller forest trees. Although coffee is not as important as it was during the eighteenth and nineteenth centuries, it remains a valuable crop because of its especially rich and fragrant taste.

I have found Puerto Rico to be an extremely appealing island. Its natural beauty and culture are important reasons for its special status. Although almost four million people live on Puerto Rico, more than two-thirds of those individuals live within or adjacent to the major cities of San Juan, Ponce, Caguas, Mayagüez, Aguadilla, and Arecibo. The countryside is far less populated and still possesses opportunities to experience Puerto Rico as it was long ago.

Several of Puerto Rico's natural areas have been set aside as preserves in an effort to protect samples of the island's biodiversity and grand scenery. Puerto Rican officials must be complimented on their far-sighted stand on resource protection. Yet many of the finest areas are being threatened by a growing population and related economic stress. Agriculture is no longer as important as it once was, as manufacturing increases in importance. The country's third largest industry is now tourism, which is undoubtedly going to increase in importance.

Puerto Ricans already are beginning to recognize these changes in their economy and are starting to plan for the day when tourism will be even more important to their well-being. Considerable efforts are under way to protect the extremely valuable but vulnerable off-shore reefs and fisheries. Underwater nature tours are included in plans for increasing tourism along the south shore. Arrangements for protecting additional wetlands and other wildlife areas are being considered.

It is important that the many unique habitats that exist on Puerto Rico be given special protection now, before the more fragile sites are degraded any further. The rare and unique birds and other flora and fauna must receive immediate protection and long-term stewardship. These are the resources that will attract tourism in the long term, and they form the basis of a sound economy for Puerto Rico now and in the future.

CHAPTER FIVE

Tortola ISLAND OF DOVES

Zenaida Dove

The view from the Sage Mountain Trail, at about 1,700 feet elevation near the summit of Tortola's highest peak, was spectacular. I had a grand, sweeping panorama of dozens of bright green islands, each surrounded by varying shades of blue. The aqua blues of the shallow waters contrasted with the magenta to sky blues of the deeper waters. The overall mosaic of greens and blues provided an almost myopic scene before me.

The island of St. John, U.S. Virgin Islands, dominated the scene to the southwest. The British island of Jost Van Dyke lay below me to the west. The smaller British islands of Norman, Peter, Salt, Cooper, and Ginger rose out of the sea like stepping stones between St. John and Virgin Gorda, the long gray-green island that lay almost directly to the east. I focused my binoculars on the southern tip of Virgin Gorda, where I could detect the jumble of huge granite boulders and grottos of the Baths, a unique snorkeling area with underwater passageways throughout the great boulders. I also could make out the observation tower near the summit of Gorda Peak (1,370 feet), the high point of the 165-acre Gorda Peak National Park. Ten miles to the northeast was the solitary island of Anegada.

Sir Francis Drake Channel separates Tortola and its adjacent cays from the "stepping stone" islands and Virgin Gorda. The channel's name was derived from one of England's most renowned sailors, Sir Francis Drake, who explored and mapped this region in 1585. The sixteenth and seventeenth centuries were the heyday of pirates, and the British Virgin Islands saw numerous smugglers and privateers taking advantage of the abundant hideaways among the islands. By the nineteenth century the British had taken control of the northern Virgins, and today the islands enjoy a semiministerial form of government. The Constitution of 1967 provides for a governor, appointed by the Crown, who, according to Arnold Highfield in *The Beautiful British Virgin Islands*, works with a "Legislative Assembly of eleven members, seven of whom are popularly elected."

The national parks of the BVIs (British Virgin Islands) are managed by a National Park Trust, a statutory body responsible to the Legislative Assembly for the stewardship of natural and cultural resources. The trust manages fifteen separate units, and eight more are proposed. Sage Mountain National Park was the first of these units, and Gorda Peak National Park is the largest, covering the entire island above the 1,500-foot contour. In addition, the Wreck of the *Rhone* is a designated marine national park that includes the sunken *Rhone*, a 310-foot royal mail ship that was wrecked off the coast of Salt Island during the hurricane of 1867. Today, it provides one of the very best diving sites in all the Caribbean.

THE SAGE MOUNTAIN FOREST

The foreground of Sage Mountain was crowded with forest, which dominated the 92-acre national park. Dense vegetation lay around me like a thick green rug that had somehow been placed around the summit of Tortola. Many of the park's trees and shrubs had been planted in an attempt to restore the area to its more natural appearance. Most of the plant species I could identify were representatives of moist forest communities, generally found only on the larger islands. Sage Mountain Park was established in

1964 to protect that last remnant of a "rain forest" community that once covered most of the central highlands of Tortola.

West Indian and broadleaf mahogany trees were most numerous. The West Indian mahogany possesses small leaves divided into four to ten pairs of shiny green leaflets, while the introduced broadleaf mahogany has larger leaves divided into six to twelve pairs of dark green, shiny leaflets. Both trees produce dark brown, woody and erect, pear-shaped fruit capsules. The wood of these trees has long been in demand for cabinets and other fine furniture. This demand undoubtedly resulted in the cutting of most mahogany trees that once occurred within the BVIs.

White-cedar, the official national tree of the BVIs, was common on Sage Mountain, as well. In spring, and sporadically during the rest of the year, this tree produces abundant showy, pink to white tubular flowers, especially about the crown, that only last a few days before they fall off and carpet the ground. White-cedar fruit are dark brown, cigar-shaped pods that hang down from among the leaves, which possess five or fewer large, palmately arranged leaflets. The size of the leaves depends on available moisture; the leaves on these trees in Tortola's moist forests are larger than the leaves of the same species of trees that occur in the drier lowlands. White-cedars also are widely used as ornamentals around houses and along roadsides.

The Sage Mountain Rainforest Trail makes a loop through some of the park's oldest vegetation. Fig and bulletwood trees were most impressive. The fig trees were easily recognized by their distinct aerial roots that often extended from their branches to the ground. Bulletwood trees, with tall straight trunks and thick brown bark, can grow to 100 feet and produce a great crown of horizontal branches. This species was selectively harvested throughout the island, and it will take many years for the protected individuals to reach maturity. But already the forest contained an impressive array of bromeliads, vines, and ferns.

The forest understory was literally filled with greenhouse vegetation. Anthuriums and philodendrons were most obvious. Giant elephant-ear vines were commonplace, winding over the ground, circling the tree trunks, and extending into the upper canopy. It took me several minutes to find a red palicourea shrub, mentioned within the park brochure. This is an ever-green with paired elliptical leaves, clusters of small tubular red flowers on the yellow stalks, and black fruit. There, too, were coco-plum shrubs, a member of the rose family, with their small, rounded, upturned leaves arranged alternately in two rows. This is the same plant that is common along the Anhinga Trail in Everglades National Park, and yet here it was in Tortola's montane rain forest.

A small stand of tree ferns was present along the Mahogany Forest Trail. I was surprised to find these little trees on the slopes of Sage Mountain; I had not seen the species elsewhere in the Virgin Islands. I found several heliconia trees along the trail, as well. These bananalike trees produce long leaves and flowers with large red bracts. Both these plants are normally associated with cloud forest communities, and their presence on Tortola suggests that Sage Mountain once contained at least a remnant of that habitat. However, other typical cloud forest plants such as dwarf palms were missing.

The little, very dark green–leaved trees, just above the parking area, were guava. Their small white flowers bloom in spring and produce little round edible fruit in summer. The fruit gradually turn from green to yellow with age and contain a bright pink pulp with numerous small seeds. Mature fruit, which look a little like small lemons, are extremely aromatic. They are used for juice and for making preserves. Also, according to Penelope Honychurch in *Caribbean Wild Plants and Their Uses*, "The leaves and buds of the guava are used medicinally in a tea for dysentery, stomach ache, worms in children and for diarrhea."

Also near the parking area is a huge mammee apple tree. I was uncertain whether this individual was natural or planted. It was a handsome columnar evergreen with glossy green, thick leathery leaves. It produces white, fragrant flowers, borne on twigs below the leaves, that bloom for one or two weeks at various times of the year. Mammee fruit are baseball-size or larger, possess thick skin, and have firm yellow to reddish flesh that can be eaten raw or used in pies and preserves. The mammee apple has a taste that I do not appreciate, but West Indians who grow up eating this juicy fruit relish the taste.

THE BIRD LIFE

A pair of **Caribbean Martins** were playing overhead while we were investigating the forest. Their loud, rather hollow whistles, "chu" or "chu chu," were audible all the while. I couldn't help but admire this pair of birds as they dashed here and there, undoubtedly in pursuit of insects that I could not detect. The male was a much darker purple color than the female, but each possessed a contrasting all-white belly. The closely related Purple Martins, which occur in North America, do not possess white bellies.

Two additional birds were taking advantage of the thermals rising from the warmer lowlands that morning, a Red-tailed Hawk and an American Kestrel. The kestrel, locally known as killy-killy or killy-hawk, after its call, appeared only briefly, then soared eastward along the ridge and disappeared. It is one of Tortola's common resident hawks, and I wondered if it was nesting somewhere in the adjacent forest. The Red-tailed Hawk, however, remained overhead for an hour or more, and I was able to admire its graceful behavior. Its wings and tail were spread out to capture the updrafts, allowing it to remain motionless over the slope. Its light underparts, dark head, black wing tips and edges, and brick-red tail provided a lovely contrast to this large raptor.

The Red-tailed Hawk is an extremely wide-ranging species that occurs from Alaska to Panama and throughout the Greater and Lesser Antilles. Some ornithologists divide the species (*jamaicensis*) into a number of forms, and the Tortola Red-tails are members of the nominant subspecies. The type locality of this form came from Jamaica. Of nine subspecies included by Herbert Friedmann in his classic book, *The Birds of North and Middle America, Part XI*, the Jamaican Red-tail is the smallest, but all of their color patterns are very similar.

There was considerable bird song within the forest that morning, but the chorus contained only five species and was dominated by one very gregarious bird in particular, the **Pearly-eyed Thrasher.** James Bond described this bird's song as "a hesitant pio-tereu-tsee with variations." It also produces a series of alarm calls and harsh "chook" sounds that are typical of other members of the thrasher family. Pearly-eyes are robin-size, all-dark birds with a reasonably heavy bill and distinct pearly eyes. Although they generally are described as an "arboreal thrasher," they can be expected anywhere, from the deepest forest and tallest trees to open gardens and fencerows. As might be expected for this family, Pearly-eyed Thrashers are true opportunists, feeding on practically anything they can swallow or tear apart. The chapter on St. Croix describes their opportunistic behavior following Hurricane Hugo.

On several occasions I have watched Pearly-eyes feed on anoles, which they capture with such tenacity and vigor that, except for the tremendous numbers of these little green to brown lizards, it is a wonder that any exist at all. A Pearly-eyed Thrasher territory may include hundreds of anoles, but these birds usually hunt only the larger anole populations, thus expending the least amount of energy. Because of the bird's aggressiveness, it also has been blamed, and rightly so, for the loss of eggs and fledglings of a wide assortment of birds. It is likely that this bird has increased in abundance following human development, taking advantage of increased access into forest interiors, where it can prey upon species that prefer less disturbed habitats.

Its situation is analogous to that of the American Crow and the Blue Jay of North America.

The brightest of the Sage Mountain forest birds was undoubtedly the little Bananaquit, or yellow breast, as it is locally known. This is a little yellow-and-black honeycreeper that feeds on nectar and sweet fruits. Its long bill is used for extracting nectar from inside flowers, but it also has adapted to civilization by feeding on sugar. In fact, it makes a habit of visiting open-air restaurants and helping itself either to open sugar bowls or torn sugar envelopes, right at the table while you are eating. Island residents often attract yellow breasts by hanging out sugar, honey, fruit, or sugar water in suitable places. The Bananaquit's wheezy "zee-e-e-swees-te" song is common throughout the Virgin Islands.

In direct contrast to the brightly colored Bananaquit is the inconspicuous **Black-whiskered Vireo,** a bird seldom seen because of its preference for the dense canopy layer of the forests and woodlands. Its songs were common in the Sage Mountain forest. This 5-inch songster is overall gray-green color with a reddish eye and a black-and-white face pattern. Its name comes from a black whisker-stripe on each side of its throat. But what this bird lacks in color, it more than makes up for by its almost constant singing. Its song consists of one- to four-note whistles that sound very much like "John Phillips," its local name.

But of all the forest birds, none were as obvious as the doves. Songs of **Scaly-naped Pigeons** and **Zenaida Doves** were abundant throughout the Sage Mountain forest. The Scaly-nape's booming song, a deep-throated "crooo-cru-cru-croooo," echoed out of the greenery. An additional pair of Scaly-napes streaked across the sky like missiles. This large pigeon is mostly slate-gray with a patch of chestnut and metallic purple color on its nape, giving it a scaly appearance. These birds are present in substantial numbers on Tortola year-round.

The smaller Zenaida Dove, locally known as mountain dove, is also present all year, but its comings and goings have posed a true mystery. George Seaman wrote about the movement of Zenaida Doves in his book, *Ay Ay: An Island Almanac:*

> This migration of doves is strongest along the more northern islands which stretch like a rough chain of jewels from Puerto Rico to the Anegada Passage. Along this route, an endless stream of doves moves eastward from dawn to dusk. . . . With that preordination of time and movement we attribute only to the immutability of galactic spheres, these small brown doves move across our spring skies with an assurance

to disturb the confidence of any agnostic. A hundred rocks and tiny cays mark the way along their turquoise path, yet each mated pair, each winging group knows its destined spot and hour. By this inscrutable trust, they move to the resurrection of their species.

Why there should be such great numbers of Zenaida Doves passing by, while it is a common full-time resident on Tortola throughout the year, is a mystery. Perhaps these birds flock together and make great circular flights. But the resident birds do not seem to decline during any specific time period. Whatever the reason, Zenaida Doves continue to reside in the forest as well as in gardens and clearings throughout the Virgin Islands.

Zenaida Doves are most evident in spring and summer, when they are courting and calling. Their song is very similar to that of Mourning Doves, but less drawn out. There are no Mourning Doves in the Virgin Islands. Zenaida Doves are medium-size doves with a short, rounded tail with rather conspicuous white patches on their outer tail feathers and on the trailing feathers of their wings.

Only the hummingbirds and Bananaquits receive more attention than the doves. The tiny **Antillean Crested Hummingbird** and larger **Green-throated Carib** can be surprisingly common around flowering shrubs. Hummingbirds are like bright green jewels among the vast array of multi-colored flowers. Preferred shrubs include the bottle brush, ixora, giant fire dart, and coral plant. Flowering trees most often utilized include the orchid tree, manjack, flamboyant, African tulip tree, and white-cedar.

I found hummingbirds to be particularly abundant at the Botanical Gardens at Road Town, Tortola's largest town and the capital of the BVIs, on one visit there in September. Established in 1979, the 2.8-acre gardens are managed by the National Park Trust as a recreational and educational facility. Different sections of the gardens are dedicated to various groups of plants: rain forest, bamboo and other grasses, bromeliads, palms, heliconias and philodendrons, and orchids.

The British Virgin Islands, a British crown colony, consists of more than fifty islands and cays within an area of 59 square miles. The principal islands are Tortola (25 square miles), Anegada (13 square miles), Virgin Gorda (8 square miles), and Jost Van Dyke (3 square miles); all the rest are smaller. But it is the smaller islands and cays where at least thirteen species of seabirds are known to nest, according to Rudd van Halewyn and Rob Norton. Those species include Red-billed and White-tailed Tropicbirds; Magnificent Frigatebird; Brown Booby; Brown Pelican; Laughing Gull;

Gull-billed, Royal, Roseate, Bridled, Sooty, and Least Terns; and Brown Noddy.

The most obvious of these is the Magnificent Frigatebird, or man-o'-war bird, an all-black bird with a long scissorlike tail, huge beak, and narrow wings that span 90 inches. Breeding males possess a bright red gular pouch which they inflate like a huge balloon during the breeding season. They can be seen over the sea and bays or soaring over the islands almost anywhere. Their dexterity and grace, evident from their dives and aerial maneuvers, are truly outstanding for such large birds. There is no mistaking these great creatures.

One should not pass up an opportunity to watch a frigatebird, especially when it is hunting. It will actively pursue and harass a gull, tern, or booby that has captured a fish and force it to drop its catch. Sometimes the pursuit is a lengthy one that covers miles and extends from several hundred feet above the sea to barely skimming the waves. Once the catch is dropped, the frigatebird will catch the prize in midair before it reaches the ocean surface.

Magnificent Frigatebirds can soar almost indefinitely on the slightest breeze. They are the most completely aerial of all birds. Their great wings give them a greater wing-to-air ratio than any other bird. They are able to soar for hours on end with rarely any movement of their wings. But for all their adaptations as aerial experts, they lack the oil glands to waterproof their plumage like most other seabirds. They must therefore stay out of the water. For example, the birds will take flying fish in flight or grab fish at the surface with their very long and strong, hooked beak, rather than diving and capturing the fish underwater.

The two tropicbirds are also magnificent creatures that demand considerable respect for their acrobatic abilities. These medium-size seabirds fly with strong wing-beats, similar to the flight of a pigeon. Peter Harrison described their flight in *Seabirds: An Identification Guide* as "fluttering wing strokes alternated with soaring glides producing butterfly-progression." When fishing, they will fly over the sea at about 50 feet elevation. Upon sighting their prey, they hover briefly and then plunge into the sea with wings half-closed like the Northern Gannet. They may remain underwater for several seconds before emerging with their prey held crossways in their bills. They will then float on the surface, with their tail cocked upward, and swallow their catch. They never fly with their prey in their bills. When feeding young, they will regurgitate their catch into the mouths of the nestlings.

Tropicbirds nest in crevices on rocky sea cliffs on the various cays. Herbert Raffaele, in his informative book, *A Guide to the Birds of Puerto Rico and the Virgin Islands,* reported that Red-bills nest from November through April and are "absent outside the breeding season." White-tails, according to Raffaele, nest from March to July and occasionally are seen "as early as December and as late as August."

Both these birds are beautiful white seabirds with straight, heavy bills, long wings, and short legs with four webbed toes. Adults sport a wedge-shaped tail that possesses two central feathers (streamers) that are greatly elongated, like long spikes. Some authors claim that sailors once referred to them as bosun birds, because they "carry a marlin spike in the tail." Others claim the bosun bird name refers to boatswain, an officer in charge of the ship's rigging, which makes sounds reminiscent of the bird's short, rasping calls.

The two tropicbirds are best identified by the markings on top of their wings. The White-tailed Tropicbird shows a black band on the inner portion of the wing that is missing on the stockier Red-billed Tropicbird. Also, Red-bills show a barred back, while the back of White-tails is all white. Both species have black primaries. Bill color alone can be confusing because both adults possess red bills.

But of all the birds found in the British Virgin Islands, none are so representative on Tortola as the Zenaida Dove. Perhaps that is partly due to the mystery that surrounds it, but it also is special to Tortola because of its namesake: the Spanish word for dove is *tórtola.*

CHAPTER SIX

St. John and St. Thomas U.S. VIRGIN ISLANDS

Bridled Quail-Dove

The **Bridled Quail-Dove** is easier to find at Virgin Islands National Park on St. John than anywhere else in the West Indies. Yet it is not an abundant and obvious bird; it blends into the forest and usually is evident only to those who understand its natural character. It is fairly common within the forested slopes in the national park, where its primary habitat is protected from development and abuse. It spends most of its time walking on the ground searching for food or perched on horizontal branches of trees at middle heights within the forest. It has developed a habit of freezing in place when disturbed and going about its business after the perceived danger has passed. At other times it will walk into the deeper shadows of the forest, where it can be next to impossible to locate; it rarely flies any distance.

This species of Columbidae, the family of pigeons and doves, is scarce or absent elsewhere throughout its range, from Puerto Rico eastward into the Lesser Antilles south to St. Lucia. On St. John, however, this rather large and plump bird can usually be found above the park roadway between Hawksnest Bay and Cinnamon Bay. Walking the roadway one morning in June, I located an even dozen individuals within less than 100 feet of the roadway. I initially detected each one by the sound of rustling leaves on the forest floor. Quail-doves forage by turning leaves in search of seeds, fruits, and insect larvae. Once detected, one simply has to remain still and watch for further movement. Shortly, the birds commence to forage. Until they move, their plumage blends so perfectly into the forest they are next to impossible to find. Only once did a bird fly off while I was watching. The bird was so close that when I stopped it immediately flushed with quick and rather loud wing-beats, then set its wings and glided away into the shadows.

I found most of St. John's Bridled Quail-Doves surprisingly tame. They usually continued feeding less than thirty seconds after their initial freeze. I was then able to watch them continue foraging over the forest floor. On occasion they would walk out of the darker shadows into lighted areas, where the sunlight highlighted their plumage like a spotlight on a stage. Then their subtle colors seemed to erupt into beautiful shades of rufous, green, and red. Their overall buff color seemed almost iridescent, and their very obvious and bright white throat and bold streak below each eye seemed to shine like jewels.

Their very distinct head-stripes tend to give them away immediately as quail-doves, because no other group of Columbids possesses that same characteristic. At first sighting they look more like quail than pigeons, but their very short legs give them a very unique appearance. They also differ from other Columbids by possessing short tails with no white markings. Their songs are also unique. Quail-dove songs were once described by Alexander Wetmore as "the humming of wind across the end of a gun-barrel—a striking sound and one whose source is difficult to locate."

The song of a Bridled Quail-Dove is like a very low pitched groan, a deep "who-ooooo" sound, like a distant foghorn. Herb Raffaele, in *A Guide to the Birds of Puerto Rico and the Virgin Islands*, described it best: "A mournful who-whooo, on one note or descending towards the end, getting loudest in the middle of the second syllable and then trailing off. Sometimes the first syllable is omitted." To me, the song of the Bridled Quail-Dove is one of those sounds that seems to be barely noticeable unless one is listening for it. Then it can be all around and everywhere at once, and it is usually impossible to pinpoint its exact location.

Although the Bridled Quail-Dove is probably present in moderate numbers throughout the forested slopes of Virgin Islands National Park, it is easiest to see along the northern shore road. Perhaps those individuals have adapted to some degree to the comings and goings along this roadway; I have even found it walking along the edges of the public parking area at the entrance to Cinnamon Bay. On one occasion I watched four groups of visitors pass within 20 feet of a feeding Bridled Quail-Dove. Each time it would freeze in place, only to resume its feeding ten to twenty seconds afterward.

In 1957, William Robertson surveyed the bird life in the newly established national park; his findings were published in the ornithological journal the *Auk* in 1962. He reported Bridled Quail-Doves "at many north coast and interior localities, but most commonly in the steep, heavily wooded valleys leading down to Fish Bay and Reef Bay." Robertson speculated that St. John's Bridled Quail-Dove population had survived earlier clear-cutting for the sugar industry due to the many inaccessible and steep guts that had not been logged. The paucity of this species on other "sugar islands" is undoubtedly due to two very different but related impacts. Sugarcane was grown on every flatland and slope possible, and so most of the island's forests were cleared for sugarcane production or cut for fuel to stoke the mills. Second, the introduction of the mongoose to those same islands for the purpose of controlling rats must have been double trouble for the ground-dwelling Bridled Quail-Dove.

THE ST. JOHN FOREST

Robertson surveyed three habitat types on St. John: dry forest and scrub, moist forest, and mangrove swamp. Except for two individual Bridled Quail-Doves found in the dry forest, all others were located in the moist forest, typical of the northern slopes mentioned above. Robertson described the moist forest community as an evergreen hardwood forest that is relatively open beneath and composed of many large trees in the mature stands.

St. John's vegetation was more thoroughly studied by Roy Woodbury and Peter Weaver of Puerto Rico's Department of Natural Resources and Institute of Tropical Forestry, respectively. They reported that the moist guts and gentle slopes often contain a "gallery moist forest" which includes the tallest trees on the island. One of those trees, *Sapium caribaeum*, related to Chinese tallow, may grow to a height of over 100 feet. The most common trees of the moist forest communities include kapok, hogplum, algarrobo, genip, and bucaro. At sea level, such as around Trunk Bay, the moist forest may contain as many as ninety-six tree species. The most common of these included kapok, hogplum, algarrobo, and samán. The shorter trees of this community are dominated by almendro, ice cream bean, soapberry, fig, ginep, caper, several cordias, and coconut palm. This community also contains numerous vines and a well-developed shrub layer that includes the introduced sweet lime and the native wild coffee, pepper, and jasmine.

There is an enormous kapok tree at Cinnamon Bay. Its great buttresses are so high that a person 6 feet tall can stand inside and not be seen. Mature kapok trees have a smooth, grayish bark, but young trees possess large conical spines on their trunks. Kapok trees lose all their leaves during the dry winter months but produce new reddish-brown, palmately compound leaves in the spring. Greenish-brown flowers appear in February and are followed by woody pods, 3 to 4 inches in length, in March. These pods produce seeds with long brownish fibers that once were used for stuffing pillows and life jackets, thus the origin of their common name.

The principal feature of hogplum trees is their very tasty fruit, which contains a huge seed; it is one of the most aromatic fruits in all the West Indies. These small yellow plums are used for jams and a liqueur. Penelope Honychurch claims in *Caribbean Wild Plants and Their Uses* that "a decoction of bud, roots, and bark was used to treat gonorrhea, used in a tea to stop diarrhea or dysentery, as a gargle for sore throats, and as an eyewash for ophthalmia."

Robertson's dry forest community was called "dry evergreen woodland" or "thicket" by Woodbury and Weaver, who reported that it covers more than 55 percent of the island. This community is usually rather dense, with small-leaved trees that are seldom more than 35 feet tall. Some of the principal dry evergreen tree species include sea grape, spindle tree, black torch, frangipani, fishing rod, jacquinia, eugenia, *Guapira fragans*, water mampoo, painkiller, black torch tree, and caper.

Whenever the forest is cleared for development and pastures, secondary vegetation is quick to reclaim the clearing. The earliest plant life to appear is usually dominated by tan-tan, *Trema micrantha*, genip, soursop, custard apple, West Indian almond, and acacias.

Tan-tan is undoubtedly one of the most prolific woody trees in the world, growing 10 feet or more in a single season. It is both a curse and a blessing: it can be a pest to gardeners, but its quick sprouting ability provides a fast soil stabilizer for controlling erosion. Tan-tan possesses twice pinnate leaves and flat, brown seedpods. It is locally called wild tamarind. Doris Jadan, in *A Guide to the Natural History of St. John*, reports that tan-tan leaves and seeds contain mimosine, a substance that "causes horses, donkeys and mules to lose large chunks of hair," but cattle, sheep, and goats can eat the plant without ill effects. She also claims that tan-tan seeds have been used locally for coffee.

Only about 2 percent of St. John's vegetation types is composed of mangrove swamp, a community that contains four mangrove species. Those four species grow within rather distinct zones that vary with the amount of saltwater they can withstand. Buttonwood occurs farthest inland, where it experiences only occasional saltwater incursion. It has shaggy and twisted bark, gnarled trunks, and pale grayish-green leaves 1 to 4 inches long with blunt to sharp tips. Next comes the white mangrove, identified by 2- to 3-inch-long, oblong, and broadly rounded leaves, each with a pair of swollen glands at the base. Black mangroves occur next. They are identified by a dark and scaly barked trunk rising directly from the ground and dark green lanceolate leaves with a sharp tip. This plant has numerous aeration roots or fingerlike pneumatophores that project above the ground from 3 to 14 inches. These soda straw–like projections allow gas exchange during periods of high water. Finally, red mangroves are the most seaward of the species, often forming a tangle of arch-shaped prop roots which hold the trunks above water level. These trees often reach 30 feet in height and may form a canopy of large opposite, thick, smooth, oblong leaves. Their trunks are often covered with bright orange crustose lichens. The prop roots attract a wide variety of molluscous and marine algae, and the intricate web of roots serves as an important nursery for a wide variety of marine life.

THE BIRD LIFE

Robertson recorded twenty-one species of nesting birds on St. John, eleven of which nested within the mangrove swamps. Fifteen species nested within the moist forest habitat, and twenty species utilized the dry forest and scrub communities. Of seventeen bird species considered winter visitors or transients, five were found in the mangroves, twelve in the moist forest, and eleven in the dry forest and scrub habitats.

The most abundant wintering bird of the mangrove swamp community is the Northern Waterthrush, a Neotropical migrant. It also occurs along freshwater streams in the interior. This species illustrates, better than any other, the connection between the West Indies and North America, where it resides during the breeding season. It summers at northern wetlands from Newfoundland westward to Alaska's northwestern slopes, nesting on the ground amid roots and overhanging banks close to water. It winters within the West Indies and throughout Mexico south to northern South America. Its distinct behavior of walking and bobbing repeatedly is evident in both summer and winter, as is its loud and sharp "chink" call note. But only in summer does it sing its wonderfully loud and emphatic song, described by Wayne Petersen in *The Audubon Society Master Guide to Birding* as "sweet sweet sweet swee-wee-wee chew chew chew; from a distance only [the] ending is clearly audible."

Other Neotropical visitors expected in the mangroves included Northern Parula, Prairie, Black-and-white, Worm-eating, and Hooded Warblers, and American Redstart. Resident West Indian birds found on St. John, more or less in order of abundance, included Pearly-eyed Thrasher, Yellow Warbler, Gray Kingbird, Scaly-naped Pigeon, Zenaida Dove, Antillean Crested Hummingbird, and Mangrove Cuckoo. In summer, the Black-whiskered Vireo can be more numerous than all the rest combined.

The mangroves on Patricia and Cas Cays, St. Thomas, also support a population of **White-crowned Pigeons,** a species that has disappeared throughout much of its range in the northern Virgin Islands. Robertson did not report it at all for St. John. James Wiley, in *Bird Conservation 2*, reported it to be endangered in the Virgin Islands, where populations have been reduced by hunting and nest robbing. Wiley adds, "There has been no open season on White-crowned Pigeons since 1960, and nesting areas are now protected, but the near-complete destruction of mangrove nesting habitat leaves little hope for a substantial recovery of the populations."

Robertson's dry forest and scrub community supported a somewhat larger bird population on St. John. He found large numbers (in descending order of abundance) of the Black-faced Grassquit, Pearly-eyed Thrasher, Common Ground-Dove, Zenaida Dove, Gray Kingbird, and Yellow Warbler. He found smaller numbers (in descending order of abundance) of the Antillean Crested Hummingbird, Green-throated Carib, Caribbean Elaenia, Caribbean Martin, Northern Mockingbird, American Kestrel, Red-tailed Hawk, Mangrove Cuckoo, Scaly-naped Pigeon, Bridled Quail-Dove, White-crowned Pigeon, and Puerto Rican Flycatcher.

The **Puerto Rican Flycatcher** is of special interest because the St. John population appears to be at the eastern edge of its range; it may have disappeared from the Virgin Islands on several occasions. It is a very shy and elusive species. A small population remains along the Reef Bay Trail, and an occasional individual will appear elsewhere on the island. The species classification is confusing because until 1983 it was considered part of the more western Caribbean form of *Myiarchus*, the Stolid Flycatcher. It was then given species status based upon Wesley Lanyon's (1967) study of vocalizations of all members of the genus. Puerto Rican Flycatchers possess a very distinct song. Raffaele described it as "whee-a-wit-whee, the two middle syllables of which are unmusical and sometimes sung independently. . . . Lanyon describes other calls including an emphatic huit, huit, a rolling pee-r-r-r and a rasping note."

Neotropical migrants reported by Robertson in the dry forest community on St. John (in descending order of abundance) included Northern Parula, Prairie Warbler, American Redstart, Black-and-white Warbler, Northern Waterthrush and Cape May Warbler (tied), Ovenbird, Barn Swallow, and single sightings of Northern Harrier, Merlin, and Yellow-billed Cuckoo.

Further, in 1987 Robert Askins and colleagues censused birds within the dry and moist forest communities during the winter months on both St. John and St. Thomas. They found heavier use of St. John's moist forest than of the dry forest, the opposite from Robertson's findings. Seven bird species were recorded in the dry forest: Yellow Warbler, Northern Parula, Prairie Warbler, Ovenbird, Black-and-white and Worm-eating Warblers, and American Redstart, in descending order of abundance. Moist forest birds included Northern Parula, Black-and-white Warbler, American Redstart, Hooded Warbler, Ovenbird, Magnolia and Cape May Warblers, Blue-winged and Worm-eating Warblers, Yellow-throated Vireo, and Prairie and Blackpoll Warblers.

Askins's St. Thomas censuses revealed only three species (compared with seven on St. John) in the dry forest: Yellow Warbler, Northern Parula, and Northern Waterthrush; and eight species (compared with twelve on St. John) in the moist forest: Northern Parula, Northern Waterthrush, Black-throated Blue, Black-throated Green and Black-and-white Warblers, Worm-eating and Hooded Warblers, and Ovenbird. These data readily illustrate the paucity of bird life on St. Thomas, which has less than 40 percent of its landscape covered with vegetation, compared with St. John's 88 percent plant cover.

The islands of St. John and St. Thomas are very different, although they are less than 3 miles apart and separated by a twenty-minute ferryboat ride across a rather deep channel. Charlotte Amalie, St. Thomas, is not only the capital city of the U.S. Virgin Islands but also contains one of the most popular yacht and cruise ship ports in the Caribbean. This harbor city is well known for its shopping and restaurants, carnival and congestion. St. Thomas's 32 squares miles have a population of about 51,000 people, 1,594 individuals per square mile. St. John's 16 square miles have a population of only 2,740 people, or 171 individuals per square mile. St. John also has fewer accommodations and stores, much less congestion, and a national park that covers two-thirds of the island. The national park also extends seaward along the northern and the south-central portions of the island.

For nature enthusiasts and history buffs, the national park provides much to see and do. The Cruz Bay Visitor Center offers an information desk, exhibits, and book and video sales. Ranger talks and walks, a historic bus tour, and an underwater nature trail are but a start.

Of the twenty-four trails available within the park, none are as rewarding to the naturalist as the 2.5-mile Reef Bay Trail. It provides close-up exposure to the moist and dry forest communities, with their variety of flora and fauna, and ends at the shoreline of remote and serene Reef Bay. Reef Bay Trail starts along Centerline Road and follows an old wagon road back and forth along the contours, gradually descending the rocky gut. Most of the trees are the same as those found on the northern slopes, but there are a few different ones. One of these is the native bay rum tree, once used for producing the famous St. John bay rum and also for seasoning stews and sauces. A member of the myrtle family, the bay rum tree has smooth gray bark and glossy, elliptic leaves that give off a rich bay odor.

Wild mammee, a spreading evergreen with stiff, thick, leathery leaves, is present as well. This native tree produces pink to rose flowers at the ends of twigs and fleshy ball-like fruit all year round. It is locally called pitch apple because of the pitch or juice that "can be squeezed from the apple-like pods after they have fallen from the tree or the green pitch apples can be boiled and used to calk boats," according to Jadan.

All along the trail, growing out of the old rock walls, are plants that are often grown in greenhouses in the United States. The few mosses, ferns, and herbs that dominate these moist sites include philodendron, peperomia, piper, strap fern, and anthurium. The anthurium can be spectacular with its large, heart-shaped leaves. Some individuals grow as epiphytes on the trees. The native piper, locally called blackwattle, was used in a tea for colds and fever, and, according to Honychurch, the native Carib Indians used it in ritual baths.

The most abundant bird along the trail is the large, obnoxious **Pearly-eyed Thrasher**. Its calls and songs are a variety of raucous whistles and vibrating caws, with shrill alarm notes thrown in now and again. It can be found from the highest vegetation to the shadowy undergrowth. Locally known as thrushee or fus for the fuss it makes, it is a robin-size bird with brown upperparts and streaked underparts, a heavy brownish-yellow bill, and whitish or pearly eyes. It has a stern countenance and a well-deserved reputation for feeding on almost any living creature plus a wide variety of fruit. Jadoan reports that it will eat any fruit except "thick-rinded items like watermelons and pumpkins."

Other birds expected along the trail include Scaly-naped Pigeon, Bridled Quail-Dove, Mangrove Cuckoo, Green-throated Carib, Antillean Crested Hummingbird, Caribbean Elaenia, Gray Kingbird, Bananaquit, and Black-whiskered Vireo. During the winter months, several North American warblers are usually present, as well. Farther on near the seashore can be found the Yellow Warbler and Lesser Antillean Bullfinch. At Reef Bay, Great Blue, Little Blue, and Green Herons are usually present, and the American Oystercatcher can occasionally be found.

The **Lesser Antillean Bullfinch** is a newcomer to the Virgin Islands, first reported for St. John at Rams Head in 1971. It has since been found throughout the dry forest areas on St. John and has even spread to St. Croix. One of the easiest places to find it is along the Lynn Point Trail, which begins just behind the Cruz Bay Visitor Center. This bullfinch can easily be confused with the smaller Black-faced Grassquit, which frequents the same habitats. The **Black-faced Grassquit** is a tiny greenish-black bird, while the heavier, all-dark Lesser Antillean Bullfinch sports a rufous chin, throat, and undertail covert.

The Lesser Antillean Bullfinch is abundant within the Lesser Antilles toward the east and south, and its recent appearance in the Virgin Islands may be a harbinger of an expanding population. The Virgin Islands are located in a central position in the West Indies, influenced by both the Greater and Lesser Antilles. Peripheral species from the west, such as the Puerto Rican Flycatcher, and from the east, such as the Lesser Antillean Bullfinch, are present in smaller numbers. But the only bird species that is more numerous on St. John than on any of the other Caribbean islands is the Bridled Quail-Dove.

CHAPTER SEVEN

St. Croix U.S. VIRGIN ISLANDS

Hurricane Hugo struck the tiny Caribbean island of St. Croix on September 17, 1989, with over 200-mile-per-hour winds (local estimate), mutilating every part of the island throughout the night. Hugo actually stalled there for several hours, with the eye of the storm centered over the western half of the island. The National Hurricane Center reported that "the eye moved over St. Croix at 0600 UTC on the 18th with a forward speed of eight knots" and surface winds "estimated at 120 knots [138 miles per hour]." When people finally emerged from their places of refuge later that morning, they found complete havoc. Overnight, 90 percent of the island homes had been severely damaged or destroyed, all the trees and shrubs had been broken and defoliated, and the remaining vegetation had been turned brown by excessive saltwater and abrasion.

It was reported time and again that the scene was "like the aftermath of a nuclear explosion." Galvanized roofing dotted the landscape. Skeletons of old structures and rusted vehicles that previously had been hidden by vegetation were readily apparent. Walls and ceilings from houses that had been intact before the storm became obtrusive eyesores in neighbors' yards. Stories of the abundant nightmarish events during the few hours that Hugo passed over St. Croix could fill many books, and some of the Hugo stories were indeed stranger than fiction.

Understandably, after such a major catastrophe there was little immediate concern about the condition of native vegetation and wildlife. Island residents were first attentive to their personal needs. Most experienced a tremendous burst of energy to restore their homes and businesses and those of their loved ones. That energy often turned to depression when they discovered that it was impossible to recreate their lives, at least in the short term, to pre-Hugo conditions. Most of their physical necessities were either destroyed or in short supply. It was many weeks before power and telephone services were restored. Eight months later, when I returned to St. Croix, people were still waiting for shipments of necessary supplies to rebuild their homes. In the meantime, they survived in one or two makeshift rooms or with complete dependency on others.

AFTER HURRICANE HUGO

Immediately after the storm, a few folks reported finding dead and dying birds. Most of these were doves and pigeons. **Scaly-naped Pigeons** and **Zenaida Doves** became yard birds wherever seed was provided. Several people also noticed the almost complete absence of hummingbirds. Although a few hummers were seen immediately after the storm, they disappeared within a few days. The complete loss of flowering plants was undoubtedly to blame. Apparently, hummingbird feeders were responsible for the few hummingbirds that did survive.

Fred Sladen was the only St. Croix resident to check on certain bird habitats soon after Hugo. He found Little Blue and Green Herons and Cattle Egrets already nesting within defoliated mangroves on the Buccaneer Hotel grounds in October. By early February 1990 he found Zenaida Doves, Gray Kingbirds, Pearly-eyed Thrashers, and American Kestrels nesting "in good numbers."

It appeared that most of the resident bird species had made it through the storm. But the questions that concerned me were, Had any species been totally wiped out? Had any population changes occurred? How long would it take for the island's bird life to recover?

Although species recovery can only be determined in the long term, I was able to visit St. Croix during the first spring nesting season, the first half of May 1990, to assess breeding bird populations and compare them with pre-Hugo conditions. This was possible because during 1987, while I was living on St. Croix, I had conducted bird surveys along four separate driving transects. I had used Robbins and Van Velzen's *Breeding Bird Survey, 1966* methods and procedures as developed by the U.S. Fish and Wildlife Service (FWS) and had summarized my data in a 1988 report. The comparisons were later published in an ornithological journal, the *Wilson Bulletin* (Wauer and Wunderle 1992).

Only one of the thirty-four bird species recorded in 1987 could not be found during 1990, the **Bridled Quail-Dove.** Although an average of 3.5 individuals had been recorded on each Rain Forest Route during May 1987, none were detected in 1990. In addition, Fred and I visited a location in Caledonia Gut, where we consistently had found this bird prior to Hugo. Although Caledonia Gut had not been cleared of downed vegetation and we were able to work our way into the canyon only for about a quarter of a mile, we did reach an area where we regularly had seen Bridled Quail-Doves before Hugo. In 1990, however, we neither saw nor heard a single bird, even though we made low whistle sounds that previously had evoked responses.

The Bridled Quail-Dove is a reasonably large Columbid that spends a good deal of time feeding on the ground, although it generally is arboreal in nature (see the chapter on St. John and St. Thomas for additional information about this West Indian species). It shares its habitat with the slightly larger Scaly-naped Pigeon, which survived the storm. Scaly-napes are strong fliers and seemingly depend upon available food within a wider range of habitats. It appears that St. Croix's population of Bridled Quail-Doves was either totally eliminated or severely reduced by Hurricane Hugo. As late as January 1993, St. Croix resident Earl Roebuck told me that he had not seen or heard of anyone else finding this bird on St. Croix since Hugo.

My transect data showed that **White-crowned Pigeon** populations apparently shifted locations from the South Shore to Salt River Bay after Hugo. Although all of the Salt River Bay mangrove habitats had been severely damaged, they still were suitable for territorial displays. White-crowns were calling from mangrove snags but were utilizing the heavier moist forest vegetation (already covered with foliage) on the adjacent hillside for nesting.

Cattle Egrets demonstrated some of the same flexibility, although the Castle Burke population, where up to two hundred birds had roosted nightly in 1978, suffered a serious decline when that habitat was badly damaged. Cattle Egret populations actually increased along the North and South Shores.

Two of eight key passerines, **Caribbean Elaenias** and **Pearly-eyed Thrashers,** increased after the storm. Elaenia increases may have partly been due to reduced tree height and foliage, which provided greater visibility. But increases in thrashers probably were due to their opportunistic personality. This bird is known to feed on every conceivable food source, from grains to meats. Post-Hugo conditions, at least early on, undoubtedly provided widespread carrion, and thrashers stressed by the storm would likely enter a breeding cycle immediately. This bird, perhaps more than any other, increased in what was previously less than preferred habitats. Their expansion into new areas may have long-lasting effects; they are aggressive competitors and predators. Conversely, Northern Mockingbird numbers declined on all four transects. One can't help but wonder about the stability of this species; St. Croix represents the extreme southeastern edge of its range.

Both of St. Croix's hummingbirds, **Green-throated Carib** and **Antillean Crested Hummingbird,** as well as Bananaquit, all nectar feeders, were decimated by Hugo and its aftermath. As a matter of fact, so were all the other primary consumers (seed/vegetation eaters), with the exception of the fruit-eating White-crowned Pigeon (most of the White-crown population may already have departed for their wintering grounds before Hugo). Significant declines also were detected in seed-eating Common Ground-Doves, Zenaida Doves, and Black-faced Grassquits. On the other hand, predators such as Red-tailed Hawks, American Kestrels, Smooth-billed Anis, and Great Egrets did reasonably well, undoubtedly because of their ability to take advantage of weakened prey species.

In summary, comprehensive increases were detected only in Rock Doves, Great Egrets, Red-tailed Hawks, American Kestrels, White-crowned Pigeons, Caribbean Elaenias, and Pearly-eyed Thrashers. A few species seemed to remain about the same: Least Terns, Zenaida Doves, Smooth-billed Anis, Gray Kingbirds, Black-whiskered Vireos, and Black-faced Grassquits. But significant population declines (of 20 percent or more) were detected for Brown Pelicans, Cattle Egrets, Scaly-naped Pigeons, Bridled Quail-Doves, Common Ground-Doves, Green-throated Caribs, Antillean Crested Hummingbirds, Mangrove Cuckoos, Northern Mockingbirds, Bananaquits, and Yellow Warblers.

Antillean Crested Hummingbird

ST. CROIX TODAY

Much of the infrastructure on the island has been restored, and the Virgin Islands government has begun a public relations blitz to entice visitors back. Tourism will undoubtedly recover. One reason for optimism at the St. Croix Chamber of Commerce is the new Salt River Bay National

Historical Park and Ecological Preserve. To be administered by the National Park Service, the developing park provides additional incentive for history buffs and nature-lovers to visit St. Croix. Although this new national park, located on the north-central coast of St. Croix, is less than 1,000 acres in size, it contains such internationally significant resources that it has been recommended for World Heritage Site designation.

The creation of World Heritage Sites evolved from the idea that certain natural and cultural sites have universal value and are worthy of international recognition, respect, and protection. Sites eligible for World Heritage Site selection (under the auspices of UNESCO) include those that (1) have had a significant impact upon history, (2) illustrate significant geological processes, (3) may be crucial to the survival of threatened plants and animals, or (4) contain features of superlative natural beauty. Salt River Bay park complies with all four criteria.

Salt River Bay and its surroundings exemplify the scenic grandeur of the Caribbean landscape, complete with aqua blue waters, white breaking surf, varied greens of the mangroves and forested hillsides, and bright blue Caribbean sky.

Historically, Salt River Bay contains the only documented site on U.S. soil where members of the Christopher Columbus expedition (the second voyage in 1493) landed and where the first known encounter between Europeans and native peoples occurred. That encounter, in which one sailor and one Carib Indian were killed, represents the cultural apex as well as the beginning of the long-term decline of the Carib civilization. The new park also contains pre-Columbian burial grounds, the ruins of a ceremonial plaza and ballpark built in the 1200s or 1300s, and two European fortresses.

Geologically, Salt River Bay is situated at the head of a great submarine canyon that is part of a submerged valley formed hundreds of thousands of years ago. Salt River Canyon is one of only a small number of well-known submerged canyons occurring in tropical settings.

Biologically, Salt River Bay contains a rare continuum of habitats. The fresh water that flows off the forested hillsides into the Salt River drainage forms a freshwater wetland before its passes through a mangrove forest and enters the Salt River Bay estuary. The Salt River Bay mangroves, which prior to Hurricane Hugo were the largest intact mangrove forest in the Virgin Islands, are expected to recover. Mangroves provide a filtering system to cleanse the water that flows seaward so that when the flow reaches the estuary it carries important nutrients that are necessary to support the seagrass beds, coral gardens, and reefs beyond. Each of these marine habitats provides important nurseries for the area's fisheries. The final stage of the continuum is a steep-sided submarine canyon that drops off dramatically to 15,000 feet.

The various habitats within Salt River Bay park, including a salt pond along the eastern shore, support twenty-seven territorial or federally threatened and endangered plants and animals. The three endangered plants include a swamp fern, Malphigia, and Vahl's boxwood. Three endangered sea turtles—green, hawksbill, and leatherback—have been found either on the beach or in the bay. Twenty-one of the area's threatened or endangered species are birds. Six species are included on the federal endangered species list: Brown Pelican, Peregrine Falcon, Snowy and Piping Plovers, and Roseate and Least Terns. The remainder include Great Blue and Tricolored Herons, Great and Snowy Egrets, Black-crowned Night-Heron, White-cheeked Pintail, Ruddy Duck, West Indian Whistling-Duck, Osprey, Clapper Rail, Willet, Royal and Sandwich Terns, White-crowned Pigeon, and Bridled Quail-Dove.

SALT RIVER BAY MANGROVES

The value of the Salt River Bay mangroves is multidimensional in that, besides providing the valuable services of keeping the marine system clean and supporting a nursery for area fisheries, they also support a substantial wintering population of North America's Neotropical migrants. During the 1986–1987 winter, Fred and I censused the Sugar Bay (one finger of Salt River Bay) mangroves on twelve occasions. We discovered a total of 20 bird species that ranged from a low of 31 individuals on October 1 to a high of 128 individuals on October 26, about the peak of landbird migration.

Five of the twenty passerines found on our surveys were full-time residents: Caribbean Elaenia, Pearly-eyed Thrasher, Black-whiskered Vireo, Yellow Warbler, and Bananaquit. More than half of the total number of birds recorded were migrants or wintering species that had traveled south for hundreds of miles from their North American breeding grounds to secure winter habitat. These included, in descending order of abundance, Northern Waterthrush, Black-and-white Warbler, Northern Parula, American Redstart, Prairie, Cape May, Hooded, and Worm-eating Warblers, Common Yellowthroat, Blackpoll Warbler, Ovenbird, Blue-winged and Magnolia Warblers, Yellow-throated Vireo, and Yellow-rumped Warbler. The value of St. Croix's mangroves to North America's songbirds is very clear.

On October 14, 1986, Fred, Earl, and I did a Big Day Count on St. Croix, recording 1,409 individuals of 78 species. The dozen most numerous species recorded, in descending order of abundance, included Gray Kingbird, Pearly-eyed Thrasher, Semipalmated Sandpiper, Barn Swallow, Rock Dove, Mallard, Common Ground-Dove, Zenaida Dove, Black-bellied Plover, Short-billed Dowitcher, White-cheeked Pintail, and Royal Tern. A few of the least expected birds included Yellow-crowned Night-Heron, Northern Shoveler, Wilson's Phalarope, Yellow-billed Cuckoo, European Starling, and Shiny Cowbird.

Prior to my arrival on St. Croix, Fred had started Christmas Bird Counts; a West End Count had been run annually since 1972, and an East End Count was started in 1986. I participated in all counts during my three years' residency. The cumulative seventeen-year total of all count species amounted to 116 birds; 41 to 78 species were tallied annually. Of the 116 birds recorded, the 24 most numerous species, in descending order of abundance, included Cattle Egret, Bananaquit, Gray Kingbird, Stilt Sandpiper, Black-necked Stilt, Yellow Warbler, Scaly-naped Pigeon, White-cheeked Pintail, Short-billed Dowitcher, Caribbean Elaenia, Pearly-eyed Thrasher, Barn Swallow, Brown Pelican and Blue-winged Teal (tied), Northern Waterthrush, Royal Tern, Green-throated Carib, Zenaida Dove and Common Ground-Dove (tied), Great Egret, Rock Dove, Little Blue Heron, Ruddy Turnstone, and White-crowned Pigeon.

We found most of the wintering shorebirds at Great Pond along the south shore or at the West End Salt Pond. Although a few shorebirds remain throughout the year, several thousand individuals descend on St. Croix in September and literally fill the shallow ponds. All of that changes dramatically in a few weeks, however, with the arrival of Peregrine Falcons. Then the majority of the shorebirds continue southward, following the Lesser Antilles to South America. Those that remain along the way must take extra care to conceal themselves among the vegetation along the edges and on the little islands.

AT OTHER TIMES OF THE YEAR

Spring migration at St. Croix is barely noticeable. The vast majority of birds that had passed through in the fall, such as the shorebirds and a few landbirds (Blackpoll Warbler is one example), return north along the continent, not through the Antilles. Spring on St. Croix is most evident by the gradual disappearance of wintering songbirds and waterfowl, the arrival of Laughing Gulls in their breeding plumage, increased numbers of singing Black-whiskered Vireos, more vigorous songs of Yellow Warblers, and eventually the "pity-pit-pit" calls of Antillean Nighthawks.

Like breeding seasons everywhere, St. Croix's fields, woods, and forests resound with singing birds. Developed areas abound with Bananaquits, Black-faced Grassquits, Zenaida Doves, Gray Kingbirds, Pearly-eyed Thrashers, and Northern Mockingbirds. The dry forest hillsides are the best places to look for Mangrove Cuckoos; their slow, throaty calls are unmistakable. There, too, can be found Caribbean Elaenias, Northern Mockingbirds, Black-whiskered Vireos, Yellow Warblers, and grassquits. Scaly-naped Pigeons prefer the moist forest communities in the canyons and in other protected sites. The "common six" birds—Cattle Egret, Zenaida Dove, Bananaquit, Gray Kingbird, Pearly-eyed Thrasher, and Black-faced Grassquit—can be found almost anywhere, from gardens to open fields. Bananaquits and Black-faced Grassquits even frequent outdoor restaurants, where they perch on the tables and railings and, in the case of Bananaquits, take sugar from the sugarbowls.

One should never leave St. Croix and the Virgin Islands without watching these little yellow-breasted Bananaquits, locally called sugarbirds, yellow bellies, or yellow breasts. One must also snorkel the coral gardens at Buck Island Reef National Monument, explore the hidden recesses and walk the ramparts of old Fort Christiansted, eat lunch at one of the restaurants overlooking aqua-colored Christiansted Harbor, and drive St. Croix's outer loop road from Frederiksted's West End to Udall Point, the easternmost edge of the United States.

CHAPTER EIGHT

Saba AN ISLAND TIME FORGOT

One moment we were in flight, staring out of the airplane at the rocky cliff face dangerously close to our right side, and then suddenly the wheels touched down and we screeched to a halt. We had arrived on Saba! Never before or since have I experienced such a landing. The runway is located at the very edge of two cliffs to take advantage of the island's one and only flat space—Flat Point. The runway length is just 1,312 feet, and only specially built STOL (short takeoff and landing) DeHaviland Otter aircraft can manage the landing. It is like landing on an aircraft carrier—one little mistake could end it all.

Actually, it is amazing that Saba has an airport at all. Saba is not only a tiny island of only 5 square miles, less than a speck in the Caribbean Sea, but it also is extraordinary because it rises to 2,854 feet elevation, higher than many of the larger Lesser Antilles. Its base consists of very steep cliffs that drop off into very deep waters. There are no beaches; there just isn't sufficient room.

The entire island is volcanic in origin, the remains of an ancient volcanic core. Except in places where the hard igneous rock is exposed to the weather, it is covered with a luxuriant growth of tropical vegetation. From a distance, Saba looks like a giant green pyramid rising out of the deep blue Caribbean Sea. Some of the locals call it the Green Gumdrop, but their more enduring name is Unspoiled Queen. According to Natalie and Paul Pfanstiehl's little book, *Saba: The First Guidebook*, early-day sailors sometimes called Saba Napoleon's Hat because of its resemblance to his tricorn. Some folks refer to Saba as Glocamorra, the place of legend, and others call it Bali Hai, or their secret island. But whatever the preference, Saba remains very much its own unique personality, virtually unchanged by today's frantic world of commercialization and hypertension.

Betty and I had taken the twenty-minute Windward Airline (locally called WinAir) flight from St. Martin. The flight had been delayed for more than an hour, so our late-afternoon arrival was most welcome. We quickly retrieved our luggage in the small terminal and stepped outside for our initial exposure to Saba.

"Welcome to Saba," read a clean and neat sign at the edge of the parking lot, with the steep-sloped island beyond. The sign was decorated with a triggerfish and a hibiscus blossom, an appropriate combination for this tiny island. Close up, at the end of the runway, high cliffs formed a backdrop to Cove Bay and stood like a mighty fortress against unwanted arrivals. These cliffs also serve as nesting sites for tropicbirds. Both the Red-billed and White-tailed Tropicbirds nest there from January through May.

We immediately claimed one of the half-dozen waiting taxis. It might be more appropriate to say that Carmen Hassell, our taxi driver, claimed us, because within minutes we were en route to the village of Windwardside and Scout's Place, where we had reservations for our two-night stay. It was immediately obvious that we were in good hands. Carmen was friendly and helpful and seemed to know every one of the island's approximately 1,100 souls. I soon discovered that Hassell was a common Saban name. In fact, Lambertus Hassell, who is said to have acquired his engineering skills from a Dutch correspondence course, was credited with the design and construction of the island's principal roadway from Juanacho Yrausquin Airport to

Windwardside. Regular air service began in 1963, the same year electricity arrived on the island.

Hassell's winding highway above Flat Point would make anyone admire the ingenuity and skill of its builders. It zigzags upward through Lower and Upper Hell's Gate (villages) with nineteen curves before topping out at English Quarter and Windwardside. We climbed 1,800 feet in about 5 miles. After Carmen delivered us safely at Scout's Place, she remained. She was minding the little bar when we went in to dinner a short time later.

The next morning was clear and bright. Mount Scenery appeared like a great green haystack dominating the little town of Windwardside. The mountain greenery was more than that of tropical vegetation that morning. The sunlight gave it a very special color like a deep velvet green, darker here and there where long drainages, locally called guts, were still filled with nighttime shadows and secrets. The scene was almost magical.

Several high-flying **Scaly-naped Pigeons** hurried across my vision and helped bring me back to the present. Nearby, **Gray Kingbirds** were calling from the tops of the stores and homes about town. The mournful calls of **Zenaida Doves** echoed along the streets. A family of Bananaquits were already searching for nectar within the bright yellow allamanda flowers growing in the Scout's Place courtyard.

Mount Scenery was beckoning me to partake of its lush beauty. I knew that I could not enjoy anything more on Saba without first adventuring into that great green world.

MOUNT SCENERY

The trail to the top of Mount Scenery begins at the edge of Windwardside. Actually, the route is less of a hiking trail than a spectacular stairway consisting of 1,046 stairs cut into the steep mountainside. It is one of the most remarkable routes in all the West Indies. From the bottom, the 1,046 steps seemed of little consequence. But it became readily apparent that the hike to the top of Saba was going to be more than walking up a long flight of stairs. The 1,046 steps gain 2,855 feet in less than 2 miles distance.

It is obvious why stairs were constructed rather than a trail, which would require numerous switchbacks and considerable scarring of the slopes. A trail would have been much longer and more costly, in both construction and maintenance. As it was, the Mount Scenery stairs climbed practically straight up the mountainside with only a few diversions. In retrospect, it seemed altogether appropriate for Saba.

The Mount Scenery trail begins in a gut filled with tropical vegetation, but even when the stairs follow an open ridge, lush vegetation abounds. Most of the plants along the lower half of the route are the same species that grow in and around Windwardside, such as bananas, mangos, soursops, and papayas. The huge mango tree that shades the start of the trail is one of the largest I have ever seen. It literally dominates the entry area.

This lower vegetation is locally called "rain forest," a term that also was used by ECNAMP (Eastern Caribbean Natural Area Management Program) in developing the *Saba Preliminary Data Atlas* (Eastern Caribbean Natural Area Management Program 1980), one of several reports resulting from a survey of conservation priorities in the Lesser Antilles by that St. Croix–based organization. However, J. S. Beard, in his classic 1944 paper, "Climax Vegetation in Tropical America," referred to this habitat type as "lower montane rain forest." Beard described it as a two-story habitat that occurs from 800 to 2,500 feet elevation.

Above the rain forest, on the upper slopes of Mount Scenery, is a very different habitat which can properly be called "cloud forest" because of its daily cloud cover, which provides sufficient moisture for the perpetuation of its extremely lush vegetation. Beard called this habitat "montane rain forest," and his description fits perfectly well: "The forest is in two closed stories, at 20 and 10 meters (54 and 27 feet) with a shrub layer formed mainly of simple-leaved dwarf palms and tree ferns. The trees have heavy crowns, branch low, and are loaded with moss and epiphytes. Leaves are simple, mesophyllous, and covered with epiphytes."

The rain forest area was filled with bird song. The most obvious of these was the little **Caribbean Elaenia,** locally called pee-whistler. This little flycatcher is very nondescript in appearance, but its behavior and character are most appealing. Only about 7 inches long, it spends a good part of its time fly-catching among the middle-level trees and shrubs. Its perkiness and upright posture, with an occasional flip of its tail, and its overall olive-gray color, except for two faint whitish wing bars, help to identify this West Indian specialty. It also has a well-concealed patch of white on the crown that it can flash when excited or during its breeding season, but I wasn't able to see that feature that morning. But its cheery song, "che-eup," repeated several times a minute, was more than enough to identify it.

Lesser Antillean Bullfinches were also active; their unique songs, five to ten "seep" notes, usually followed by a buzz, were heard several times at the start of the trail. This species has learned to feed at tables in outdoor restaurants, where it is rarely shy, but in the wild it is often hard to find. The males are coal-black except for a rufous throat, eyeline, and undertail covert. Females are nondescript gray-brown with a rufous blush on their wings.

We reached the cloud forest about midway to the summit. It was evident first by the abundance of tree ferns. We had found a few in lower, more protected places along the trail, but suddenly this giant fern was everywhere. It is a fascinating plant with a fibrous trunk and huge frondlike leaves that grow from the top of the trunk in a spiral arrangement.

Wild heliconias were abundant as well. I identified at least two kinds, both with long paddle-shaped leaves and large red or yellow bracts that reminded me of lobster claws. The true flowers are hidden inside the horny bracts that are able to catch and hold water. These native plants are closely related to the introduced banana trees that were common farther down the mountain.

All the heliconias and bananas produce an abundance of nectar, and two of the Caribbean's largest hummingbirds, the Green-throated and Purple-throated Caribs, take advantage of this available supply of nutrients. Although the **Green-throated Carib** is widespread throughout the Lesser Antilles and ranges west to eastern Puerto Rico, the slightly larger **Purple-throated Carib** occurs only in the Lesser Antilles from Saba southward.

Unlike most other hummingbirds, male and female caribs look just alike; there is no sexual dimorphism. At first glance the Purple-throated Carib appears to be just a large, all-dark hummingbird. But in proper light it is a truly gorgeous bird with a deep purplish-red throat and breast, blue-black belly and upperparts, greenish-blue feathers below the tail, and glossy green wings. All other West Indian hummingbirds possess blackish wings.

The Purple-throated Carib's most impressive feature, however, is its long, decurved bill. It is this wonderful organ which allows it to feed on the sheathed heliconia flowers. I watched one individual feeding on heliconias along the trail, approaching each flower from below and probing into each of the bright red bracts one at a time. K. H. Voous, author of *Birds of the Netherlands Antilles*, wrote that the "female tends to have [a] bill longer and more strongly curved than [that of the] male." Assumedly, the female is able to utilize larger and deeper heliconia flowers than the male.

The Purple-throated Carib also is able to make long-distance overwater flights. There are a few records of the species on St. Croix, U.S. Virgin Islands, a distance of about 95 miles directly west. Saba is the nearest island with a population of these unique hummingbirds.

Saba also possesses another avian duo, **Pearly-eyed** and **Scaly-breasted Thrashers.** Like the Green-throated Carib, the Pearly-eyed Thrasher's

Purple-throated Carib

range extends from throughout the Lesser Antilles west to Puerto Rico. However, the Scaly-breasted Thrasher occurs only from Saba southward.

Pearly-eyes are abundant throughout the Virgin Islands, where they utilize every habitat type available from the rain forest to gardens and mangroves (see Chapters 6 and 7). Scaly-breasts are much more selective, preferring the wetter upland forests, and rarely are found in the drier habitats.

On Saba, the two species seemed equally abundant in the rain forest, but while Scaly-breasts declined with lower elevation, Pearly-eyes increased.

These two thrashers look alike at first glance but are quite different when they can be seen in good light. The larger Pearly-eyed Thrasher is generally streaked with brown on its throat and neck, while the Scaly-breast, true to its name, has grayish-brown barring on its throat and underparts. This pattern gives it a scaly appearance. In addition, the usually distinct white eye of the Pearly-eye helps to separate it from the Scaly-breast, which has a rarely noticed brown eye.

In addition to these two members of the thrasher family, there is yet a third thrasher that inhabits Saba's cloud forest environment, the **Brown Trembler.** This bird is the strangest of the three. Its name clearly describes its fascinating behavior of trembling when agitated or excited. It then droops its wings and shakes all over, and the shaking may last for several minutes. Otherwise, it is a rather plain-looking bird, about midsize between the Pearly-eyed and Scaly-breasted Thrashers, with brownish upperparts and lighter underparts and an extremely long bill.

At several places along the Mount Scenery trail we were able to look down into the streets of Windwardside to see how it hugs the little ridge above the sea. It wasn't until then, from that bird's-eye perspective, that I realized that almost every rooftop in Windwardside was a brick-red color. For that matter, so were the vast majority of rooftops everywhere else on the island. The contrast of red roofs, bright green vegetation, and deep blue sea was bewitching.

Clouds covered much of the mountaintop and obscured our view by the time we reached the summit. It was wet and chilly, with little puddles of rainwater scattered about. It was easy to understand the meaning of "cloud forest" from the very different conditions, all within a couple of hours. The tree ferns and other mountaintop vegetation were dripping wet.

The return trip was far more difficult than our slow, plodding, uphill hike had been. On the way up, we had stopped numerous times to admire a flower or bird or to appreciate a particularly scenic view. Once I discovered an all-dark snake about 2 feet in length that was scurrying across the steps just ahead of us. I had tried to find it in the trailside vegetation to attempt to identify it, but once off the trail I couldn't locate it in the thick vegetation. Later, when I asked about the snake's possible identification, I was told it more than likely was the nonpoisonous West Indian Racer of the genus *Alsophis*.

At another point we stopped to watch a Red-tailed Hawk soaring reasonably close by. This bird was a reminder of the distant connection between

North America and the West Indies. It is the same Red-tailed Hawk species that is so common on the continent. Its broad wings and brick-red tail were spread out to catch the thermals that were beginning to climb the slopes from the warmer lowlands.

Voous summarized Saba's bird life by pointing out that twenty-six of the fifty-eight known species are resident or breed there and only twenty-four species are Neotropical migrants from North America. Twelve species are seabirds. One seabird, the Audubon's Shearwater, has become something of a celebrity to Sabans.

The Audubon's Shearwater is locally called wedrego, a name derived from one of its incredulous nighttime calls which has been interpreted as "where-do-we-go, where-do-we-go," hence wedrego. George Seaman, in *Every Shadow Is a Man*, wrote: "To hear his wild repertoire on a moonlit night as he flies back and forth from land to sea is an indelible experience. Laughs, cries, groans, shrieks are the mating language of the wedrego."

Wedregos are true seabirds that spend their entire life at sea, except for a few weeks each year when they nest on some rocky, isolated island of the West Indies. At that time, they select burrows in rocky crevices and lay a single egg that is tended by the pair. Also at that time of year they forage only at night, leaving their burrows after dark to feed on flying fish and squid, which they capture on or near the surface. At other times of the year they occur in flocks, flying swiftly over the waves and barely shearing the tips, hence their name, Shearwater. They can fly with great agility, either with rapid wingbeats, gliding, or fluttering. In calm air their wheeling flight is very much like that of a swift. This crow-size bird is dark brown above and has a white belly, chest, and throat, and it has large white underwing patches on its otherwise dark-brown wings.

We descended out of the clouds at about the halfway point from the summit of Mount Scenery; dark shadows dotted the landscape. When we strolled through town it was with a different appreciation of this little Dutch village. We passed the Honey Bee Kindergarten, almost across the road from Scout's Place. We paused a few minutes to listen and discovered that English was the main language. It seemed rather odd that Sabans speak more English than Dutch, which should be their native tongue. Saba is, after all, one of the Netherlands Antilles. Carrol Fleming, in *Adventuring in the Caribbean*, provided a thumbnail sketch of Saba's history: "Columbus sighted the island in 1493. Saba has lived under sixteen different flags; the island changed hands twelve times in the seventeenth and eighteenth centuries alone. Holland ended up with it in 1816 and it has been Dutch ever since. English, the spoken tongue, remains the legacy of early settlers from the Shetland Islands."

THE BOTTOM

On our second morning we departed Scout's Place again right after breakfast, but instead of climbing up the mountain we struck out westward, following the cement roadway in the direction of The Bottom. The road follows the terrain along the steep hillside, in and out of the various guts. Tiny **Black-faced Grassquits** scurried away from the roadside as we approached. **Gray Kingbirds** sang their loud "pitirre" calls from various tree snags. **Pearly-eyed Thrasher** songs were the most evident, providing a variety of harsh calls and shrieks. A **Black-whiskered Vireo** added its voice to the morning songfest. It had a much sweeter song, a three-syllabled series of whistles, very much like that of its look-alike North American cousin, the Red-eyed Vireo. It differs only in its black whiskers, a dark line that extends from its bill downward along the edge of its throat. The National Geographic Society *Field Guide* provides excellent illustrations of the two species.

We detected the very low and mournful calls of **Bridled Quail-Doves** on two occasions as we walked along the roadway. The call of this very secretive bird is slightly louder in the middle and then trails off. It is so low in pitch that some people are not able to hear the call at all. On the rare occasions when this plump bird is discovered in the open, the broad white line below the eye is its most distinct feature. It has a reddish back and lighter underparts and very short, heavy legs. I have found it on St. John and St. Croix by listening for it walking among the dry leaves. It will rarely fly but usually will walk away when approached. See Chapter 6 on St. John and St. Thomas, U.S. Virgin Islands, for more information about this tropical bird.

The Bottom is Saba's administrative center, but it is barely larger than Windwardside. It is part of the Netherlands Antilles, which includes Saba, St. Martin, and St. Eustatius in the Lesser Antilles and Aruba, Curaçao, and Bonaire along the north coast of South America. Administrative overview is provided by a lieutenant governor who lives at The Bottom in the large wooden house next to Wilhelmina Park. He presides over the Island Council, which oversees local problems and developments. The administrative center for the Netherlands Antilles is located at Willemstad, Curaçao. Saba shares one delegate with St. Martin and St. Eustatius to the twenty-two-member council in Curaçao.

The Bottom is located 820 feet above Fort Bay, where there is a single pier for use by transportation barges, diving boats, visiting sailboats, and the like. Diving among Saba's adjacent coral reefs offers unique experiences that coral reefs in shallower waters cannot provide. Twenty-five separate dive spots, including an enormous "tree" of black coral, form part of the island's underwater appeal.

We walked around the town for a couple of hours and enjoyed an iced tea at Cranston's Antique Inn. We learned that this inn and restaurant was a government guest house in 1955 and housed Queen Juliana of the Netherlands during her visit. Outside on the street were women selling crafts. They were eager to show us samples of their beautiful drawn-thread work that included bunwarmers, scarves, handkerchiefs, baby bibs, and more. Carmen met us in front of the inn at noon, and we rode back up the hill to Windwardside. We ate lunch at Captain's Quarters and then headed for the airport for our afternoon flight.

Our flight was delayed, but the extra time allowed me to walk down the runway toward the high cliffs to see what birds might be present. Black-faced Grassquits flew ahead of me along the runway. A lone Barn Swallow swooped down in search of insects. An American Kestrel flew up from the end of the runway and streaked off across Cove Bay to settle on the top of one jagged precipice.

Several Magnificent Frigatebirds were soaring over the slope above the cliffs. Their great wingspan and narrow body were unmistakable. Then I could see a number of Brown Boobies fishing the Cove Bay waters. These birds were all brown above with an all-brown head and neck and a white belly and abdomen. I watched them fishing by high dives that sent them fully below the surface, where they remained for several seconds before flapping out and upward to circle before diving again, sometimes from as high as 60 feet. There were more than twenty individuals.

The smaller, all-white birds with solid black wing tips and a bright red bill were Red-billed Tropicbirds. I counted thirteen of these incredible creatures, flying much faster and more agilely than the more plodding boobies. Most of these birds were too far away to see them well, but on one occasion a lone bird made a wider than normal circle and came across the bay to where I was able to see its features much better. What a beautiful bird it was! Its most outstanding feature was its long white tail-streamers, which were as long as the rest of the bird's body. Its back was finely barred with black against its snow-white body. But I could also see its bright red, surprisingly large bill and the heavy black line that runs over the eye from the bill onto its neck. It called out, a shrill "careek, careek," as it turned back, almost as if to say farewell, or maybe it was responding to my WinAir aircraft, which was rolling down the runway in my direction. I hurried back to the terminal, and we soon boarded WinAir for our return flight to St. Martin. Our departure provided only part of the excitement of our arrival. Our aircraft became airborne almost immediately, and I watched the Unspoiled Queen fade away in the distance.

CHAPTER NINE

Anguilla

TRANQUILLITY WRAPPED IN BLUE

Bananaquit

From the air, the extreme flatness of Anguilla is readily apparent. The island is an ancient coral reef that just barely pokes out of the Caribbean Sea. Numerous living reefs surround the island. The highest point above sea level is Crocus Hill, only 213 feet elevation. Numerous shallow harbors still support an economically viable fishing industry for fish and lobsters, and in recent years many of the island's thirty-plus white-sand beaches have been developed for tourism. Today, Anguilla offers the visitor a relatively quiet, out-of-the-way place to soak up the sea and sun without the hassles of the larger, more-developed islands. Anguilla is very much like what St. Martin, Antigua, and the eastern half of Guadeloupe must have been like thirty years ago. Some Anguillians recognize that advantage. The motto on my apartment brochure read, "Tranquillity Wrapped in Blue." From my perspective, the long-term success of Anguilla's tourist industry will depend upon whether the Anguillians can retain that feeling of isolation or whether they will attempt to compete with the other islands and destroy the special atmosphere that currently exists.

Betty and I arrived on a Coastal Air flight direct from St. Croix after a two-hour flight, but most of the island's visitors enter through nearby St. Martin, and many of those folks come to Anguilla for day trips only. Although we stayed in a small, very clean, and attractive apartment (the Syd-Ans) in the village of Sandy Ground, we visited several of the more exclusive and also more expensive hotels during our four-day stay. We were happy with the Syd-Ans apartment, which our taxi driver had recommended, and were terribly disappointed with the very slow breakfast service and unfriendly waiter we experienced at the Malliouhana Hotel, sometimes considered to be one of the finest in the Caribbean.

Malliouhana was the Carib Indian name for the island, but when Columbus passed by in 1493 he named it Anguilla, Spanish for eel, because of its resemblance to that long fish. The British arrived in 1650 and, in spite of two attempted invasions by the French, remained in full control. A nonbloody revolt occurred in 1967 that required a British peacekeeping force, and in 1976 the approximately 7,000 Anguillians were granted domestic self-government.

We rented a jeep and drove every road on the island. Of course on an island of only 34 square miles, less than 16 miles from tip to tip, there was not a great deal of choice. We found that about one-third of the island's terrain consisted of coral terraces and bare limestone rock, much of it worn into deep, sharp pockets by the continuous salt spray and grinding sand. The rest of the landscape seemed to contain a thin layer of soil that could hardly support adequate crops. We found only a few patches of corn and peas and a few worn pastures with sorry-looking cattle and goats.

BIRD LIFE

As might be expected on a coral island with many salt ponds and bays with seagrass beds, the bird life consisted largely of those species associated with the sea and salt ponds. Because of the timing of our visit in midsummer (July 1–4), the birds we saw were representative of resident species, not migrants or winter visitors from North America. Of thirty-six kinds of birds recorded, sixteen were land birds, thirteen were seabirds, and seven were water birds.

The yards and gardens of homes and the abundant plantings at the various hotels contained the largest variety of land birds. The most abundant of these included Zenaida Doves and Common Ground-Doves, Green-throated Caribs and Antillean Crested Hummingbirds, Caribbean Elaenias, Gray Kingbirds, Pearly-eyed Thrashers, Yellow Warblers, Bananaquits, Black-faced Grassquits, and Lesser Antillean Bullfinches. We also saw smaller numbers of Mangrove Cuckoos, Caribbean Martins, and Black-whiskered Vireos. Cattle Egrets were present in fields, and we found American Kestrels at a variety of locations.

Of all those land birds, none was so obvious as the **Zenaida Dove**. This mid-size dove was almost everywhere, from the village streets and overhead wires to the lawns and fields. Its soft, cooing song, almost identical to the Mourning Dove, which does not occur in the Lesser Antilles, was commonplace. It is best identified by its rounded tail edged with white and the white trailing edge on its secondary wing feathers. It is generally a rather stocky dove that is brown above and vinaceous below; breeding birds usually show cinnamon color on their head and neck. It is a lovely bird that is too often taken for granted because of its abundance. See Chapter 5 on Tortola, Island of Doves, about its behavior there.

The only other dove on Anguilla is the tiny Common Ground-Dove, barely half the size of the Zenaida Dove and without any white on the body or wing. Instead, the wing primaries show obvious rufous color in flight. Adults also possess a scaly-looking breast. Their song is also very different, a soft "oo-a" ascending on the last syllable. These doves often congregate at freshwater puddles after rain; the flock may include several dozen individuals. Then they strut around like some kind of fancy gamecock, with their tails cocked up and running at each other, no doubt to claim superiority.

The Yellow Warbler was surprisingly common throughout the island, from the hotel grounds and beach forests to the arid brushland and mangroves. This little all-yellow bird, with faint reddish streaks on its breast, is mistakenly called canary or yellow bird, but it is the same Yellow Warbler found in North America. This is the only all-yellow bird that occurs on Anguilla, expect for the possible exception of an escaped pet.

James Bond, in the chapter on West Indian Wood Warblers in Griscom and Sprunt's book, *The Warblers of North America*, called the Yellow Warbler the "most widespread and familiar warbler in the West Indies." He also pointed out that there was considerable racial variation, that males in the Lesser Antilles often have chestnut crowns. Only one of the several birds I observed showed any chestnut color on the crown, but they all sang their typical, cheerful song, described by Bond as "wee-chee-wee-chee-chee-wur."

Just behind our apartment at Sandy Ground was a large salt pond with a long, narrow ditch that separated the pond from the apartment complex.

The far section of the pond was part of a salt production operation. Snowy Egrets and Little Blue and Green Herons were present most of the time in the near ditch, stalking prey or waiting quietly for some choice morsel to wander by. One morning a lone adult Yellow-crowned Night-Heron was present, probably not yet finished with its nighttime hunting activities. I found another individual perched among the sea grapes at Rendezvous Bay.

The most common resident bird at the Sandy Ground salt pond was the Black-necked Stilt. A dozen or more individuals, including several reasonably large youngsters, were present at all times. With the least disturbance they would fly up and make a wide circle, calling all the while, before settling back down in the same general area. Their loud and incessant "kek kek kek" calls went on and on. I decided that the Black-necked Stilt would make a wonderful "watchdog." The clamor these birds raise can be startling, and they seem to stir up all the other shorebirds that might be present. When they finally alight they usually raise their black, pointed wings high up vertically over their head before folding them deliberately over their immaculate plumage. They may even bob up and down by bending their knees.

Another fascinating trait practiced by Black-necked Stilts is "belly-soaking," the transporting of water by wetting the plumage to cool themselves as well as their eggs and chicks. Ehrlich and colleagues in their book, *The Birder's Handbook*, point out that more than a hundred belly-soaking trips can be made in a single day.

These extremely long-legged birds are easy to identify because of their black back and bill and snow-white underparts, set on a pair of bright red stilts for legs. They also have a large white spot over each eye. Juveniles look just like the adults but are not so dark.

Our trip to the West End produced a few more water birds, including White-cheeked Pintails at Rendezvous Pond, more Black-necked Stilts, four Lesser Yellowlegs, and two adults and one immature Willet at the West End salt pond. One of the three adult White-cheeked Pintails was a female with nineteen fairly large ducklings. The presence of nineteen ducklings with one hen was a little surprising because pintails normally produce broods of only five to twelve ducklings. However, it isn't uncommon for one hen to "watch" youngsters of other hens at various times. I was especially pleased to find this West Indian duck with so many offspring, because populations of this native species have declined throughout much of its range.

This bird is very different from the Northern Pintail, which is so common on the North American continent, as well as in Europe and Asia. The White-cheeked Pintail is the southern relative that is native to South America, the Greater Antilles, and the northern Lesser Antilles. It looks a little like the female Northern Pintail, with a broad white patch on its cheeks and throat. It also possesses red streaks on its upper bill and a green rather than brownish wing spectrum. It is a very distinguished bird.

We found a lone American Oystercatcher on the rocky shoreline at Sandy Hill Bay. The area was strewn with broken whelks. Oystercatchers, sometimes called whelk-crackers, after their feeding behavior, are rare in the Lesser Antilles. They are crow-size shorebirds that utter a loud, shrill cry, "weep, weep, weep," when startled. They possess an all-black head and chest, white underparts, grayish-brown back, pink feet, and a bright red bill. The size of the bill gives them an almost awkward appearance, but their extremely large and heavy bill is used to chip mussels and barnacles off seashore rocks and to split open whelks, clams, and other shellfish.

SEASHELLS

Until we moved to St. Croix, I had paid little attention to seashells. Other than picking up an especially colorful shell along the California beach or on Padre Island, Texas, I had more or less left shell collecting to others. But our sudden emergence into the West Indies kindled an interest that had apparently lain dormant for many years. Betty and I began to collect seashells wherever we traveled. During the three years we lived on St. Croix and traveled to all the West Indies, we collected and I identified and cataloged more than 550 species of seashells. All of these were collected from the drift along the beach or, in a few cases where the beach was reasonably steep, underwater where the base of the beach flattened out. Such was the case at Anguilla.

Each day we stopped at likely looking sites to briefly walk the beach and snorkel the adjacent waters. We were surprised how many of the best beaches contained hotels and condominiums and were essentially closed to nonpaying visitors. Nevertheless, we sampled several of these without asking; a middle-aged white couple is usually assumed to be a paying customer.

We hunted seashells (circling the island) at Captain Bay, Shoal Bay (fairly good), Long Bay, Meads Bay, West End Bay, Cove Bay, Rendezvous Bay, Little Harbor, Sandy Hill Bay, and Mimi Bay. Of all these sites, we had the greatest success at Rendezvous Bay, but only after we discovered that the beach was too steep for the shells to be naturally washed out into the surface; we found them in 2 or 3 feet of water at the base of the slope.

We found more than fifty species of seashells during our stay on Anguilla. Percy Morris's book, *A Field Guide to Shells of the Atlantic*, was indispensable. Later at home I used R. Tucker Abbot's *American Seashells* to double-check my identifications.

Another surprising find on the Rendezvous Bay beach was a dead juvenile porcupinefish, only about 5 inches long and with dozens of sharp spines. I couldn't tell how it had died (there were no marks of injury), but it was bloated like a football. One of its methods of defense is to inflate itself by taking in either water or air to make itself larger than it would otherwise be; this action also stretches the skin and projects the defensive spines outward. Porcupinefish are actually more adept than the closely related pufferfish at inflating themselves. They also have a toxic skin secretion.

Just above Rendezvous Beach was a narrow woodland of short trees, shrubs, and vines that, by crawling under the canopy, provided wonderful shade out of the dazzling sun on the white beach and aqua waters. The dominant woody plant was sea grape, a common species along the coastlines throughout the West Indies. The same species grows along the southern coasts of the eastern United States, where it is little more than a vine or low-growing shrub. In the West Indies it can be a 20-foot tree. Most obvious are the very large, almost plate-size, roundish leaves with dark red veins. Its name comes from the edible berries that, although acid-tasting, are eaten outright or are used for preserves. Penelope Honychurch in her book, *Caribbean Wild Plants and Their Uses*, stated, "The Caribs used this species for making weapons. The gum was used for varnish. The wood, which is still used today for making furniture, is a striking deep red and very hard." She also mentions that the bark is used in a tea for diarrhea.

Sitting in the shady canopy, I was suddenly aware that I was not alone. Less than a dozen feet away, perched on a vinelike branch of sea grape, was a **Caribbean Elaenia.** How long this little flycatcher had been there I'll never know. But once I discovered its presence I was able to look it over very carefully. In spite of the bird's rather drab appearance, it was a personable neighbor. Twice it dashed out for a passing insect, snapping up its prey with a loud clap of its bill. The rest of the time it stayed nearby, it didn't utter a sound. Elaenias usually are fairly noisy birds, and their harsh "che-up" or "wi-wi-eup" calls have given them the common name of pee-whistler or cheery-cheer. It apparently decided not to tempt its human neighbor with a sample of its vocal renderings.

Once, after it returned with an insect it had captured, it raised its crest ever so slightly and I was able to see a tiny patch of white on its crown. Otherwise, it has dark olive-gray upperparts with two lighter wing bars and lighter gray underparts. It possesses a subtle beauty not easily evident except by such a close-up examination.

Each morning at dawn I left our apartment and walked the beach at Road Bay. Fishermen were always ahead of me, either preparing for the day's activities or slowly motoring their boats out of the bay and past the jetty. Seabirds were always present, either flying about, sitting on the jetty or beach, or bickering with one another as most gulls and terns seem to do. The most common of the seabirds was always the Laughing Gull, the only gull present. Its all-black head, red bill, dark gray back, and snow-white underparts, neck, and tail made this bird easy to identify. The only tern present inside the harbor was the Royal Tern, somewhat longer and thinner than the Laughing Gull and with only a black cap and a yellow-orange bill. Both birds were sitting together on the beach one morning. Their fishing habits are very different. Laughing Gulls skim the water's surface, picking up various food items, or feed upon fish carcasses they discover on the beach. Royal Terns, on the other hand, fish by diving into the sea, often fully submerging, to capture fish that they spot by flying or hovering overhead.

Farther out to sea, beyond the bay and jetty, were a number of the more pelagic terns: Sandwich, Least, and Bridled. The Least Tern undoubtedly nests on some of the island's undisturbed beaches or clearings. It usually occurs in large colonies, but it is a species that has declined throughout much of its range, so its presence on Anguilla was good news for those of us who appreciate seabirds. This is the smallest of all the terns, barely 9 inches long, and with a black cap and a black wedge on its primaries that is evident in flight. Breeding birds possess an orange-yellow bill tipped with black. It is otherwise an all-white bird with a deeply forked tail. It has a very distinct call, a high-pitched "kip" or a harsh "chir-ee-erp."

A pair of Brown Pelicans left their perch on the far end of the beach and flew off toward the sea, where they would fish some school of passing fish. Then a Brown Booby soared over the bay, only a few feet above the quiet waters. The aqua colors of the bay reflected upon the white underparts, giving it a truly beautiful and striking pattern. Every morning two or three Magnificent Frigatebirds were seen soaring over North Hill at the end of the bay. These huge, marvelous creatures look all the world like an ancient archaeopteryx. With a 90-inch wingspan, long forked tail, and huge beak, they are able to soar hour after hour on even the slightest of breezes. They are even able to sleep on the wing.

Magnificent Frigatebirds, perhaps more than any other of Anguilla's bird life, truly represent the pelagic character of the island. Anguilla evolved from the sea. Magnificent Frigatebirds are significant and highly visible members of that environment.

CHAPTER TEN

St. Martin

A NORTHEASTERN GATEWAY

Pearly-eyed Thrasher

The Great Salt Pond at Philipsburg at one time must have been a marvelous habitat for water birds, especially during spring and fall. I imagine it teeming with millions of migrants en route either north or south along the chain of islands that form the great arc between North and South America. Perhaps as many as two dozen species of shorebirds could have been found there at one time. Sandpipers, plovers, curlews, godwits, dowitchers, turnstones, snipes, and stilts—all undoubtedly stopped to rest and feed before continuing their journeys. Their survival depended upon the availability of adequate food at key staging areas along their route. St. Martin's Great Salt Pond was one of those crucial stops.

The Great Salt Pond today is only a fraction of what once existed there before Philipsburg, the capital city of Dutch Sint Maarten, began to expand, filling the pond to make room for more and bigger hotels and stores. So instead of finding nutrient-rich salt marsh and mudflat habitats, today's migrant shorebirds find a landfill that is gradually eating up the valuable staging area that once existed. Instead of finding plenty of food to replenish the fat expended on their long overwater flights from North America and to prepare them for the next phase of their journey, they find only trash and ruin. Further, the expanding population of human beings has also introduced house cats and dogs and encouraged rats, Cattle Egrets, and gulls, all the species that are there for a free handout. Those human-induced creatures also prey upon the declining shorebird populations.

I walked the south and east shores of Great Salt Pond one fall morning in the midst of the southbound migration, expecting to find great numbers of shorebirds. Instead I found only a couple of hundred individuals of only a dozen species: Black-bellied and Semipalmated Plovers, Killdeers, Lesser Yellowlegs, Spotted, Semipalmated, Western, Least, and White-rumped Sandpipers, Ruddy Turnstones, Short-billed Dowitchers, and Common Snipes. Hundreds of Cattle Egrets and several Laughing Gulls were foraging among the garbage. Barn and Cliff Swallows were fly-catching above the rotting debris.

Most of the shorebirds present that day had come from as far away as the Arctic tundra in Alaska, where they nest. Twice annually they make the great trek between their summer and winter homes. The little Semipalmated Plover, for example, builds its tundra nest among tufts of alpine grass and patches of lichen. Southbound birds follow a route that takes them toward the East Coast of North America, where they gather in great staging areas along the bays of Nova Scotia and New Brunswick. Most of those individuals follow the coastline south to Florida and cross the Caribbean Sea to Central and South America. A second group travels over water to the West Indies, where they gather again in staging areas at salt ponds on Hispaniola and St. Croix or in the Lesser Antilles. Although a few individuals remain all winter, the bulk of the migrants continues southward to the nutrient-rich bays of Central and South America. In spring their northbound journey begins as early as March and generally follows the same route they took southward.

Semipalmated Plovers are plump little shorebirds that run about on the mudflat or beach, head held high, searching for insects, crustaceans, mollusks, and the like, which they grab up with their short bills. They possess white underparts, except for a single dark band across their upper chest, dark brown upperparts, except for a white band that forms a collar, and a white forehead and indistinct eye line. They also have orange-yellow legs and bill, tipped with black, and partially webbed feet (difficult to see in the field), from which they derive their name, semipalmated.

The Short-billed Dowitcher is a breeding bird of the peatlands of the northern boreal forests. Eastern birds overwinter along the East Coast and south through the Antilles into Mexico and Central America. Dowitchers are medium-size shorebirds with a long, straight bill which they use to probe for food in the mud. Their feeding habits consist of rapid jabbing motions. In flight they show an obvious white wedge from their back to tail. When disturbed, flocks often wheel in tight formations and may fly high in the sky before returning to feed.

Many shorebirds are hunted along their migration routes; gunners in the West Indies share equal responsibility for the demise of shorebirds and other species. Professor K. H. Voous, author of *Birds of the Netherlands Antilles*, pointed out that shooting has had considerable impact on several St. Martin birds, although he did not particularly include shorebirds: "Uncontrolled shooting has led to the extermination of the Red-tailed Hawk, which was persecuted all over the island for being a 'chicken-hawk.' Game birds like the Zenaida or Mountain Dove have seriously decreased in numbers or have practically (Scaly-naped Pigeon) or wholly (White-crowned Pigeon) disappeared owing to excessive shooting."

THE ISLAND

The vacationing public has discovered the West Indies only since the early 1960s, and a few of the large, flat islands have become staging areas of a very different sort. St. Martin's Juliana Airport provides daily air service to most of the West Indies, with connections to all the North American terminals from Toronto to Miami. Travelers to all the Windward Islands, the northern Lesser Antilles, pass through St. Martin. The result is a major infrastructure, including everything from overnight accommodations and restaurants to shopping centers, discos, and casinos, all built around the tourist industry.

St. Martin has become known for its abundant white-sand beaches and shopping. The *St. Martin Events* tourist guide claims that the island has thirty-six white-sand beaches, "more than 500 restaurants serving at least a dozen international cuisines," an eighteen-hole "championship golf course," "more than 500 duty-free shops and boutiques," and "several thousand St. Maarteners delighted to welcome you to their sun-drenched island home."

In our quest to visit all the West Indies, Betty and I spent two days on St. Martin, directly after two quiet and lovely days on Saba. There we had hiked up Mount Scenery into the cloud forest, walked the mountain road to The Bottom, and thoroughly enjoyed Saba's solitude and wildlife (see Chapter 8). What a change of pace we found on St. Martin! The taxi ride from Queen Juliana Airport to Hotel Pasaggrahon in Philipsburg was like a taxi ride through crowded streets in dozens of cities in North America. Our hotel, however, was very adequate, an old home located right on the beach on a narrow strip of land that separates Great Bay from the Great Salt Pond, or what is left of the Great Salt Pond. We were able to walk out onto the street and shop in either direction to our hearts' content. My "shopping" amounted to walking along the street past the various historic structures of downtown Philipsburg, namely the town hall and post office, and back to Hotel Pasaggrahon.

St. Martin is also different from its neighboring islands in that it is divided into two political territories. The southern portion of St. Martin (13 square miles) is Dutch and is called Sint Maarten, while the larger northern part is French (21 square miles) and is called Saint Martin. The division of the land resulted from a Dutchman and a Frenchman who, after fortifying themselves with adequate drink, walked the entire border of the island. Their meeting place at the opposite side of the island marked the boundary; the Frenchman was the faster of the two. The name of the island came from Christopher Columbus, who, on St. Martin's Day in 1493, claimed the island for Spain and named it in honor of the saint.

The island is divided topographically as well as politically. Although the entire island has a limestone base, the northern half is hilly, reaching 1,391 feet elevation on Pic du Paradis, and possesses dry forest habitat in the few areas that have not been cleared for agriculture and grazing. The dominant vegetation of these isolated forests includes gumbo limbo, white cedar, and several species of eugenia, as well as an abundance of vines, lianas, and bromeliads.

THE GREAT LOOP ROAD

We spent an entire day driving a rental car around the great loop road from Philipsburg northeast to Oyster Bay and Babit Point, then north to Grand Case and to Bell Point, the northern end of the island. We returned via Grand Case Beach, Pointe Arago, through the French capital city of Marigot, and then made a loop around Simpson Bay Lagoon, Rouge Beach, Long Beach, and back toward Philipsburg past the airport. It was a long and enjoyable day of sightseeing and stopping at various locations to watch birds. Voous reported that 107 species have been recorded on St. Martin; 40 of these are resident and breed. The remainder are migrants or winter visitors. There is no way to know how many species have been eliminated by overuse of their habitats.

I recorded only twenty species during the approximately eight-hour loop trip. The **Pearly-eyed Thrasher** was the most common bird that day. This robin-size bird is overall gray-brown with dark brown streaks on its throat and breast, white tips at the end of its tail, and a pearly-white eye. Its abundance around gardens and fencerows attests to its ability to adjust to our domination of the environment. Pearly-eyes are more numerous around the abundant introduced trees and shrubs than they are in their native forests.

All members of the thrasher family have a reputation for being aggressive, but the Pearly-eyed Thrasher is not only aggressive against potential competitors but eats the eggs and young of many other songbirds, as well. It also preys on various lizards and insects and almost every living creature it can kill and consume within its very broad range. See Chapter 5 for additional information about this aggressive bird.

Other songbirds found on our loop trip included **Gray Kingbirds,** usually fly-catching from utility poles or perched on the wires; Barn Swallows over the pastures; Bananaquits, locally called yellow-bellies because of their all-yellow underparts; Yellow Warblers singing from the scattered mangroves along the coastal areas; Lesser Antillean Bullfinches; and Black-faced Grassquits.

Like the Pearly-eyed Thrasher, the Bananaquit, bullfinch, and grassquit have also learned to get along in the human-influenced environment. These three little birds frequent outdoor restaurants, where they actually feed at the tables. The bullfinch and grassquit come for pieces of bread and other handouts. At the Oyster Pond Restaurant, where we ate an excellent lunch, these two species landed on our table during the meal. They were apparently eager to finish anything I might choose to leave and were well conditioned to their clean-up duties. Because they have a similar appearance (rather stubby with a short, heavy bill), people sometimes think that the smaller grassquit is only a young bullfinch, but this is not the case. The **Lesser Antillean Bullfinch** is an inch larger than the **Black-faced Grassquit.** Both are all dark; males are a slaty-black color, but the bullfinch male possesses a distinct rusty-colored throat and undertail covert. The smaller grassquit lacks the rusty color and its back tends to be greenish in the right light. Females are distinguishable by size and the bullfinch's much heavier bill.

Other land birds found on our loop drive included American Kestrels, the same little falcons so common throughout most of North America, and a few Common Ground-Doves. These tiny, short-tailed doves frequent farmyards and villages.

Water birds found that day included Brown Pelicans, Brown Boobies, Laughing Gulls, and Royal Terns over the bays and Great Blue and Little Blue Herons, Greater and Lesser Yellowlegs, and Common Moorhens at various ponds.

Only the inaccessible cliffs and the off-shore keys retain any resemblance to the valuable habitats that once existed on the island. Point Blanche, the peninsula southeast of Philipsburg, still is utilized by Red-billed Tropicbirds for nesting. Locally known as tropics, breeding pairs of these long-tailed seabirds can usually be found there from December to May, and their wild flights are a thing to behold.

Courting tropics usually are heard before they are seen. Their calls are shrill rasping or a series of fast clicking sounds in flight. They often fly together in unison in wide circles over the sea beyond their nest sites. Their flight is extremely swift, but they will suddenly glide for a long distance, then fly upward at a sharp angle before diving down toward the sea, only to pull out just above the waves. They will then gain altitude to about 300 to 500 feet and circle again before repeating their wild dives.

Tropicbirds are true seabirds that spend most of their lives at sea, coming to land only to nest. Their entire food supply is retrieved from the sea by diving into a school of fish and capturing their prey underwater, always held crossways in their bill. They swallow their catch either underwater or at the surface and never carry their food in their bill. Nestlings are fed regurgitated food that the adults store in their crop or throat.

The most outstanding feature of the Red-billed Tropicbird is its extremely long tail, which trails its 20-inch body by 20 to 25 inches. Its bright red bill and snow-white body, combined with black lines behind the eyes, black barring on its back, and black wing tips, make it one of the most spectacular birds in the West Indies.

Several other seabirds frequent the various keys that lie between St. Martin and St. Barthèlemy (locally called St. Barts), only a dozen miles to the south. Following a review of Caribbean seabird literature and direct observations, Rudd van Halewyn and Robert Norton reported that eleven species were known to nest on St. Martin's little rocky keys: Manx Shearwater (rare), Red-billed and White-tailed Tropicbirds, Brown Pelican, Laughing Gull, Gull-billed, Roseate, Bridled, Sooty, and Least Terns, and Brown Noddy.

During our loop drive, we encountered many more hotels under construction than we found examples of undisturbed habitats. We observed a wide range of recreational activities ranging from sunbathing on the many beaches, snorkeling, sailing, windsurfing, and parasailing to golf, tennis, and fishing. The option of nature study on St. Martin, however, is fast declining. It is sad that St. Martin has chosen an industry that is so poorly controlled and that will degrade the one truly unique resource—the Great Salt Pond— that, in the long term, could help the island's economy.

When competition for sun and sea reaches its peak in the West Indies, those islands that protect their natural resources now will undoubtedly have fewer economic problems than those areas that exploit their natural features for the artificial advantages of the short-term benefits of tourism.

CHAPTER ELEVEN

Antigua ISLAND IN THE SUN

The view from Antigua's Shirley Heights offers a smorgasbord of the West Indies. From the promontory almost 500 feet above the Caribbean Sea, the scalloped coastline is readily apparent to the south and north. To the east are the island's rolling hills, with their abundant fields, scattered homesites, and occasional patches of gray-green brushlands. Below the promontory in the foreground are English and Falmouth Harbors, great indentations of blue-green waters. These harbors were responsible for Antigua's head start in its race toward civilization.

Antigua's harbors have long been considered the best protected anchorages in all the West Indies. English Harbor was headquarters for Great

Britain's Caribbean fleet between 1707 and 1899, throughout the Napoleonic Wars. England owned the island until Antigua's independence on November 1, 1981. English Harbor is now one of the best yacht harbors in the world.

The dockyard at the head of English Harbor is known as Nelson's Dockyard, named for the famous British admiral, Lord Horatio Nelson. Between 1784 and 1787, then Captain Nelson was stationed in the Leeward Islands but only occasionally visited Antigua, according to Brian Dyde in *Antigua and Barbuda: The Heart of the Caribbean*. Dyde wrote that Nelson "was in no way connected with Antigua" during that time and that Nelson hated Antigua, "calling it a 'vile spot' and 'this infernal hole.'" Nevertheless, the naval dockyard was named for that most famous sea captain, admiral, and English lord.

Nelson's Dockyard and the adjacent Shirley Heights have become the centerpiece of Antigua's historic past and, since 1984, the country's first national park. Nelson's Dockyard National Park extends for about 7 miles along the southeastern coast from Carlisle Bay to Mamora Bay. Many of the park's historic structures have been restored so that park visitors can wander through workshops, the paymaster's office, and sail loft to acquire a better understanding of the way things were in the early eighteenth century.

The Admiral's Inn and restaurant was constructed of millions of ballast bricks from historic sailing ships. The fourteen-room hotel contains hand-hewn beams and four-poster beds. The Admiral's House is a museum with an assortment of Admiral Nelson's memorabilia. The Capstan House and Copper and Lumber Store have been made into a time-share apartment complex. The Clarence House, once the home of the English Duke of Clarence, who later became King William IV of England, is visible across the harbor. It is now the country home of the governor and is open to visitors only on special occasions.

At the mouth of English Harbor are the ruins of two forts. Fort Berkeley commands a small rocky flat on the north side of the entrance and the much larger Fort Shirley dominates the cape on the south side. Fort Shirley, named after General and Sir Thomas Shirley, governor of the Leeward Islands in Antigua from 1781 to 1791, was built during that period to protect the British naval presence at English Harbor.

Betty and I spent several hours walking among the ruins of Fort Shirley, examining the surrounding flora and fauna and generally admiring the scenery. The extensive network of stone walls was part of the old barracks, and we also visited the remains of the officers' quarters and what was once a powder magazine. Fort Shirley not only provided excellent protection to the harbor below but also a marvelous wide-angle view across the

Caribbean. Far to the south, about 40 miles away, was the island of Guadeloupe, covered with low-lying clouds.

I couldn't help but think how different Guadeloupe is from the smaller and lower island of Antigua. The high, forested mountains of Guadeloupe are cloud-covered much of the time, resulting in more than 300 inches of annual rainfall in the Soufrière region (see Chapter 13 on Guadeloupe). Antigua's annual rainfall of only 45 inches gives the island a semi-arid environment. The vegetation on Cape Shirley is a fairly good representation of this semi-arid habitat. J. S. Beard, in his 1944 paper, "Climax Vegetation in Tropical America," called it "cactus scrub." This vegetation type makes up almost one-fifth of Antigua's total area of 108 square miles, according to Allen Putney's *Survey of Conservation Priorities in the Lesser Antilles.* Except for small stands of mangroves along the northeastern coast and a minute patch of dry woodlands in the east, all the rest of the island's landscape has been altered from the original vegetation. Beard's description of the cactus scrub habitat fits Antigua very well: "open vegetation dominated by column cacti and prickly-pear, with scattered gnarled bushes, micro- or leptophyllous, often thorny, and terrestrial bromeliads." He further stated that "the ground is not grassed but frequently shows bare soil."

Looking southward we saw scattered, low-growing shrubs, a tall, thorny, cylindrical cactus of the genus *Cephalocereus*, and green rosettes of succulent leaves, many of which contained tall woody stalks, like a giant asparagus. These were the native century plants or agaves. The century plant name is derived from the belief that these plants take one hundred years to bloom, which is not the case. All century plants bloom at fifteen to twenty-five years of age, and, like other members of the daffodil or amaryllis family, they die immediately after blooming. New plants start from sprouts or seeds that fall from the flowers during their last great rush to glory. While blooming, the tall stalks produce large, dinner plate–size flowers that attract many of the island's birds and insects.

During March and April, flowering century plants provide a lush banquet of avian delights. Hummingbirds, Bananaquit, and Antillean Euphonia come to sip the sweet nectar from the flowers. Other birds come to feed on the abundant insects that are attracted to the sweet flowers: Gray Kingbird, Caribbean Elaenia, Northern Mockingbird, Yellow Warbler, and Lesser Antillean Bullfinch. Still others—Red-tailed and Broad-winged Hawks and American Kestrel—frequent the area to prey on those birds that come to feed at the century plants.

The **Antillean Euphonia** is one of Antigua's most appealing birds. It is a chunky little tanager with a multicolored plumage of blues, yellows, and greens. Locally called mistletoe bird, after its preference for mistletoe berries, it has a soft, euphonic "tuk tuk" call.

Both the Red-tailed Hawk, with its brick-red tail, and the similar but somewhat smaller Broad-winged Hawk, with a barred black-and-white tail, were present over the ridge and at Nelson's Dockyard during our stay. I couldn't help but wonder how these two very similar species of broad-winged raptors were able to exist together on Antigua. Although almost every island in the West Indies possesses a population of Red-tails, Broad-wings occur only on Cuba, Hispaniola, Puerto Rico, and Antigua and from Dominica southward. They skip Jamaica, all the Virgin Islands, the eight Lesser Antilles north of Antigua, and Montserrat and Guadeloupe, which lie between Antigua and Dominica. This is a very strange pattern of distribution that does not relate solely to island size, topography, or vegetation.

I watched the soaring Broad-winged Hawk for several minutes as it floated along the slopes above the harbor. Broad-wings in North America usually are forest birds and rarely soar so completely in the open. Yet I couldn't detect any features on this bird that were any different from the hundreds of Broad-wings I had seen in the eastern United States. However, Herbert Friedmann, in his 1950 book, *The Birds of North and Middle America, Part XI*, reported that the Antiguan birds are "lighter and smaller than any of the other subspecies" and that the Antigua Broad-winged Hawk is resident only on the island of Antigua. The Antigua Broad-winged Hawk, therefore, although only a subspecies, is the island's only endemic bird.

Most of Antigua's human visitors are more interested in sun, sand, and sea than the island's flora and fauna, and few are disappointed. Antigua boasts of having 365 beaches, "one for every day of the year," along its 90-mile-long coastline. Many of those beaches are among the finest in all the West Indies. There also are plenty of hotels and other accommodations that range from exquisite, for those willing to pay the price, to moderately priced rooms with slightly less prestige. The restaurants also run the gamut. One night Betty and I splurged and ate at the French restaurant, Le Bistro, where we enjoyed one of the half-dozen best meals we experienced all the time we lived in the West Indies.

During all our daylight hours on Antigua we drove the roadways, walked the trails and beaches, and attempted to explore areas that might provide the greatest exposure to the island's natural and cultural resources. It didn't take long to realize that the vast majority of the landscape had been in agriculture at one time or another. I expected to find lots of sugarcane fields but instead found vast areas planted with sea island cotton. Sugarcane fields were few and far between; today sugarcane is planted only for local production of sugar, molasses, and rum.

When sugar was king, however, on Antigua and on all of the other West Indian islands that possess fertile flatlands and an adequate rainfall, sugarcane fields often reached to the highest hilltops. If the forests were not cleared for agriculture the trees were felled to fuel the sugar mills. On Antigua, a series of catastrophic droughts was responsible for the demise of the sugar industry. Antigua's last sugar mill closed in 1972, three decades after it had all begun. Remnants of hundreds of rock mills still jut out of the Antiguan landscape, mute skeletons of the island's glorious past.

Cotton growing, particularly in the drier eastern half of the island, has provided an alternative. A textile industry has begun, but the economy has not recovered. The best hope for Antigua, according to many Antiguans, is tourism. Some argue that the tourist industry has the greatest chance of restoring a stable economy. There is no shortage of beaches. The island's semi-arid climate, with temperatures that range throughout the year between 72 and 86 degrees Fahrenheit and without the influence of cloud-covered mountains that are common on most of the larger West Indies, is perfect for sunbathing and swimming. Additionally, the island's scalloped coastline provides niches for accommodations and restaurants so visitors can appreciate the remoteness of their environment. Antigua also has one of the major airports and one of the best deep-water ports in the Lesser Antilles. Both are products of World War II, when the United States constructed the two ports for defensive reasons. Both sites have been improved upon and provide Antigua with an infrastructure to support tourism. Air service includes daily flights into V. C. Bird International Airport direct from the United States and Canada and all the key West Indies. Antigua is also the home base for LIAT, an important airline that flies throughout the eastern Caribbean. Tourism currently provides over three-quarters of the island's income.

Antigua's road system provides access to the entire island and, for the most part, is in good to adequate condition. We rented a car at the airport and drove to as many of the out-of-the-way places as we could find. We discovered that Antigua contains three distinct districts, each with very different topography. The highest elevations lie in the northwest, where the Shekerley Mountains contain three peaks over 1,000 feet: Sugar Hill (1,160), McNish (1,120), and Boggy Peak (1,319), the island's highest. The Shekerley Mountains are of volcanic origin, undoubtedly part of the ancient chain of volcanoes that created many of the Lesser Antilles. (See Chapter 15 for additional details about this geologic feature.) Dyde pointed out that although these mountains are often green and the drainages can carry fast-flowing streams during wet periods, these features can be misleading; there are no tropical forests or permanent streams on the island.

Just north of the Shekerley Mountains is a 3-mile-wide plain created in part by the alluvium from the mountains. To the north of a line from St. John's Bay to Willoughby Bay is a hilly environment of limestone origin. A steep limestone escarpment is evident at Willoughby Bay. This portion of the island was once a coral reef.

MORE BIRD LIFE

On our second day we explored the eastern portion of the island, driving to Indian Town Point, Emerald Cove on Nonsuch Bay, and Half Moon Bay. En route we stopped at Potworks Dam, the island's largest freshwater reservoir, with the hope that we might find some water birds. Although I walked along the northern shore for a good part of a mile, I found only a few species: Great Blue and Tricolored Herons, Great Egret, White-cheeked Pintail, Blue-winged Teal, Common Moorhen, Killdeer, and Greater Yellowlegs. All of the birds spooked easily, and I wondered if they were hunted as heavily as they were in the French islands.

I did get reasonably close to a Great Egret that was fishing along the shoreline. I watched it for several minutes, poised with its large yellow bill pointed downward, as quiet as a porcelain statue. Then suddenly it thrust its sharp bill into the water, almost at its feet, and withdrew a small fish, about the same size as its bill, which it immediately swallowed. It moved on down the shoreline several feet, then struck the same pose, waiting for another snack to venture near enough for its next lethal strike. Small feathers on its wing tips moved ever so slightly in the slight breeze, but otherwise its snow-white plumage and long blackish legs were again frozen in time.

Two species of ducks flew up from the near edge of the shoreline a couple of hundred feet ahead of me. Blue-winged Teals were winter visitors from North America, but the pintails were full-time resident birds that occur throughout the Caribbean, except in the southern Lesser Antilles. White-cheeked Pintails are very different from the Northern Pintails so common in North America. White-cheeks possess snow-white patches on their throat and neck that extend up onto their cheeks, a bluish bill with a bright red streak at the base, and an overall mottled body. They lack the extremely long pintail of their northern cousins and have a bright green rather than brownish wing speculum. Also, the sexes are similar, rather than possessing separate plumages like Northern Pintails.

Nonsuch Bay provided us with the greatest diversity of bird life that day. We found three species of seabirds fishing the bay waters. Royal Terns were most active, flying back and forth over the bay waters at about 30 to 40 feet high, then suddenly plunging downward into the water with a great splash. On several occasions they emerged with a little silver fish in their bill that they swallowed almost immediately. I couldn't help but admire the birds' clean white plumage and contrasting black cap and smudge of grayish color on their upper wings that turned blackish near the tips. Their long, orange-yellow bill gave them almost a stately appearance.

Other seabirds found at Nonsuch Bay included Brown Pelican, surprisingly common, and Magnificent Frigatebird, sometimes known as man-o'-war bird, with its great, long wings, forked tail, and long, hooked bill. On one occasion I watched a frigatebird pursue a Royal Tern that had just emerged from the bay waters with a fish in its bill. The chase was a wild one, up and down, this way and that. Then suddenly the tern dropped its catch, and before the little fish hit the water the frigatebird had scooped it up in its bill and swallowed it. The chase had lasted less than three minutes, but I had witnessed some incredible maneuvers. I was especially impressed with the dexterity of the much larger frigatebird.

Most sightings of these great birds are of soaring birds, high over the sea or along the sea cliffs, and one seldom has the opportunity to appreciate its skill in pursuit flying. But when I watched one perform its typical behavior of harassing smaller seabirds so that they will give up their catch I got a very different perception of its personality. It truly is an oceanic predator. No other tropical seabird has its large size and dominance.

We found the greatest number of land birds within the various gardens and landscaped areas adjacent to the hotels. Although the avian diversity was rather low, it was obvious that a few species have learned to take advantage of the variety of introduced trees and shrubs. Those few species, however, were surprisingly abundant.

Bananaquits, the yellow-bellied birds with a black head and bold white eyeline, sometimes called sugarbirds because of their love of sugar and nectar, were everywhere flowers were in bloom. Their wheezy "zee-e-e-e-swees-te" calls were commonplace during the morning hours and only slightly less so during the rest of the day.

The little **Black-faced Grassquit** was just as abundant, spending most of its time searching for seeds on the ground or in grassy places in fields and in gardens. It, too, sings a buzzing song, a two-syllabled "tik-zeeee"

White-crowned Pigeon

sound, but it is not so drawn out as the Bananaquit. Both of these little birds can usually be found at outdoor restaurants, where they feed on sugar or crumbs.

The larger **Lesser Antillean Bullfinch** is similar to the Grassquit, but males possess a rusty throat and chin patch and undertail covert. It, too, has learned to feed on crumbs in outdoor restaurants but is less abundant than the smaller grassquit and Bananaquit.

The common dove of Antigua is the **Zenaida Dove**, a Mourning Dove look-alike, except for its broad white outer tail-feathers. Since there are no Mourning Doves in the Lesser Antilles, any medium-size dove found on Antigua will be the Zenaida Dove. The tiny Common Ground-Dove is also present throughout and can easily be identified by its tiny size and rufous wing-patches in flight.

The larger **White-crowned Pigeon** was also present in fairly large numbers. On most of the West Indies this species is confined to the mangrove forests, but on Antigua I discovered several birds carrying nesting material or actually building nests within the foliage of mango trees along the highways and in downtown St. John's. Apparently, Antigua's White-crowns have adapted to this additional habitat, and they seemed to be doing very well. White-crowns are beautiful pigeons with a dark gray plumage offset by a conspicuous white crown. In the Shekerley Mountains I found **Scaly-naped Pigeons** present, as well. This is an even larger pigeon, often called red-necked pigeon, that is also overall dark gray, but without the white crown. Instead, it has a hind neck that in good light shows a beautiful chestnut and metallic-purple color.

I was especially pleased to find these two pigeons so common; their abundance indicates that they are not being persecuted on Antigua as they are on the adjacent French islands, where these birds are rare or missing altogether.

The most beautiful birds of the gardens and hotel grounds are the hummingbirds, and the tiny **Antillean Crested Hummingbird** is almost everyone's favorite. Although it is less than 4 inches tall, the male possesses an obvious crest that, when seen in good light, is a vivid green color. Its entire upperparts are green and its underparts are dark gray-brown. It also sings an emphatic "pit-chew" song, often from a high perch. Females are rather drab birds without a crest. It is known to nest four or five times annually, usually laying two tiny eggs within its thimble-size nest. This tiny hummingbird is very special. Scientists have named it *Orthorhyncus cristatus*, or the "bird with an upright crest." It is the only species of this endemic West Indian genus.

The much larger **Green-throated Carib** is also present and is also a beautiful bird with its green back and violet-blue breast, but it does not have the personality of the little Antillean Crested Hummingbird. Both sexes of this large hummingbird look alike, except females tend to have slightly longer and more curved bills than the males.

Visitors to Antigua will soon learn these birds. They are common and help to welcome all who open their eyes to their colorful surroundings.

CHAPTER TWELVE

Montserrat THE EMERALD ISLE

Montserrat Oriole

The faint, almost indistinguishable bird song came from the wall of forest vegetation farther up the hillside to the left of the streamflow. I tried to squeak louder, with my lips on the back of my hand, hoping to entice the perpetrator closer. There it was again, and somewhat nearer. It definitely was an oriole song; the sweet, melodic whistle notes could be nothing else. Yet the song was shorter, less drawn out than that of the look-alike Black-cowled Oriole. Again, the melodious whistles, even closer. I suddenly was nervous in anticipation. The song seemed now to be coming from near the top of a tangle of vines only 100 to 125 feet from where I was standing. I trained my binoculars on the top portion of the vegetation. I was positive of the bird's location; if only it would come out into view. I made spishing noises like an agitated wren, trying to attract the oriole into the open. Instead, I heard an emphatic "chuk" call. Then another. And then, as if by magic, the oriole appeared exactly where I was looking. My first **Montserrat Oriole,** a bird that occurs nowhere else in all the world, only on this tiny Caribbean island of Montserrat. It remained in view only for 10 to 15 seconds, then it moved back into the dense vegetation, and a few seconds later I detected it flying away in the opposite direction.

I was jubilant! I wished that I had someone to share my excitement with, but I was alone. The sighting was extra special for me because I had come back to Montserrat for the one purpose of finding this bird. It was my second attempt. Betty and I had visited Montserrat two years earlier, and I had searched for this endemic bird all during our three-day stay, but to no avail. So I had returned in May 1989. I had taken a taxi from the airport to Runaway Ghaut (the local name for ravine), walked up the short roadway to Olveston Spring, and in less than an hour had found the bird of my quest. It was a worthwhile stopover.

MONTSERRAT

There is a Montserrat legend that claims that any visitor who drinks from the Runaway Ghaut stream will return.

> If you drink from that burn,
> You will surely return.

I was not aware of the Runaway Ghaut legend on my first visit, but it wasn't likely I would have drunk from the streamflow even if I had. The condition of the spring is much like that of so many other places where the "delicious" free-flowing waters have been "developed" for the local water supply. The spring source had been dug out and contained. Pipes had been laid from the spring to a large storage tank located just below, at the end of the road. Secondary pipes protruded grotesquely from the storage tank to carry water to homes and businesses elsewhere.

The forest beyond, however, seemed relatively undisturbed. It was part of five forest preserves that collectively encompass more than 18 percent of the island's land surface, all of the forested slopes above 1,500 feet elevation. However, according to Wayne and Angela Arendt, "The significance of having 5 forest reserves is greatly reduced. . . . the vegetation on two of these 'reserves' (Silver Hill and St. George's Hill) has been almost completely destroyed by agriculturists and developers. Even elfin woodland on the highest peaks continues to disappear at the hands of agriculturists."

The Arendts had lived on Montserrat for seventy-six days during 1984, May 14 to July 29, to study the status and ecology of the Montserrat Oriole. This oriole is the country's national bird and is depicted on stamps and numerous publications. Montserrateans are justly proud of its unique status. The 1984 study was funded by the Montserrat government, Montserrat National Trust, and U.S. Agency for International Development. The Arendts had selected eight study sites, based on earlier sightings and adequate habitat. Olveston Spring in Runaway Ghaut was one of these sites. They briefly describe the immediate vegetation in their study report as follows: "Regeneration riparian vegetation and plantation tree species dominate the scene. Common tree species include: rubber tree (*Ficus elastica*), ashwood (*Casearia sylvestris*), white manjack (*Cordia sulcata*), Spanish-oak (*Inga laurina*), and hogplum (*Spondias nombin*)."

The rubber tree is one of the banyon-type figs, familiar to most travelers in the tropics. It has large, leathery, glossy leaves with many parallel veins and long red terminal buds. Pitchpine sweetwood is a member of the laurel family. It is evergreen and produces dark blue to black fruit (drupes) that are valuable for wildlife. Ashwood is closely related to Brazil's true guassatunga tree (Flacourtia family), which produces beautiful white flower clusters from the leaf axils.

White manjack is most often a thick, brushy plant that produces many white flower clusters and gooey berries year-round; it is a favorite of pigeons, doves, and all the other fruit-eating birds. Spanish-oak is a member of the mimosa family and produces conspicuous yellowish, powder-puff flowers and huge "big bean" seedpods. The flowers are rich in nectar and are excellent hummingbird attractants. Hogplum produces olive-size fruit that are prized by wildlife and humans alike. The ripe orangish-colored fruit (drupes) produce a sweet scent and can be eaten alone or used for jams and liqueurs.

The Montserrat Oriole was discovered by Fred A. Ober while he was on a collecting trip to the Caribbean for the Smithsonian Institution in 1880. Taxonomist George N. Lawrence, who prepared the initial description of the bird, named it for Ober: *Icterus oberi*. Lawrence described the new species thus:

Male: Head, neck, upper part of breast, back, wings, and tail black; lower part of breast, abdomen, under tail-coverts, and rump light brownish chestnut, with the concealed bases of the feathers of a clear light yellow;

the thighs are yellow, with a wash of chestnut; edge of wing and under wing-coverts yellow; bill black, with the sides of the under mandible bluish for half its length from the base; tarsi and toes black.

Besides *Icterus oberi*, Montserrat possesses at least two other endemic vertebrates and two plants. Although there are no unique mammals, there are two lizards: galliwasp and anole. The galliwasp (*Diploglossa montisserati*) is a tropical species that looks much like a skink with very short and weak legs. It is closely related to alligator and glass lizards but can be recognized by the ringlike arrangement of its scales. The anole (*Anolis lividus*) is the small green "chameleon" that occurs everywhere on the island. It can change colors rapidly and dramatically from deep green to brown to almost black. Unlike the galliwasp, Montserrat's anole is covered with minute granular scales. The male possesses a movable throat appendage which it exhibits in fanlike fashion when it is excited or on its territory. The two endemic plants, *Rondeletia buxifolia* and *Xylosma serratum*, are known only from the Great Alps Falls area.

Betty and I had flown to Montserrat, via Antigua, in early February 1988 as part of our efforts to visit all of the West Indies. We had landed at Montserrat's Blackburne Airport, on the windward side of the island, after a fifteen-minute flight from Antigua, 30 miles to the north. Montserrat's landing strip is too small for larger aircraft, so all incoming flights must originate on nearby Antigua (three flights daily).

I had reserved overnight accommodations at the Coconut Hill Hotel within the town of Plymouth, located on the western side of the island. The road across the mountain provided us with a good first look at the diversity of this beautiful island. As our taxi moved upward we left the lower and drier windward side and emerged into greener and more tropical uplands. The higher peaks were covered with clouds, which no doubt helped to account for the bright green slopes. We could better understand the term "Emerald Isle of the Caribbean" that is so often used to describe Montserrat.

Actually, there is another very good reason that Montserrat has claimed the Emerald Isle title. The island's first European settlers were Irish. Irish and English Catholics, fleeing religious persecution from the nearby and Protestant St. Kitts, settled there in 1632. The next year, more Catholic refugees arrived from Virginia, where they had experienced similar persecution from Episcopalians. Sixteen years later, in 1648, Montserrat received another Irish infusion when Oliver Cromwell, following his victory over King Charles I, banished Irish political prisoners to Montserrat. That act not only increased the island's population but enhanced its Irish character as well. The Irish brogue is still evident among the citizenry.

Irish influence is present throughout the island. Howard Fergus, author of *Montserrat: Emerald Isle of the Caribbean*, mentions several other examples: "A carved Irish shamrock still adorns the gable at Government House. The island's flag and crest show a lady with a cross and a harp. The lady is Erin of the Irish legend." Examination of a Montserrat map further illustrates the Irish influence. Irish place-names abound. Some of the obvious ones include Cork Hill, Delvin's, Duberry Hill, Fogerty, Galway's Estate, Irish Ghaut, Katy Hill, Killiecronkie Spring, Kinsole, Riley's Estate, and St. Patrick's.

The name of the island, in comparison, seems almost out of character. Its name originated with Christopher Columbus, who passed along the eastern shore on his second voyage in November 1493. Although he did not stop there, he wrote in his diary that the profile of the island reminded him of the serrated peaks surrounding the Santa María de Monserrate Monastery outside Barcelona, Spain. Before Columbus, the Carib Indians called the island Alliouagana, meaning "land of the prickly bush." Archaeologists believe that the island was uninhabited in 1493; the Caribs had already eliminated the more peaceful Arawaks by then.

As we descended the western slope of the island, our driver described the capital city of Plymouth as "too busy and too many people" for him. Apparently, relativity also applies on Montserrat. He lived near the airport and only ventured to town when he had to. We learned later that the population of this capital city was about 4,000; Montserrat's total population was about 13,000, including an estimated 2,500 retired North Americans.

Montserrat is now a British crown colony. Government is carried out by a governor, appointed by the crown, and by local government officials. The economy has moved sharply toward tourism and away from agriculture during the last twenty years. Agriculture has been on a continual decline since the rich sugar production years of the eighteenth century. Tourism in 1986 amounted to more than 25,000 visitors and accounted for 30 percent of Montserrat's gross national product.

Our taxi driver deposited us at the Coconut Hill Hotel, a quaint one-hundred-year-old structure within the town of Plymouth. The hotel was one of the moderately priced hotels, "located in a quiet residential area within an easy walk to the beach and with views of the same. A casual atmosphere prevails on the park-like grounds that surround the one-time mansion," according to Kathy Strong's *Caribbean Bed and Breakfast Book*. Although the Coconut Hill Hotel was old and somewhat run down, it was very adequate for our needs. The bed was comfortable; the food was good; the hotel grounds did provide a relaxing place to visit; the proprietor made arrangements for a rental car.

Our principal objectives on Montserrat were to see the island and to visit its more out-of-the-way natural areas rather than to spend time in town and along the beach. All the Caribbean islands possess sand, sea, and sun, so seeing only those repetitious features on Montserrat would, for us, be a waste of time. We aimed at better understanding its natural character, its varied habitats, and its special flora and fauna.

It was obvious from the very start that Montserrat is volcanic in origin; it is one of the several Leeward Islands considered part of the inner volcanic arc of the Lesser Antilles. Although there have been no major eruptions on Montserrat since 1640, fumaroles, which emit sulfurous fumes, still occur within the Soufrière uplands. Three distinct mountain ranges exist on the 39-square-mile island. The island's general topography was best described by long-time Montserratean Howard Fergus thus: "Three lofty, green-clad mountain ranges flaunt the skyline. The northern range, the Silver Hills, ends in a bold headland; the southern range descends in a cliff to the sea, which abounds in break-away boulders. The tallest range, the Soufrière Hills, rises to 3,002 feet above sea level at Mount Chance, whose summit is almost always obscured by clouds."

We visited the Soufrière Hills on one of our three days. We discovered two completely different habitats, both accessible by trail: Galway's Soufrière and Great Alps Falls. We began our day with a drive south along the coastline from Plymouth to St. Patrick's, where we turned into the mountains on the Galway's Soufrière road. In passing the little village of St. Patrick's, I couldn't help but wonder what kind of celebration those folks must have on St. Patrick's Day. With such a name the town leaders must plan an appropriate affair.

Just above St. Patrick's village is the remains of Galway's Plantation. Founded by Irishman David Galway in the 1660s, the site was partially restored during the 1980s, and today it is an excellent example of an early-day sugar plantation. The numerous structures and extent of the complex provide the visitor with an excellent perspective of the complexity of operating such a sugar plantation during the eighteenth century. The exhibits include cattle, windmills, a large sugar-boiling house, a reservoir and cisterns, cemeteries, slave quarters, and the great house. Although almost every island in the Caribbean has sugar plantation remains, few possess the spirit of true independence, of interrelated village life, as does Galway's.

The paved roadway continues beyond Galway's, following the mountain ridge upward to a small parking area at the edge of a sulfurous pit that emanates foul smells and steam. A trail enters the yellowish hollow, where one can view close up the rocky fissures filled with the boiling brew. The scene leaves no doubt about Montserrat's volcanic origin and that another eruption is indeed possible and only a matter of time. J. Davy, an early British visitor, described the area as "horror in the lap of beauty," according to Fergus. It reminded me of a smaller version of Yellowstone Canyon in Yellowstone National Park.

Beyond the sulfurous pit, a trail winds upward to the southern flank of the Soufrière Hills and then continues across the mountain to Roche's Estate. Betty and I followed the trail upward to the high point, less than 2 miles, to where it skirts a beautiful forest. The main reason for visiting this area was another attempt to find the Montserrat Oriole. Arendt reported finding the bird "especially common" near the upper forest. But in spite of searching this area for a couple of hours, we were unable to find the bird.

We were impressed, however, with the wet forest habitat we found there. Great stands of bamboo were magnificent. The abundant tree ferns demonstrated that we truly were in a moist forest environment. Taller trees included trumpet-tree, matchwood, and miconia. The latter species is a member of the Melastomaceae family, abundant in the tropics and easily recognized by the parallel venation pattern of its broad, elliptical leaves. Trumpet-tree is also a common tropical species with large palmate leaves that are deeply lobed into seven to eleven sections. The underside of the leaves is whitish, and when the leaves are blown by the wind, the color flickers from green to white. That characteristic helps to identify the tree from a considerable distance. All of the woody plants found there were early invaders, demonstrating the secondary nature of the forest. Recent clearing activities were evident by the new pineapple field found at the edge of the forest. As much as an acre had been cleared and planted with pineapples that seemed to be doing very well. Small fruits were growing from the centers of the spiny green leaves.

In spite of squeaking and spishing along the forest edge, I could detect no orioles. I did attract a few other resident species, however. Most numerous was the ubiquitous Bananaquit, and three **Pearly-eyed Thrashers** came out to see what the commotion was all about. The look-alike **Scaly-breasted Thrasher,** a Lesser Antillean species, also appeared. It is surprising that these two similar species can occur together, and I believe that a study of the two birds' requirements would make a most worthwhile thesis. For further comments on these two West Indian endemics, see Chapter 8.

A pair of **Purple-throated Caribs** came dashing out of the forest at one point. One remained for several minutes, perched a dozen yards or so away, and allowed us an excellent look at this large, beautiful hummingbird. It flicked out its tongue a couple of times, as if to test the air or to capture, reptilelike, a tiny passing insect. It left just as suddenly as it had appeared, disappearing into the green forest.

Movement to the right of where it disappeared caught my eye. I was certain it was a warbler but wasn't sure of the species. A few seconds later (the result of low spishing), a gorgeous male Black-throated Blue Warbler emerged from the forest into full view. It remained long enough for me to watch it feed on insects by gleaning them from the foliage and once by flying out to capture its prey on the wing. It also preened its lovely feathers and at one point bathed in tiny water droplets clinging to the leaves. The deep blues and contrasting colors, most evident when shafts of sunlight settled on the bird like a heavenly spotlight, were phenomenal.

I couldn't help but wonder about this and other Neotropical migrants wintering on Montserrat. Although I found only Black-throated Blues, Northern Parulas, and Northern Waterthrushes during my visit (Yellow Warblers are a common resident species), several others are known to over-winter in the Lesser Antilles. James Bond, in *The Birds of the West Indies*, also includes Black-and-white, Prothonotary, Magnolia, Yellow-rumped, Black-throated Green, Yellow-throated, Prairie, Kentucky, and Hooded Warblers, Louisiana Waterthrush, Ovenbird, Common Yellowthroat, and American Redstart.

Montserrat's native forest appeared adequate to support a significant population of wintering warblers. Timothy Johnson reported in his 1988 monograph, *Biodiversity and Conservation in the Caribbean: Profiles of Selected Islands*, that Montserrat's virgin and secondary forest cover amounts to from 2,500 to 3,500 hectares (6,250 to 8,750 acres) and adds that "the inaccessible parts may not have been disturbed since the abolition of slavery in 1834."

The Great Alps Falls Trail begins in the bottom of a deep but arid drainage (White River) beyond St. Patrick's and the tiny village of Shooter's Hill. We found several local youngsters at the trailhead, all willing and eager to "guide" us to the falls. It took considerable discussion to convince these lads that we preferred to be alone so that we could slowly bird our way along the route, rather than have someone pointing out the obvious features and taking too much of our attention. There is one junction along the route which did cause some confusion, and we purposely took the ridge trail to the right of the drainage for about 1 mile to an old orchard, knowing it was not the proper trail. Our intention was to find additional oriole habitat, but we were not successful.

When we returned to the canyon-bottom trail the route was easy to follow the rest of the way, a total of about 2.5 miles. The White River Valley route provided a varied environment from open desert to cooler riparian habitats. The falls themselves are located at the head of a deep and beautiful box canyon and drop 72 feet into a sparkling pool. We found Black-faced Grassquits, Pearly-eyed Thrashers, Smooth-billed Anis, Zenaida Doves, Antillean Crested Hummingbirds, and a pair of American Kestrels (locally called killy-hawk) along the more open route. Once inside the canyon, **Scaly-naped Pigeons** were by far the most numerous species. They undoubtedly were visiting the area to drink from the stream that flows along the sheltered canyon bottom.

FOX'S BAY BIRD SANCTUARY

Because of its volcanic origin, Montserrat claims no white-sand beaches. Its beaches are black as coal, but in the right light the grains of sand can sparkle like diamonds. We discovered this fact when we visited Fox's Bay Bird Sanctuary, established in 1979 by the Montserrat National Trust, only 2 miles north of Plymouth. The long but narrow beach extends for more than a mile north of Bransby Point. The widest portion fronts a mangrove swamp. The 6-acre sanctuary also contains a shallow saltwater pond surrounded by mangroves and manchineel trees.

I followed a trail along the southern edge of the mangroves. In a few places, by creeping through the first line of vegetation, I could see some distance into the wetlands. Common Moorhens were the most numerous birds detected, but I discovered a lone Caribbean Coot, as well. Its fully white frontal shield, above the bill, was conspicuous for a few seconds only. Then it sighted me and swam farther back into the pond out of sight. At another opening I found a Sora and was able to watch it feeding along the edge of an emerged pile of debris. A few minutes late, five Blue-winged Teal suddenly exploded from the water reasonably close by when I shifted position. I detected the sharp "chips" of a Northern Waterthrush on two occasions as I moved slowly along the pathway. At one point I spished up a Northern Parula. Most of the time, however, spishing produced only Pearly-eyed Thrashers, Bananaquits, and Yellow Warblers.

I was pleased to find Fox's Bay Bird Sanctuary. It is good evidence that the people of Montserrat are aware of the value of such refuges for overwintering songbirds as well as the well-being of the human population of the island. Mangrove habitats are just as important as the upland forests to both migrant and resident species. (See Chapter 7 for further information about the value of mangroves to Neotropical migrants.) I commend the Montserrat National Trust for its efforts. The trust also has published a nice little book titled *Birds of Montserrat*, authored by Peace Corps volunteer Allan Siegel.

BACK TO RUNAWAY GHAUT

After two days I still had not found a Montserrat Oriole. I decided to spend my last morning back at Runaway Ghaut in a last-ditch effort to find this elusive species. I had visited with local birder Bert Wheeler, who did not have a better suggestion.

Dawn of February 4 found me back at Olveston Spring in Runaway Ghaut. The bird chorus that morning was dominated by Pearly-eyed Thrashers; they seemed to be everywhere. Their very loud and boisterous whistles drowned out many of the other bird songs. The higher-pitched songs of Bananaquits and the buzzing calls of Black-faced Grassquits were also audible. The very loud and shrill songs of Lesser Antillean Bullfinches were evident, as well.

Once I observed a **Forest Thrush** in flight from one edge of the forest to another, and I watched it sing its soft, musical song from a far-off perch. It was barely audible against the din of thrasher cacophony. On another occasion I discovered a pair of **Brown Tremblers** chasing each other through the forest. I watched one "tremble" in its unique fashion, tail up, wings out, and shaking as if begging food from an adult. Farther to the right, where drier second forest was dominant, a pair of Mangrove Cuckoos sang their very distinct, guttural "ga-ga-ga-ga" notes. Overhead, I detected several Scaly-naped Pigeons as they flew from their roosting sites to feeding trees elsewhere. A pair of American Kestrels wheeled over and disappeared beyond.

Still I did not detect the bird of my quest. Once I thought I heard a series of call notes along the row of vegetation below the water tank, but when I searched the area I couldn't find any bird that might have been the perpetrator. I did find a Green-throated Carib, which posed several seconds for me. Walking back up toward the spring, I discovered a lone **Antillean Euphonia** perched at the top of a mango tree just below the roadway. The light was right, and I stood transfixed by the beauty of this little bird for several minutes.

After stumbling through the mud at the spring flow and circling along the edge of the forest for more than an hour, I was finally forced to give up. Maybe I had accidentally drunk from the spring and, as the legend states, I was destined to return.

POSTSCRIPT

Hurricane Hugo caused severe damage to Montserrat in September 1989, affecting every living thing on the island. Much of Plymouth and the other villages were destroyed. Roads were made impassable and communication systems were put back to conditions experienced by the early settlers. It was only through monumental efforts and assistance from dozens of friendly countries that the Montserrateans were able to rebuild their lives.

What about the birds and other natural resources on the island? What about the Montserrat Oriole, the national bird? It undoubtedly suffered a severe blow, but like all the other native creatures it somehow made it through the storm. Arendt reported to the Society of Caribbean Ornithology in 1994 that it had moved to more protected ghauts following the storm. The population is expected to fully recover and will again be the subject of birding quests. The Montserrat Oriole will continue to attract naturalists from throughout the world.

CHAPTER THIRTEEN

Guadeloupe

A GREEN LAND WITH BEAUTIFUL WATERS

The **Guadeloupe Woodpecker,** locally known as *tapeur* (from French *taper,* "to tap, strike, bang, beat") and to scientists as *Melanerpes herminieri,* occurs nowhere else in the world than on the French Windward Island of Guadeloupe. The Guadeloupe Woodpecker is not only very different in appearance from any other of the world's more than two hundred woodpecker species, but it is the only member of the Picidae family (woodpeckers, piculets, and wrynecks) that occurs within any of the Lesser Antilles. Even on Guadeloupe its range is limited to the forest communities below 2,000 feet elevation. It is most numerous on the moist eastern slopes and rare in the drier lowlands along the coast.

Guadeloupe Woodpecker

At first sighting, the Guadeloupe Woodpecker appears entirely black. But in good light its reddish-purple chest and belly are more obvious and provide a marked contrast to its glossy-black back and head. It has a subtle beauty that is unusual for woodpeckers. Ornithologist Lester Short, in *Woodpeckers of the World*, also points out that the "males are somewhat larger and distinctly longer billed," but the sexes look alike.

In watching this bird within the moist forest habitat above the little village of Domaine Duclos, it reminded me most of the Lewis' and Acorn Woodpeckers of the western United States, without the lighter collar and the red face or crown. It is similar in size and behavior. I watched a pair of Guadeloupe Woodpeckers sally off a snag after passing insects and then fly with deep wing-beats to a second nearby snag. On landing one bird made a deep "chuuur" call, then bobbed its head just like an Acorn Woodpecker. These three woodpeckers are closely related, according to the AOU *Checklist of North American Birds*. The AOU lists eighteen *Melanerpes* woodpeckers within North and Central America and the West Indies and places the Guadeloupe Woodpecker between the Lewis' and Acorn Woodpeckers.

My May visit to Guadeloupe was for the express purpose of finding and observing the Guadeloupe Woodpecker, the island's only endemic bird, and also to visit Guadeloupe's large national park, Natural Park of Guadeloupe. Betty and I had flown to Guadeloupe's Raizet Airport from San Juan, Puerto Rico, rented a car, and spent the next four days touring the island. Although it rained a good part of the time, we were able to visit all the principal habitats and even climb to the 4,813-foot summit of La Soufrière, the centerpiece of the national park and Guadeloupe's highest peak.

We spent most of our time on Basse-Terre, the western portion of Guadeloupe, which is often described as the "western wing of a giant butterfly." Guadeloupe is often referred to as the "butterfly island" because of its shape. The eastern wing is Grand-Terre, the smaller, lower, and more heavily developed portion of Guadeloupe. The two sections are separated by La Rivière Salée, a narrow strait with a connecting highway bridge.

We turned west off Highway N1 at Versailles onto Highway D23, the cross-mountain road that intersects Highway N2 on the west coast at Mahaut. In only a few miles we turned north toward the village of Prise d'Eau, where a secondary road goes west to Domaine Duclos and a research station, Station de Recherches de Zoologie. This station is situated at the base of Route Forestière de Grosse Montagne, an unimproved roadway that cuts through the forest and crosses the mountains to join up with the Trace des Crêtes trail on the western slope. We were able to drive only a short distance above the research station.

The lower portion of Route Forestière de Grosse Montagne is where Jon Barlow of the University of Toronto had found a small population of the endemic and perhaps now extinct Guadeloupe House Wrens several years earlier; I was curious whether any of these rare birds could still be found. This bird was first thought to be extinct as early as 1914, but it was rediscovered by M. J. C. Roche near Cacao in 1969, and Barlow recorded four singing males above the research station in May 1973. But in spite of walking up and down the trail for several hours, I was unable to locate any Guadeloupe House Wrens. However, the moist forest habitat along the lower portion of Route Forestière de Grosse Montagne produced a full complement of the island's moist-forest bird life. Guadeloupe Woodpeckers were reasonably common there. Most flew off as I approached, but one individual let me approach to within about 60 feet. Its very dark plumage initially helped to conceal it on the dark-colored snag.

Other birds recorded along the trail included Scaly-naped Pigeon, Mangrove Cuckoo, Black and Lesser Antillean Swifts, Purple-throated Carib, Lesser Antillean Flycatcher, Caribbean Martin, Forest Thrush, Scaly-breasted Thrasher, Brown Trembler, Plumbeous Warbler, Bananaquit, Black-faced Grassquit, and Lesser Antillean Bullfinch.

Of these additional fourteen species, none were as exciting to me as the **Plumbeous Warbler,** a species with which I had not previously been acquainted. I found that its behavior was very different from that expected of a warbler. It seemed to move through the thick vegetation at all heights in wrenlike fashion, creeping around the trunks of the trees and skulking within the deep shade of the abundant vines, all the while twitching its tail from side to side. It was an active and rather aggressive bird; on two occasions I watched it chase away Bananaquits that had apparently come too close to its territory. Once it raised its tail like a wren and uttered a wrenlike rattle.

Although the Plumbeous Warbler is never going to win a beauty prize, I found it to be a lovely creature. Its upperparts are a rather plain slaty-gray color, with a bold white eyeline and suborbital spot (between eye and bill) and two distinct white wing bars. Its underparts are overall gray with lighter patches on the throat. Its tail is longer than is shown in the illustration in James Bond's *Birds of the West Indies*, giving it a wrenlike character in the way it flipped its tail about. Bond describes its song as "a short, but rather melodious, 'pa-pi-a.' Call-note a simple 'chek.'" But in *The Warblers of North America*, edited by Ludlow Griscom and Alexander Sprunt, Jr., Bond wrote that the Plumbeous Warbler's song "may be described as a short, rather plaintive 'de-de-diu' and is one of the few bird sounds heard in the rugged mountains of Guadeloupe."

At one point while I was watching a Plumbeous Warbler moving through the vegetation, a very different bird suddenly appeared within my field of vision. A slight adjustment of my binoculars brought a middle-sized *Myiarchus* flycatcher into sharper focus, a **Lesser Antillean Flycatcher.** Although I had never before seen this bird, I knew immediately what it was. All the *Myiarchus* flycatchers look essentially alike, except for subtle differences: body and bill sizes and various color combinations on their tails and wings. They can be difficult to identify. In fact, the Lesser Antillean Flycatcher was considered to be a Stolid Flycatcher until 1983, when that bird was split by the AOU into four separate species: Stolid Flycatcher of Jamaica and Hispaniola; La Sagra's Flycatcher of Cuba, the Bahamas, and Grand Cayman, and now found regularly in winter on Elliott Key, Florida; Puerto Rican Flycatcher of Puerto Rico and St. John (rare); and Lesser Antillean Flycatcher of the Lesser Antilles from Barbuda south to St. Lucia. Wesley Lanyon (1967) was the first to divide these four species, but he recognized their close relations by referring to them as a "superspecies."

NATURAL PARK OF GUADELOUPE

We spent two nights in the southwestern corner of Guadeloupe at Les Relais de La Soufrière, a clean and very pleasant hotel on the upper edge of the village of Saint-Claude, about 45 miles from Raizet Airport. Saint-Claude is situated just above the capital city of Basse-Terre at 1,875 feet elevation on the western slope of La Soufrière.

A narrow mountain road climbs out of Saint-Claude and snakes upward for another 4 miles to a parking area at the foot of the volcanic summit of La Soufrière. This area is but a small part of the 74,000-acre Natural Park of Guadeloupe, which extends north to south along the upper slopes of Basse-Terre for about 23 miles; its width varies from 2 to 5 miles. Allen Putney, in the final report of the *Survey of Conservation Priorities in the Lesser Antilles*, reported this area to be the largest remaining wildlands within any of the Lesser Antilles, and it includes almost 5,000 acres of relatively undisturbed rain forest.

Rain forest habitat dominates the roadsides between Saint-Claude and the Soufrière trailhead and forms a broad belt of dense vegetation between approximately 1,000 and 2,300 feet elevation. This habitat is reminiscent of a huge greenhouse: philodendrons, anthuriums, epiphytes, and creepers are abundant.

Ecologist J. S. Beard called this lush environment "lower montane rain forest" in his 1944 paper, "Climax Vegetation in Tropical America." Beard wrote that this habitat possesses two tree strata, a canopy layer about 70 to 100 feet high and a lower story 10 to 50 feet high, with leaves predominantly simple in structure. The principal plants of Guadeloupe's key habitats are listed in the national park booklet, *The Natural Park of Guadeloupe: Walks and Hikes*. Dominant canopy trees listed for the rain forest include white chestnut, résolu, carapate, marbri, and yellow mangrove. Shorter trees include laurel, yellow laurel, yellow bois doux, and Isabelle bois doux.

Scattered patches of cloud forest also occur in the area, especially in depressions, where clouds tend to form almost daily. Cloud forest habitat also has two closed layers, at 60 and 30 feet, and a shrub layer dominated by simple-leaved dwarf palms and tree ferns. Beard wrote that cloud forests possess trees with "heavy crowns, branch low, and are loaded with moss and epiphytes."

Above the rain forest is a very different environment of low shrubs and stunted trees that are locally regarded as "high-altitude savannahs" and described in the national park booklet as "stunted forests drenched by humidity (236–394 inches of precipitation), lower temperatures (54–59 degrees F yearly average), excessive haze and choking of the soil." Principal plant species listed for this habitat include mountain mangle, mountain olive, marbri, bois canon, mountain palmetto, and mountain caca-ravet. Beard called this habitat by its Spanish name, *páramo*, and described it as "almost devoid of woody vegetation and covered mostly with stemless plants having enlarged root-systems and coriaceous [leathery] leaves, arranged usually in basal rosettes."

The *páramo* habitat covers all of the summit and higher ridges, most of which are composed of various forms of igneous rock derived from past eruptions of La Soufrière. The most recent major eruption occurred in 1976, and there are numerous fumaroles on the upper slopes and at the summit that still spout steam and gases, a good reminder of the mountain's dramatic origin.

On a grander scale, Guadeloupe's La Soufrière is but one of many volcanic peaks within the Lesser Antilles that are part of a chain of volcanoes that, along with coral reefs, are responsible for the very existence of the islands. Guadeloupe is composed of both land-building materials. Grand-Terre is primarily limestone from ancient coral reefs, and Basse-Terre is primarily volcanic in origin.

The evidence of volcanism was everywhere around us as we climbed the winding trail to the summit. Huge pinnacles of black volcanic lava jutted out of the slopes like some kind of Pleistocene forest. In the morning mist that swirled around us, the black pinnacles of lava, partly clad in green, looked very much like a scene from a make-believe fairyland. A number of eroded gullies provided further proof of the soft volcanic soils of the mountain peak. In the harder rocky areas, it was difficult to determine if the great vertical cracks were from erosion or fumaroles that ran deep into the molten earth. Vegetation on these black rocky slopes was dominated by green and yellow mosses and lichens, with an abundance of little ferns and fleshy succulents, many rosette forms.

The view of the surrounding *páramo* was reminiscent of a huge green rug that had been laid between the rain forest and the rocky crags of the summit. Passing through that carpet of greenery, I stopped now and then to identify the wildlife. But except for four species of birds, La Soufrière's summit was limited to the green world of chlorophyll.

The most numerous of the four bird species found along the trail was the little **Black-faced Grassquit.** It seemed to make up for its size and rather drab appearance by its activity. Birds were singing all around us, perched on the ground or on various low plants and also on the lava pinnacles. They sang their songs, buzzing "tik-seeee" sounds, over and over again. I watched one very dark male that sang from four separate posts. I assumed that at that late-May date this bird was on territory and warning other grassquit males away.

The slightly larger **Lesser Antillean Bullfinch** was also present in numbers along the trail. It too is a short, plump, all-black bird, but males possess a rufous-red chin, throat, and undertail covert. Females are overall dark olive-gray with some brown on their wings. Their songs are very different from the Black-faced Grassquit. Bond described the bullfinch song as "a simple twittering, with an occasional harsh petulant note or a shrill tseep-tseep; also a shrill trill."

One of the gullies along the trail contained a few shrubs, and this is where I found a pair of Plumbeous Warblers. The gully must have been 500 yards above the rain forest habitat, where the species is reasonably common, but for some reason this pair had chosen the almost bare gully on the steep upper slope. I watched for other Plumbeous Warblers along the trail, but no more were seen.

The fourth member of the avian foursome was a lone **Purple-throated Carib** that was feeding on a bright red flowering shrub. This bird, too, can be expected within the lower patches of cloud forest, and this lone wanderer was undoubtedly taking advantage of the nectar-filled flowers present on the *páramo*. See Chapter 8 for a description of this marvelous hummingbird.

The top of La Soufrière is cratered, and deep fumaroles still carry steam and rotten-egg smells from the bowels of the earth into the atmosphere. Standing on the edge of one deep fissure, we could detect gurgling sounds, evidence of the great temperatures that existed far below. The summit also provided incredible views in all directions. Far below to the west was the tiny village of Saint-Claude, and farther down was the city of Basse-Terre. Beyond lay the great Caribbean Sea. To the east I could see a series of ridges that stretched downward to the Atlantic Ocean shore. Northward was the broad mountain park of Guadeloupe. Far beyond, toward the northeast, was the other Guadeloupe, the flatlands of Grand-Terre.

I spent my second morning walking through the rain forest, following the roadway above Saint-Claude. The morning was wet, with dripping water everywhere. The dawn chorus of birds was just beginning as I entered the canopied roadway. The volume of song was reminiscent of the tropics of Central America, but I soon realized that only eight species were contributing to the chorus.

The most distinct song that morning was the deliberate one- to four-note whistle of the **Black-whiskered Vireo.** This is the Caribbean analog to the Red-eyed Vireo of North America, generally the same size and appearance except for the black whisker-line that runs from its bill downward below the cheek. Its loud songs echoed from the forest, and from any one point on the roadway I could detect three or four singing birds. Also like its North American cousin, it sings throughout the daylight hours, so after the morning chorus declines it often is the only bird song still evident. The dominance of this bird was most obvious that morning.

The other abundant songs that morning included the screeches and squawks of the **Scaly-breasted Thrasher.** Bond wrote that its voice is "like that of a mockingbird, but softer and more hesitant." That morning in the Guadeloupe rain forest, its voice did not impress me as being soft and hesitant. The birds must have been at the height of their vocalization, which might be described as loud and even piercing. I was able to observe several of these noisy thrashers perched on the larger branches of trees 20 to 30 feet above the ground. It has a rather thrushlike stature but with grayish-brown plumage and a black, rather short bill, short at least for a thrasher. Its name is derived from its scaly-looking breast, which contains many dark horizontal streaks against a gray background.

Lesser Antillean Bullfinches and Black-faced Grassquits were also in full song that morning. The majority of the bullfinch songs came from the forest, but the grassquits preferred the roadsides. I saw six or eight individuals up and down the roadway, spaced out every 100 feet or so as if they were on a territory. Plumbeous Warblers were fairly common, as well. They joined the chorus with their rather short but melodious song, "pa-pi-a." Several Purple-throated Caribs were present, too, usually zipping by in high gear or feeding on the flowering heliconias that hung out of the forest over the road's edge.

Suddenly I discovered a medium-size, all-dark bird perched in the open, about 30 feet away, trembling as if frightened by my appearance. Its wings hung down and were shaking like two rags. I knew immediately I had found a **Brown Trembler,** one of the West Indies' most interesting birds. I focused my binoculars on the bird and watched its strange behavior. The trembling continued. Suddenly it turned and flew off into the forest, but I had been able to observe it for several minutes and was amazed at its strange behavior. I wondered if such a behavior, typical when the bird is stressed, shortens its lifespan. All members of the thrasher family are aggressive and belligerent. Only this one has developed a trembling behavior, useful to amaze some creatures, like humans, but I wondered how effective it would be to distract a predator. Perhaps its trembling would be perceived as a trembling leaf among the dense foliage. The bird's colors of brown above and a lighter brown below would undoubtedly help it blend into its surroundings. The Trembler's most distinct feature is its very long and slightly curved bill. It undoubtedly utilizes this long tool to extract insects and other small creatures from cracks and debris. But although I have seen tremblers on numerous occasions within their rather small range, from Saba to St. Vincent, I have never been fortunate enough to watch them feeding. All of my sightings have been of birds that apparently saw me first and were either totally still or trembling like a leaf in the wind.

POINTE DES COLIBRIS

The eastern extension of Grand-Terre is a rugged peninsula of land called Pointe des Colibris. This portion of Guadeloupe is very different from the lush highlands of the Natural Park of Guadeloupe. Instead, the point is a wild combination of sandy beaches and rugged limestone rocks, some standing in tall spirals and others stretched out over the terrain. Trails pass through a littoral wooded area, follow the shoreline, and crisscross the hillside.

Caribbean Elaenia and Black-whiskered Vireo songs rang out of the stunted woodlands. A pair of Tropical Mockingbirds chased one another about the opening along the trail. I stopped to look at this bird, which is so similar to the Northern Mockingbird of North America and the Greater Antilles. But the tail of the Tropical Mockingbird is darker, with larger, more contrasting white corner patches; it somehow makes the tail more obvious. Tropical Mockingbirds also lack the distinct white wing-patch of the

Northern. Their songs are somewhat similar, but these mockingbirds also produce "a few clucks and wheezy notes; unlike the well-known Northern Mockingbird," according to Robert Ridgely and Guy Tudor (1989). They also contend that Tropicals rarely mimic other birds.

The range of the Tropical Mockingbird is fascinating. It occurs in Mexico south of the Isthmus of Tehuantepec, throughout Central America, and south to northern South America, then northeast to Trinidad and Tobago and northward through the Lesser Antilles as far as Guadeloupe. It does not get to nearby Montserrat or farther north but stops suddenly at Guadeloupe. The range of the Northern Mockingbird extends east only to St. Croix, U.S. Virgin Islands, leaving all of the northern Windward Islands without either species.

I followed the trail over the rugged limestone ridge to where the Atlantic breakers were washing up onto the contorted shoreline. From this easternmost corner I could see an amazing number of seabirds fishing the deeper waters about a quarter of a mile out. I sat on a black rock bench, binoculars in place, and gazed out to sea. Sooty Terns were most numerous, but there were also a few Brown Noddies, and I counted five tropicbirds farther out that I was never able to identify either as Red-billed or White-tailed Tropicbirds, and one lone Brown Pelican. All of these birds nest on Guadeloupe, according to Rudd van Halewyn and Robert Norton (1984). Other seabirds reported for the island include Manx Shearwater, Laughing Gull, and Roseate and Least Terns.

Guadeloupe is a French island, actually an Overseas Department of France since 1946, but its people, culture, and mores are the result of a harmonious blending of European, African, and East Indian origins. The island's original name, Guadalupe, came from Columbus, who claimed the island for Spain in 1493, during his second voyage to the New World. France acquired the island in 1815 and changed the name to the French spelling of Guadeloupe. However, the native inhabitants, the fierce Carib Indians, called it Karukera, meaning "Island of Beautiful Waters." To most visitors today it is indeed Karukera, a very green land surrounded by beautiful waters.

CHAPTER FOURTEEN

Dominica THE NATURE ISLAND

Dominica is the most mountainous of all the West Indies. In proportion to its size, Dominica's impressive peaks, ridges, and ravines make it more rugged than Switzerland. Its dissected topography contains more than 350 rivers and streams. Although several West Indian islands contain higher elevations, the steepness of its slopes gives Dominica a personality all its own. This rugged character makes access into its hinterlands particularly difficult. The island's roadways generally follow the coastline and cross the mountains only in a few places. Although the capital city of Roseau is only 18 airline miles from the island's Melville Hall Airport near Marigot (on the opposite side of the island), the narrow, winding roadway requires more than two hours to travel. The mountainous terrain also provides the central mountains with a certain amount of protection that would not have been possible if there was greater access.

Approximately half of the island is more than 1,000 feet above sea level; the highest peak of Morne Trois Pitons reaches 4,699 feet elevation. These highlands comprise the major portion of the 2,736-acre Morne Trois Pitons National Park, which, in conjunction with the larger 8,800-acre Northern Forest Reserve, with its 4,686-foot Morne Diablotin, dominates the greater part of Dominica's mountain landscape. Allen Putney, in his 1982 *Survey of Conservation Priorities in the Lesser Antilles,* reported that these areas contain over 2,000 acres of moist forest habitat (more than anywhere else in the Lesser Antilles), 3,680 acres of rain forest (second only to Guadeloupe), and 2,360 acres of cloud forest. The combined montane forests are the most extensive in all the West Indies, covering up to three-quarters of the island. These lush forests are directly related to the island's extremely high rainfall. The mountainous interior receives over 250 inches annually. The coastal city of Roseau, located in one of the driest parts of the island, receives about 80 inches annually.

Because of the extent of Dominica's relatively undisturbed forest system, it has received considerable ecological study over the years. During the 1940s, Oxford forester J. S. Beard mapped the island's vegetation, and his 1944 paper, "Climax Vegetation in Tropical America," provided a baseline for numerous followup studies of tropical vegetation. In 1988, P. G. H. Evans further summarized Dominica's major vegetation types, listing the major woody plant species of two montane habitats: rain forest and montane thicket/elfin woodland. Evans's dominant rain forest species included gommier, chataignier petit coco, chataignier petite feuille, carapite, bois diable, and balate (at higher altitudes). Dominant montane thicket/elfin woodland species included bois bandé, laurier rose, mauricif (montane thickets), palmiste montagne in palm brakes, and kaklin (elfin woodland).

In 1988, Timothy Johnson summarized Dominica's important fauna and flora in an International Council for Bird Protection (ICBP) monograph, *Biodiversity and Conservation in the Caribbean: Profiles of Selected Islands.* Johnson pointed out that Dominica possesses four single-island endemic vertebrates (two birds and two lizards) and several regionally endemic vertebrates: twelve bats, nine birds, six reptiles, and two amphibians. Of approximately one thousand flowering plants, six species and two varieties are endemic.

This high degree of endemism illustrates not only the island's rather pristine conditions but also that Dominica has been spared the effects of the mongoose, an introduced mammal that is common almost everywhere else in the West Indies. Because the island's mountainous terrain does not lend itself to extensive agriculture, sugarcane was never a significant crop. When all the "sugar islands" introduced the mongoose to control rats and other pests, Dominica did not. The result of the introduced mongoose was far more damaging to those islands' fragile ecosystems than expected. Mongooses feed on almost everything, from garbage to birds and reptiles; many of those islands' unique wildlife either disappeared or declined drastically. Rats adjusted to mongoose predation simply by foraging at night while the mongooses slept; they began to nest in trees out of reach of the nonclimbing mongooses. Most islands now consider the mongoose their number one pest.

FINDING DOMINICA'S TWO ENDEMIC PARROTS

My principal reason for visiting Dominica was to find the country's two endemic birds. Both are Amazon parrots, the **Red-necked** and **Imperial Parrots.** The Imperial Parrot is the largest of the genus, and both are considered endangered by the ICBP.

We left our vehicle along the muddy track at the upper edge of a banana plantation. The July morning was chilly and humid, and the vegetation was still dripping from the night's heavy rainfall. The sun was trying desperately to poke its way through the gray overcast. Paul Butler led the way. Our party of six trudged up the muddy slope across soggy banana leaves and between the blue plastic bags used to protect the young fruit from pests.

A pair of **Scaly-naped Pigeons** sprinted across the sky and disappeared into the mist. Below us, along the lower edge of the banana grove, I detected the wheezy songs of Bananaquits. I couldn't help but think how appropriate it was to find these little honeycreepers in a banana plantation. They feed on the sweet nectar produced by the flowering plants.

We quietly followed Paul to where a trail entered the forest. Then one by one we ducked into the undergrowth and entered an entirely different, shadowy green world. We trudged onward, following a more defined trail now. Although there was little movement evident around us, besides our party of intruders, I began to hear bird sounds inside the forest. Most were muffled by the tangle of vegetation, but ahead I identified the very distinct song of a House Wren. Although once considered a separate species, it has since been lumped with the same House Wren species so common in North America. Off to the left I heard squawks I attributed to Scaly-breasted

Thrashers. A Black-whiskered Vireo song echoed through the mist. Beyond I heard the low, cooing songs of Scaly-naped Pigeons.

Then, only a dozen feet ahead of us, a rabbit-size mammal darted across the trail. To the right were two more, frozen in place to avoid discovery. These were agoutis, large, long-legged rodents with bristly hair. They were very ungulatelike in appearance, with a large head, short ears, a short tail, and bulging jaws, almost like a javelina of the American Southwest. There are several species of agoutis in Central and South America, and those found in the Lesser Antilles were introduced by pre-Columbian Indians. Scientists believe that the entire Antillean population, which has evolved into four separate subspecies, were all derived from the Brazilian species, *Dasyprocta aguti*. According to mammalogist E. Raymond Hall, the Dominican subspecies of agouti is *noblei*.

Agoutis are generally diurnal. During the day they live within the forest undergrowth and feed on fruits and nuts. At night they sleep in dense brush, under fallen trees and vines, or in unused dens. They often are hunted for food and have been greatly reduced or eliminated on most of the islands. Hunters can attract agoutis from their hiding places by tossing stones into the air; the falling object sounds like a falling fruit to the agoutis, which then come out to feed.

The trail suddenly emerged into an open vista with a deep ravine below and a steep green slope beyond that ran onto a higher ridge 300 to 400 feet above. Another slope climbed upward and disappeared into the mist. In the foreground was a wooden platform that someone had built on a tree that leaned out over the deep ravine. Not only did the platform appear insecure and downright flimsy, but the route to the perch was incredibly dangerous as well.

Paul spoke for the first time in several minutes. "This is where we will see the sisserous." Sisserou is the local name for the Imperial Parrots. He added, "The platform was built by researchers as an observation deck for watching the parrots up and down the ravine. You are welcome to try it out!" No one accepted. I have done some crazy things in my life to see wildlife, but nothing could entice me to use that wooden perch hanging out a hundred feet or more over the Picard River gorge. I decided that if my chance to see parrots depended, literally, on climbing out on a limb, I would forsake the opportunity.

We shifted our positions to a comfortable stance in preparation for what could be a long wait. The ground was too muddy to sit on. According to Paul, this overlook provided our best opportunity for seeing Dominica's

Imperial Parrot in its natural habitat. The smaller Red-necked Parrot (known locally as jacquot) has a much broader range throughout the Northern Forest Reserve. But the entire population of Imperial Parrots, estimated in 1988 by Evans at only about sixty birds, is confined to the montane rain forest along the northwestern slope of Morne Diablotin. The best view of that area is where we were located, above the Syndicate Estate banana plantation.

It is unlikely that the Imperial Parrot population was ever very large, but they once ranged throughout Dominica's forested highlands. These birds have been used for food and pets since pre-Columbian times. But after Hurricane David in 1979, when much of their southern habitat was destroyed, the surviving birds converged in the northwest, where they remain today. The Red-necked Parrots continue to utilize approximately 60 percent of their original range, and their population includes about five hundred birds, according to Butler. But the Imperial Parrots have not done as well. Their numbers continue to decline, largely due to clearing of their essential habitat for Dominica's growing banana industry, and also due to continued shooting of the birds for food and trapping for the pet trade. The most recent estimate (1995) is approximately one hundred birds, according to Butler.

The decline in Dominica's parrot populations appears to have been put on hold, however. This about-face has been due primarily to the efforts of the Forestry Division, which has been assisted in the past by Paul Butler, who initiated a program of "Promoting Protection through Pride." Butler, called the "Lee Iacocca of Caribbean conservation" by Chris Wille in a 1991 article in *American Birds*, uses every gimmick imaginable to sell children and their parents on the value of protecting their natural heritage. By dressing like parrots, encouraging local calypso musicians to play original songs about the parrots, and broadcasting their message on billboards, bumper stickers, and T-shirts, they were able to convince industry to use the Imperial Parrot as a symbol in advertising. The official flag of the independent state of Dominica prominently displays the Imperial Parrot, which has since become the country's national bird. Butler's unique brand of conservation, funded primarily by RARE (Rare Animal Relief Effort, headquartered in Philadelphia), has succeeded elsewhere and has great potential on Dominica. (See further details on Butler's efforts in Chapter 17.)

A Broad-winged Hawk suddenly appeared over the ravine, circled once or twice, and then dropped beyond the ridge into another ravine. Then a thin rattle call attracted my attention to the shrubs just below our overlook. I moved a few feet closer for a better look. I could see movement through the wet shrubbery, and it took several minutes of watching before I could

Imperial Parrot

identify our visitor as a **Plumbeous Warbler,** one of Dominica's unique birds that the island shares only with nearby Guadeloupe and Marie Galante. This warbler is very wrenlike in its behavior of creeping about the undergrowth; it even flips its tail about. The Plumbeous Warbler is best identified by its slate-gray body (lighter underparts) with a white eyeline and spot between the bill and eye, two white wing bars, and white tail spots.

The flutelike song of a thrush suddenly burst upon us and we all gazed upward, beyond the wooden perch, toward the end of the tree limb. There, only about 70 feet away, was a **Rufous-throated Solitaire,** in full song and apparently oblivious of the admiring watchers below. It is an incredible bird with a wonderful song. It remained only another couple of minutes before it flitted off to another perch beyond our view, but we continued to hear its flutelike warble. Mockingbird-size, this solitaire has a slate-gray back and light gray underparts, except for the bright rufous throat and undertail coverts. Its broad white tail stripes were obvious, as well. With binoculars I was able to see the white spots at the base of the bill and below the eye. But its flutelike song is what truly sets it apart as something very special.

Several Red-necked Parrots converged on a group of trees directly across the ravine. Paul identified the trees as gommier trees, full of seeds and fruit, a favorite of the Dominican parrots. Red-necks arrived from various directions in pairs or in small flocks of four to seven birds. We all focused our binoculars on these birds, hoping that one would suddenly become an Imperial. Then suddenly, almost directly above us, a larger parrot soared by on open wings, and Paul called out, "Sisserou!" I immediately focused my attention on this larger parrot. Then two additional Imperials came from our left, crossed over our ridge, and joined up with the first bird. Their larger size was unmistakable. They circled the feeding trees once and then dropped into the upper canopy and disappeared.

I continued to watch that area for their reappearance, and although movement was evident on two or three occasions, I wasn't able to clearly see the birds again. Our sighting had been short, but their size and color pattern were distinct. I had clearly seen their purplish-violet underparts, red patches at the bend of the wings, and greenish back. As the birds circled over the ridge I had detected a dark band across their necks. We looked at each other in congratulations; it was an exemplary experience.

We waited another hour, hoping that others would appear, but we did not see any more sisserous. We did see more Red-necked Parrots, coming and going over the far ridge, including two pairs that flew up the ravine to within a couple of hundred feet of us before banking to their left and gliding into the same group of fruiting gommier trees on the opposite ridge. In flight I was able to clearly see the parrots' large red neck-patch (actually on their upper chest), distinct red wing-patch, and violet-purple face and forehead. I could also see their whitish eye-ring and bill. Their overall plumage was mostly deep green, so once they landed in the trees with equally green foliage they were next to impossible to find.

The sun was beginning to poke through the clouds as we emerged from the forest into the banana field. We heard more Bananaquit songs, and the "tseep-tseep" songs of the Lesser Antillean Bullfinch were all around us. Then I detected the very distinct euphonic "tuk-tuk" song of an **Antillean Euphonia.** We detoured slightly from the direct route back to our vehicle, tracking the repetitious "tuk-tuk" songs. Then directly ahead of us at midelevation on one of the few remaining forest trees, perched above a small bundle of mistletoe, was the little songster. What a beautiful bird it was! Less than 5 inches long, the male Antillean Euphonia sports an olive-green back with a metallic-blue neck and crown and a yellow-orange forehead. Its underparts are yellow-green with a blue-green throat. The duller female was inside the clump of mistletoe, feeding on the succulent little berries. This little tanager was split from the more widespread Blue-hooded Euphonia of Mexico and Central America by the AOU in 1983. Our sighting was a fitting climax to an early morning visit to Dominica's endemic parrots.

LOGISTICS

Our small party of naturalists was staying near Portsmouth at Sunshine Village, clean, beachfront cottages operated by Alfred and Irene Eckert. The overnight cost of $44 (double) was quite reasonable, considering it also included a delicious dinner of "mountain chicken." Mountain chicken is actually a large native frog, locally called crapaud and known to scientists as *Leptodactylus fallax*, that is common within the middle elevation scrublands of the island. I later learned that crapaud is a foam-nester that at the onset of the rainy season lays its eggs in a nest constructed of glandular secretions whipped into a froth that looks like beaten eggs. The tadpoles live in the liquefied center of the nest until rains enable them to swim into nearby pools. Adult crapaud legs, battered and fried, are delicious.

The Sunshine Village location provided opportunities to visit several of Dominica's more interesting sites on the northern half of the island: a nearby mangrove swamp and Cabrits National Park, the Syndicate Estate and the adjacent slopes of Morne Diablotin, and the abundant beaches and bays along the northeastern Atlantic coastline.

Our visit to Cabrits was especially interesting because Forest Service employee Colmore Christian was our guide to the eighteenth-century Fort Shirley, located on the crest of a hill overlooking Prince Rupert Bay. The entire garrison contains the ruins of more than fifty major structures. The surrounding vegetation was dominated by the beautiful purple-red flowers of the tree locally called savonette. Penelope Honychurch, in her fascinating little book, *Caribbean Wild Plants and Their Uses*, claims that Carib Indians used the roots of this midsize tree as a fish poison. The closely related lancepod tree of tropical America was used by the Mayans to make a fermented drink used in religious ceremonies.

The northern highway turns east at Portsmouth and crosses the foothills to the Atlantic side of the island. Then it becomes the Coast Highway, which runs south to Marigot before turning southwest across the central foothills between Morne Diablotin and Morne Trois Pitons.

Below Marigot is the Carib Indian Reserve, where Indian baskets, grass mats, and various shell crafts can be purchased at a little roadside store. Carrol Fleming described the Carib Reserve in her book, *Adventuring in the Caribbean*, as "the last enclave of a proud people still governed by a tribal chief." Below the highway is the village of Salybia, located within a beautiful setting among green trees and with the bright blue backdrop of the Atlantic Ocean.

MORNE TROIS PITONS NATIONAL PARK
AND THE SOUTHERN COAST

Farther south is Emerald Pool, located inside the eastern edge of Morne Trois Pitons National Park. A five-minute walk from a parking area, the trail passes through a lush grotto of rain forest to a beautiful emerald-green pool of water at the base of a low waterfall. It is an exquisite scene, well worth the time and effort required.

The forest at Emerald Pool seemed to me to represent the best example of undisturbed rain forest that I had seen anywhere within the West Indies. The tall forest trees were filled with epiphytes and vines, creating a picture that could easily have been transposed from the African jungles. Bird sound included a half-dozen or so forest species. But the most notable birds there were a pair of **Forest Thrushes** that came so close I was able to look them over without the aid of my binoculars. It was by far the best look I have ever had at this deep forest species.

The Forest Thrush is robin-size with contrasting brown, white, and yellow features. It is largely brownish with large, white, teardrop-shaped spots, edged in brown, on its chest and belly, a bright yellow bill, eye-ring, and legs, and an all-dark eye and tail. When I later looked at the Forest Thrush illustration in James Bond's book, *The Birds of the West Indies*, I was amazed at the similar pose of the bird at Emerald Pool. The colors of the live bird, however, were more iridescent and richer than those in the book.

I watched one individual perched on an open limb at eye level, frozen in place as it looked me over. It gave a loud and rather sharp "chuk" call that reminded me of the softer "chuck" call of the Hermit Thrush, a North American relative. The second bird suddenly sang a soft and musical trill, like a series of low, waffling flute notes. The first bird immediately responded by flying off toward the song. A second later I found the two birds perched side by side.

We made Hotel Cherry, in the heart of Roseau, our base of operations during our stay in the south. One early morning, Ted Dale and Mike Walsh (two friends from St. Croix) accompanied me on a long walk along the Caribbean coast to the southwestern point of the island, Scotts Head, that juts northward into Soufrière Bay. The view from the top of Scotts Head, looking north across the water toward Roseau, with its bright green forested backdrop, was truly spectacular.

Bird life that late March morning included all the common lowland species. **Caribbean Martins** were especially abundant over Roseau and the bay front; their purple back and white belly gleamed in the sunshine. A pair of Tropical Mockingbirds guarded a well-manicured lawn at the edge of town. Magnificent Frigatebirds, Zenaida Doves, Gray Kingbirds, Caribbean Elaenias, Scaly-breasted Thrashers, Bananaquits, Black-whiskered Vireos, Black-faced Grassquits, and Lesser Antillean Bullfinches were all present in substantial numbers. Fewer numbers of Green Herons, Broad-winged Hawks, one Spotted Sandpiper (a migrant no doubt), Common Ground-Doves, Mangrove Cuckoos, Smooth-billed Anis, Antillean Crested Hummingbirds, House Wrens, Yellow and Plumbeous Warblers, Streaked Saltators, and Carib Grackles were also present. And at the very top of Scotts Head, sitting alone on an old weathered snag, was a Merlin. This little falcon of the boreal forests seemed out of place in the Lesser Antilles, yet I knew that it normally winters in these islands. It may already have been en route northward from its wintering grounds in South America. My sighting was but a snapshot in time.

My friend Sandra Isherwood, who had organized both of my visits to Dominica from St. Croix, had once lived on Dominica and had friends throughout the island. We visited many of her old haunts, including La Guiuave for refreshments (I tried the local sorrel drink); La Robe Creole

Restaurant, where we had a superb lunch; the Botanical Gardens, which had not fully recovered from the impact of Hurricane David in 1979; and Papillote (French for "little butterfly"), with its excellent outdoor restaurant (great flying fish meal) in a garden setting and with an adjacent hot pool for lounging, all located below beautiful Trafalgar Falls.

Dominica Forest Service Director Félix Grégoire (now [1995] Permanent Secretary, Ministry of Agriculture) visited with us after dinner and presented us with a slide program on the work under way to manage the island's very significant natural and cultural resources. The following day we accompanied Forestry Officer Dave Williams on a tour of Morne Trois Pitons National Park. This 17,000-acre park, just over 9 percent of the island, was established in 1975. It includes the virgin forest of the 1,000-acre Archbold Preserve, donated by American J. D. Archbold.

As we climbed onto the slopes of Morne Trois Pitons, the montane rain forest was spread out before us. Some of the trees reached 100 feet in height and 10 feet in diameter. One hundred and sixty-seven tree species have been recorded in the park, and sixty different species were found on one 10-acre study plot. The park's numerous features include four volcanoes and two freshwater lakes, including Boiling Lake in the Valley of Desolation, where there are numerous fumaroles and hot springs. Boiling Lake, a remnant of the mountain's volcanic past, is considered the second largest boiling lake in the world. The last major eruption occurred in 1880.

We also visited Freshwater Lake, a beautiful highland area that was under development for a new hydroelectric project. Road construction and clearing along the west side of this unique lake were already under way. I couldn't help but question the logic of the Dominican government in degrading this natural feature and creating a new threshold for additional development and the introduction of exotic life that will only increase the decline of the island's montane forest. Dominicans must be vigilant or they will lose their current superiority as a true nature preserve. Nature can usually overcome natural catastrophes if the flora and fauna are not subjected to the many technological advances of an over-energetic civilization.

The great open bowl that holds Freshwater Lake showed much evidence of Hurricane David in 1979. This portion of the natural park had been severely damaged by the storm; 100 percent of the forest had been flattened. The once-mature forest was little more than a dense thicket; a few trees had reached 20 feet in height. An interpretive trail had been built from a parking place onto the eastern slope above the lake to allow visitors a closer inspection of the slowly recovering forest.

On my second visit in March, I imagined that the plant life was already more dense and taller than when I had seen it fifteen months earlier. I walked the trail to a little clear stream that was feeding the lake. I wondered if it would be that clear on my next visit, after the hydroelectric project was completed.

The bird life within the stubby forest was confined to a lone Antillean Crested Hummingbird, several Lesser Antillean Bullfinches, and a surprisingly large number of Plumbeous Warblers. The large number of these black-and-white warblers within the stunted forest was unexpected. There were more Plumbeous Warblers there than I had seen in the mature montane forests and lowland forests elsewhere on the island.

Is it possible that the Plumbeous Warbler has evolved over time as a "disturbance species," preferring second-growth vegetation like that at Freshwater Lake? Hurricanes are no doubt part of its natural history. That concept would be a most interesting one to study and a wonderful excuse to spend more time on this wonderful nature island.

CHAPTER FIFTEEN

Martinique ISLAND OF FLOWERS

Martinique's first inhabitants called their island Madinina, meaning "island of flowers." When Christopher Columbus visited Madinina in 1502, he wrote that the island is "the best, richest, and sweetest country in the whole world." Today, Martinique, the French name since it was claimed by France in 1674, is one of the most popular tourist destinations in the Caribbean. It is famous for its cuisine, music, dance, and natural beauty. For nature lovers, Martinique can boast that one mammal, one bird, and five reptiles are single-island endemics; additionally, one mammal, eight birds, four reptiles, and one amphibian are regionally endemic. However, many of these unique species are in danger of extinction.

The **Martinique Oriole** is one of those single-island endemics; it occurs nowhere else in the entire world. It has been found within all of Martinique's forest types, from the dry scrub in the lowlands to the moist forest habitats in the mountains. Although it is widespread, it has never been common, and since 1988 it has been regarded as threatened, according to N. J. Collar and P. Andrew (1988). Rob Norton, Betty, and I searched for this lovely bird in several parts of the island on various days before we finally encountered it in the cloud forest at Pitons du Carbet in the north-central highlands.

That late summer morning was cool and cloudy, with fog clinging to the wet slopes. The mountain road (Highway D1 between Gros Morne and St. Pierre) was lined with flowering shrubs and trees that sometimes formed a gallery over the highway. Hundreds of little **Black-faced Grassquits** skittered off the roadway as we passed by. These all-dark birds with dull greenish underparts and a buzzing "tik-zeeee" song may be Martinique's most common bird. They occur everywhere from open areas within the mountain forests to the fields and diverse human ecosystems in the lowlands. They have adapted to human habitations to the extent that they frequent outdoor restaurants, where they often attempt to share tidbits from meals.

Just beyond the village of Treu Matelots the roadway passes through a portion of the Parc Naturel Regional de la Martinique, an extensive national park that is divided into a number of preserves and recreation areas. This is where we first encountered the beautiful **Rufous-throated Solitaire**. A pair of these birds were sitting in the center of the roadway, and we were forced to brake sharply to avoid hitting them. As soon as they flew up I was able to identify them from their butterflylike flight and contrasting rufous and gray underparts. It is a marvelous bird that is overall gray except for the rufous throat, upper chest, and undertail covert and with extensive white on the outer tail feathers and less obvious white below the eyes and on the chin.

The Rufous-throated Solitaire is one of the most delightful birds in all the West Indies. A member of the thrush family, it has a song that is not soon forgotten. David Lack described its song in *Island Biology Illustrated by the Land Birds of Jamaica* as "sustained clear liquid notes, some with the character of musical glasses, others trilled, uttered over a very wide range of frequencies, often at harmonic intervals of several tones, and sometimes the bird even appears to sing two sustained notes simultaneously." The local name for this solitaire is *siffleur de montagne*, French for "whistler of the mountains."

Most sightings of Rufous-throated Solitaires are of birds perched high in the treetops, either singing their wonderful flutelike songs or feeding on tiny fruits, sometimes hovering in midair to reach less accessible ones. But the bird's broad beak and surrounding bristles suggest that it also feeds on insects. Like other New World solitaires, Rufous-throats place their cup nest of moss on or near the ground, often on a bank or the side of a cliff.

Very soon after we entered the national park area we encountered a dozen or more hunters spaced out along the roadside, each packing a shotgun and staring upward into the forest canopy. Although throughout our approximately four-hour stay in the area we did not hear any shots, we also did not encounter a single dove or pigeon, birds that usually are common within similar habitats on islands where hunting is not sanctioned. On Martinique, we discovered that hunting is a popular and destructive pastime.

We found a stretch of roadway, just south of the junction of Highways D1 and N5, that was not patrolled by hunters and appeared to contain relatively undisturbed habitat. We parked our rental car at a little pullout at the base of a steep mountainside and then walked down the roadway. Both sides of the highway were filled with lush vegetation. The most obvious plant species was tree ferns, with their large lacy foliage at the top of a dark stalk, 20 to 30 feet high. Trumpet-trees, with their deeply lobed leaves arranged like a many-pointed star, towered overhead. The undergrowth was also crowded with ferns, reminding me of an arboretum. Bright red flowers of turk's caps were scattered along the roadsides.

Almost immediately Betty discovered a pair of **Blue-headed Hummingbirds** feeding amid the turk's cap flowers. What an incredibly beautiful bird it was! Like most hummingbirds, the males are the most colorful; females are usually more subtly colored to provide for better camouflage while tending the nest with less chance of attracting predators. The Blue-headed male is a wild combination of deep greens, purples, and blues, with red on the basal portion of its lower mandible. The male's most outstanding feature is the brilliant blue, actually a deep violet-blue, of its head and throat. Below the violet-blue throat was a bib of mottled blue. The rest of the body was emerald-green, except for the purplish-blue tail and blackish wings. It is undoubtedly one of the world's most gorgeous birds.

The Blue-headed Hummingbird is unique even within the world of hummingbirds. Of approximately 315 hummingbird species known to science, it is the lone representative of the genus *Cyanophaia*. Sometimes known as Antillean Emerald, it is found only on Martinique and nearby Dominica, where it occurs primarily at middle elevations within the montane forest and partly open countryside.

A second and more common hummingbird, the **Purple-throated Carib,** was also present, feeding on the turk's cap flowers and among the flowering bromeliads growing on the branches of various trees. This larger humming-bird is dark overall but in good light shows a deep purple-red throat and chest, deep blue-green undertail covert, and green wings. See Chapter 8 for additional information about this species.

We continued our search for the Martinique Oriole, walking farther down the roadway. We came to a place where the steep forested slope gave way to a relatively flat area filled with moss-draped vegetation. Suddenly Rob called out, "There it is, an oriole!" I swung around from observing a Scaly-breasted Thrasher just in time to see an oriole fly from one tree to another in the flat. I immediately focused my binoculars on the place where the bird had disappeared, about 100 feet away, and waited. After another thirty seconds it reappeared, and I was able to watch it work its way up onto a heavy branch into the open. It was a fairly small oriole with a brown to chestnut head, neck, and chest, black back and tail, and orange color, almost orange-rufous, on the underparts, upper wings, and rump. It reminded me immediately of the Black-cowled Oriole of the Greater Antilles and Central America, but I knew that this bird, as well as the look-alike Montserrat and St. Lucia Orioles, was split off from that species. The AOU regards all four birds as members of one superspecies.

Guy Mountfort, in his 1988 book, *Rare Birds of the World*, stated that the Martinique Oriole is "reported to be in serious decline." James Bond, in his 1985 edition of *The Birds of the West Indies*, wrote that it was "most numerous in semi-arid hills in the southern half of Martinique." We could not, however, find the bird in the southern lowlands, only in the central mountains. As difficult as it was for us to find it, I cannot help but concur with Mountfort's assessment.

Throughout our stay in the moist uplands, I could not help but be on the lookout for Martinique's endemic fer-de-lance, a snake that is considered to be one of the world's most poisonous reptiles. Although it is extremely rare, it receives a great deal of attention. According to herpetologist Raymond Ditmars, the snake's name originated in the Creole-French West Indies, in spite of being utilized for the same group of snakes wherever they occur from southern Mexico to South America. In the West Indies the fer-de-lance occurs only on Martinique and nearby St. Lucia. These snakes can be huge, up to 6 feet in length. They reside throughout the forested portions of the islands, although they are extremely secretive and rarely seen. The fer-de-lance is nocturnal and hides out in deep shade and hollows during the daylight hours. Ditmars includes a fascinating description of the species hunting its prey on Martinique in his book, *Snakes of the World*. He also describes the snake as follows: "coloration is olivaceous gray, crossed by dark bands narrowly margined with dull yellow or greenish—the bands widen as they extend downward."

NORTHERN MARTINIQUE

We continued west on Highway D1 across the central mountains to where it terminates at St. Pierre and the west coast highway (D10). There we turned north, followed Highway D10 along the coastline, and made a grand loop of the Pele Mountains (4,584 feet). Low clouds hung over Pele like a great shroud. We saw eroded valleys and stark hillsides everywhere. Several streams flowed under the highway and cut across black silt beaches. All of this was evidence of the cataclysmic blast that in 1902 split the side of Mount Pele and poured lava and fire out onto the capital city of St. Pierre. The city and its 30,000 inhabitants were destroyed within three minutes. A lone survivor, a prisoner in the city's well-built dungeon, was discovered four days later. The Museum of Volcanology, with its photographs and relics, is well worth visiting in the rebuilt St. Pierre. The capital was moved to Fort-de-France.

The north coast highway provides plenty of views seaward. Dominica rises out of the sea only 25 miles northward across the Canal de la Dominique. The few beaches in the north are narrow and consist of black or dark brown sand and silt. The waters beyond are deep and treacherous. On one stop near La Prêcheur we watched approximately seventy-five Brown Noddies feeding a quarter-mile offshore. Near St. Marie we found about sixty Sandwich Terns feeding just beyond the entrance to a pretty little bay.

EXOTICS

Late afternoon found us back in the vicinity of Le Lamentin Airport, on the adjacent racetrack (Hippoderme) grounds. We had been told that the Martinique Oriole was sometimes found in this area. Although we searched the adjacent trees, we found no orioles. Instead, we discovered that the tall grasses around the racetrack were filled with little finches, two of which were African species that had been either released by pet owners or introduced through natural means such as wind and dust storms, which often reach the West Indies from West Africa.

Within two hours we found hundreds of Red Bishops and a pair of Bronze Mannikins (African species) and a couple dozen Grassland Yellow-Finches, a species that was introduced to Barbados from South America and that has spread northward into the Lesser Antilles. The male Red Bishop, in breeding plumage, is one of the world's showiest creatures. This scarlet-and-black bird is best described by Serle, Morel, and Hartwig in *A Field Guide to the Birds of West Africa* thus: "Black crown and sides of head. Scarlet upperparts. Brown wings and tail. Tail short and concealed by long scarlet upper and under coverts. Scarlet throat and chest. Black breast and belly. Orange sometimes replaces scarlet." It is a member of the weaver family, known for weaving elaborate nests attached to shrubs or trees on the African savannah. Earlier in the day we had discovered eight Village Weavers, another African species, along with their active nests, along the northwest coast. That record apparently was the first for Martinique, an indication, perhaps, of the close relationship between the West Indies and the African continent.

LA CARAVELLE PENINSULA

Rob and I also explored Martinique's La Caravelle Peninsula, a finger of land that juts northeast into the Atlantic for about 6 miles. The habitat of La Caravelle Peninsula is very different from the lush montane forests to the north. Dry woodlands dominate the terrain except for the stands of mangroves that edge the southern lagoons. The eastern half of La Caravelle Peninsula is a nature preserve, one of the scattered pieces of Martinique's nature park. A trail runs from a small roadside parking area southward to Ferret Point for a distance of about a mile.

Songs of Caribbean Elaenias and Yellow Warblers were abundant that summer morning. Pearly-eyed Thrashers added their voices to the chorus. A Lesser Antillean Flycatcher whistled "e-oo-ee" from the thicket of green. A pair of Scaly-naped Pigeons flew across the sky, their reddish necks gleaming in the morning light. A Zenaida Dove flew ahead of us; the broad, white tips of its outer tail-feathers were obvious.

We left the trail near the bottom of the hill and worked our way through the dense shrubbery to the bottom of a broad gut with a reasonably bare understory and a rather dense canopy. This habitat was close to the coast and was more of a littoral woodland than the vegetation along the ridge-top. This is where we expected to find one of Martinique's rarest birds, the White-breasted Thrasher.

Movement in the shrubbery just ahead of us riveted our attention; we froze in place, binoculars at the ready. Nothing! I spished ever so quietly. Again. All of a sudden a pair of Streaked Saltators appeared out of the foliage. We gazed at these birds with full appreciation because they were trip-birds for us both, but we were also disappointed because they were not what we had expected. Streaked Saltators are similar in size to the

White-breasted Thrasher, about robin-size, but they are very different birds. Saltators are arboreal finches with heavy beaks. In fact, the local name for this species is *gros-bec*. They were a dull greenish color with a white eye-line and white throat bordered with black. Streaked Saltators occur from northern South America northward into the Lesser Antilles as far as Guadeloupe. Their song is a loud "tchew-tchew-tshew, tcheeer," according to Robert Ridgely and Guy Tudor.

We decided to remain where we were for a time rather than search elsewhere; this habitat was very different from any other we had seen on Martinique. Caribbean Elaenias were all around us; their "k-up" calls sounded again and again. We also heard a clear "ture-too-too" song, a musical caroling. In spite of searching the surrounding areas for this bird we could not find the singer but assumed at the time that it was an oriole. Only later did we observe a Bare-eyed Robin singing this same song. This is another northeastern South American species that occurs in the West Indies only on Martinique.

While trying to locate the above songster, slowly winding through the woodland, I noticed two brown blobs underneath two huge umbrellalike leaves, side by side. On closer inspection the two brown blobs turned out to be bats, hanging upside down with their hind feet attached to ribs of the leaves; their wings were folded and they apparently were asleep. These bats looked exactly like the common myotis bats I was familiar with in the southwestern United States. Later, after reading a paper on the bats of the Lesser Antilles by J. Knox Jones (1989), I decided I had probably found *Myotis martiniquensis*, or Schwartz's myotis bat, the island's only endemic mammal. Jones lists twenty-four bat species for the Lesser Antilles, ten of which occur on Martinique.

Rob and I remained in place within the littoral woodland habitat, watching each shadow. We both felt that we had glimpsed birds there that we had not yet identified. Then, almost directly above our heads on an open branch, we spotted a **White-breasted Thrasher.** A second one appeared, and for more than a minute we were staring at one or the other of these elusive birds. Then they both were gone. It was as if they had given us a brief show, or maybe they had come to look us over, and then, satisfied, had departed. As much as we continued to search we could not locate the birds again. But our brief observation was excellent. My notes, which I wrote immediately afterward, read: "bright white breast, dark back with hint of mask, eye reddish, bill long and hooked." Bond adds that the species also "twitches its wings; tail rarely cocked," which we did not observe. I have read nothing else about this bird that suggests it has a hooked bill.

White-breasted Thrasher

To the scientific world, the White-breasted Thrasher is known as *Ramphocinclus brachyurus* and considered threatened with extinction. Mountfort wrote that the species "has suffered severely on Martinique from the popular passion for hunting small birds. Neither the bird nor its habitat is protected and it is now rare and restricted to a single peninsula on the northeast coast of the island, where mongooses, rats and hunters still prey on it."

MORE WANTON KILLING

A few days later, Betty and I experienced another dramatic example of wanton killing of birds. Our day began with a drive to the airport so that Rob could catch his return flight home to the Virgin Islands. Then we drove east to the coast and south on Highway N6 to the southernmost peninsula and Savane des Pétrification. This portion of Martinique contains low arid hills, mangrove forests, salt flats, and a large salt pond, known as Etang des Salines.

The southern portion of the peninsula reminded me of numerous other tropical wetlands. However, the government had installed a number of camping and picnic sites among the scattered sea grapes and other trees near the point. By midmorning the area was crowded with a hundred or more campers, picnickers, swimmers, sunbathers, and the like. But immediately adjacent to this area, all within a radius of a quarter-mile, were hunters. Several individuals were walking along the shore of the salt pond, gun at the ready, watching for any shorebird or waterfowl that dared come within shooting distance.

Betty and I spent almost three hours in the area and located only three shorebirds, two Semipalmated Sandpipers and a lone Whimbrel. The Whimbrel was dragging an injured leg that was barely hanging in place. All the time we were there we could hear shots in the distance. The recreationists seemed to be oblivious to the shooting that was going on so close by.

The pond and the arid habitats should have been full of bird life. It was late summer, when West Indian salt ponds normally teem with shorebirds. Instead, there were almost no birds to be found. A Caribbean Elaenia, a lone Tropical Mockingbird, a few Carib Grackles, four passing Barn Swallows, and a Gray Kingbird were all I recorded.

A few days later, on returning home to St. Croix, I wrote a letter to the island administrator and another to the Fort-de-France newspaper. Both letters were transcribed into French. Neither organization had the courtesy to respond. I end this chapter with a copy of my letter to the island administrator:

Dear Sir:

My wife and I have just returned from an eight-day visit to the island of Martinique, and we wish to say that we enjoyed a wonderful stay. We drove most of the island's principal roads and visited the mountain forests and the beaches. Of sixteen West Indian islands we have so far visited, we found Martinique to be the most beautiful, cleanest, and apparently best managed. You are to be commended!

However, we found one issue that disturbed us both a great deal! We were amazed that Martinique still allows the indiscriminate hunting that we found under way at numerous areas along the shoreline and in the mountains. We are not against hunting of wildlife that takes the appropriate amount of an area's wildlife production. But the excessive shooting of birds, such as pigeons, waterfowl, and shorebirds, that only pass through Martinique in migration should no longer be condoned. Songbirds and many other species are seriously declining throughout the

Western Hemisphere. The shooting of those threatened species as they pass through Martinique will have serious consequences on the various species elsewhere. I suspect that Martinique hunters already have detected this general decline in their hunting success.

Please look into this most serious practice and take the necessary steps to let the world know that Martinique has also acquired a mature conservation policy.

I hope that on my next visit to your beautiful island I will not be threatened by shooters lining the roads and that wild birds will be part of Martinique's natural beauty.

Most sincerely,
Ro and Betty Wauer

CHAPTER SIXTEEN

St. Lucia ISLAND OF MYSTERY

St. Lucia! The name is a mystical and lovely one for a beautiful island. Many claim that St. Lucia is the most beautiful of all the West Indies. I wouldn't argue the point. Historians tell us that Christopher Columbus named the island on December 13, 1502, the feast day of St. Lucy, as he passed by the island on his fourth voyage. He never did come ashore. The island's rugged coastline discourages landing, although there are a few good harbors, and in the sixteenth century the fierce Carib Indian residents were also significant deterrents.

For me, St. Lucia is very special. Its appeal is partly due to the rugged physical beauty of the island. Its rocky and jagged appearance gives it a rather forbidding character. The steep slopes and deep canyons, including the renowned Pitons that rise dramatically out of the Caribbean Sea on the island's west side, help to shape that mystique. Inland, lush forests clothe most of the island, and the resultant greenery gives it a luxuriant appearance. Actually, the effects of these natural characteristics make much of St. Lucia's uplands largely inaccessible to all but the most persistent visitors, thus protecting many of its outstanding resources. The results are more endemic birds than occur anywhere else in the Windward Islands.

The best example is St. Lucia's **Semper's Warbler.** It is undoubtedly the island's best-kept secret and one of the rarest species in all the West Indies. This endemic species is so difficult to find that it has not been positively recorded for several years. There have been only five records during the last forty years. It may, in fact, be extinct, although that is unlikely; there is still plenty of good habitat remaining that has not been unduly disturbed by human encroachment. But since the bird's call, song, and nest are unknown, all of the searching undertaken to find it in recent years has failed. Yet a local forestry officer claims to have seen a warbler fitting the description, one he had never seen before, as recently as 1989.

Semper's Warbler (*Leucopeza semperi*) is a reasonably large warbler with dark gray upperparts and whitish underparts, according to James Bond's *The Birds of the West Indies*. Bond's illustration depicts a short-tailed, heavy-billed bird that is remarkably undistinguished. He places it between St. Vincent's Whistling Warbler and North America's Ovenbird. The 1983 AOU *Check-list of North American Birds* places it between Cuba's Oriente Warbler and North America's Hooded Warbler. It is clear that ornithologists have little understanding of this species. It is a true mystery bird.

Besides Semper's Warbler, St. Lucia possesses three other endemic birds: St. Lucia Parrot, St. Lucia Oriole, and St. Lucia Black Finch; and four endemic subspecies: St. Lucia Nightjar, House Wren, White-breasted Thrasher, and Forest Thrush. An additional twenty-one of St. Lucia's bird species are considered West Indian endemics.

Fred Sladen and I spent three days on St. Lucia in late May 1989 searching out the endemic birds and enjoying the island's raw beauty. Our time was spent mostly in three areas: Edmond Forest, above Soufrière; Piton Flore, within the Castries Waterworks Forest Preserve; and Louvet Estate and Grande Anse, along the east coast. We recorded a total of sixty-two species of birds.

Edmond Forest lies within the greater Central Forest Reserve (approximately 2,900 acres), which includes most of the island's southern highlands. Access to the forest is easy; a parking area at the forest boundary is only 8 miles from the center of Soufrière. Although the entrance road is extremely rough, we found that the trail, which begins at the parking area and runs through the forest all the way across the mountains, is well maintained. It provided us with a wonderful introduction to St. Lucia's rain forest environment and its bird life. It was there, during the morning of May 29, that we found three of St. Lucia's endemic birds.

The trail enters the Edmond Forest rather abruptly, going from an open forest-edge habitat to a closed canopy one. Almost immediately inside we detected the "pree-e-e" song of a **Lesser Antillean Pewee.** Although it took us a few more minutes to locate this little flycatcher amid the undergrowth after its emphatic calls had announced its presence, we found this species reasonably common throughout our stay in the forest.

I had seen this Caribbean endemic on a few earlier occasions, at Guánica in Puerto Rico and on Guadeloupe and Dominica, but we found that the St. Lucia birds looked very different. They possessed a surprisingly bright cinnamon-colored belly and a yellow lower mandible. All of the Lesser Antillean Pewees I found on the other islands are extremely dull in comparison. I could not, however, detect any variation in their songs. Should St. Lucia's Lesser Antillean Pewee be given separate status?

A little farther into the forest we detected the fast, bubbling notes of a House Wren. This little bird was more difficult to find, requiring us to coax it out of its dense green world with quiet spishing sounds. It eventually came to within 6 or 7 feet of us, although it remained cautious as it worked its way closer amid the dense shrubbery. American House Wrens have been divided into a number of subspecies, and this one (considered endangered) occurs nowhere else but on St. Lucia. Nearby Guadeloupe's endemic form has not been recorded in recent years and may be extinct; see Chapter 13 for additional information.

Some ornithologists claim that the St. Lucia House Wren population is declining. Timothy Johnson's conservation profile on St. Lucia in *Biodiversity and Conservation in the Caribbean* reported that this bird was "formerly believed to be restricted to the Grand Anse valley in the north-east, but recently found elsewhere at Caille Des, Olouvet, Marquis, and Petite Anse, although no longer present at Chastenet, Piton Flore or Edmond Forest where it was once widespread." We recorded what seemed to be three territorial individuals during that first morning in the Edmond Forest.

It was while we were observing the House Wren that I was attracted to movement along the grassy edge of the trail, 12 to 15 feet ahead. Shifting my attention to the new site, I discovered the first of several **St. Lucia Black Finches** that we were to find. It probably had initially been attracted by our spishing sounds, and we found it busy feeding on grass seeds, which it gleaned by jumping onto each grass stem and pulling it to the ground, where it fed on the seed heads. It reminded me at first of the abundant Black-faced Grassquit but was almost twice that size and possessed a much heavier bill. It had an overall dark appearance in the shadows, but when it worked its way into the sunshine its shiny black back, especially around the head, contrasted with its buffy underparts and pink legs and feet. A truly lovely bird! It also had a strange habit, especially for finches, of flipping its tail, almost flycatcherlike. On one occasion we heard it sing a song not unlike that of a Bananaquit; Bond described it as a "wheezy 'tic-zweee-swizewiz-you.'"

As we progressed down the trail, we detected the melodic whistle-notes of an oriole; I later wrote in my field notes that its song reminded me of a drawn-out "hiccup-a hiccup; Orchard Oriole–like." We found a pair of the endemic **St. Lucia Orioles** feeding on the fruit of a fig tree some distance off the trail and were able to admire these birds for several minutes. At first glance they seemed very like the Black-cowled Oriole of the Greater Antilles, Central America, and Mexico; they possessed a similar color pattern. But that St. Lucia bird was a black and orange male; females are black and yellow. We found this lovely bird several other times in a variety of habitats during our visit.

About a mile into the forest the canopy opened up on the right so that we had a good view of the adjacent slopes. Although we had heard the beautiful songs of distant **Rufous-throated Solitaires** almost as soon as we had entered the forest, this new vantage point provided us with a marvelous view of a pair of birds perched on open snags a couple of hundred feet away. We watched them sing their wonderful songs, apparently oblivious of our admiring stares. This bird possesses one of the most exquisite songs in the entire bird world, although it lacks the contrasting plumage of many other West Indian specialties. David Lack, in *Island Biology Illustrated by the Land Birds of Jamaica*, points out, however, that it is "the only solitaire with any rufous colouring." See Chapter 1 for further details about its plumage.

Several Scaly-naped Pigeons flew overhead along the open slopes, and three Lesser Antillean Swifts streaked by not far above the treetops. We also saw a pair of Black Swifts for a few seconds as they approached from down the valley, wheeled overhead, and then disappeared back down the valley from where they had come. A Broad-winged Hawk made a tight circle over the far ridge. Then suddenly we were watching three parrots flying across the open sky. Their rapid wing-beats, green bodies, and conspicuous red wing-patches, from only about 200 feet away, identified them as yet another of St. Lucia's endemic birds, the **St. Lucia Parrot.**

This species is one of the West Indian birds that have declined dramatically in recent decades. Although once widespread throughout all of St. Lucia's 235 square miles, it is now restricted to approximately 49 square miles in the southern mountains. But unlike some of the other West Indian parrots, the population of this species—*Amazona versicolor*—has begun to recover. It has increased from a low population of about 100 birds in 1976 to as many as 250 individuals in 1986.

The reasons for the bird's recovery are very clear and are principally due to a dramatic attitude change on St. Lucia by government officials and the public alike. Laws were changed to protect the valuable watersheds and the parrots. A 1977 law made it illegal for anyone to shoot parrots or destroy their essential habitat. According to Rosemary Low, in a 1987 article in *Bird Talk*, this law carries a "maximum fine of $5,000 and a reward of up to $5,000 to anyone reporting a shooting. A law prohibiting the destruction of trees in the forest reserve carries a $2,000 fine for the first offense, a $3,000 fine for the second offense, and a jail term of one year for a third offense." Most important was a companion public education program that was started in 1979 under the direction of Paul Butler, who was working for the St. Lucia government. Butler, with equal support of the local Forestry Department, began several new initiatives. Low described this innovative program as follows:

> In 1979, the St. Lucia parrot was declared the national bird, an event accompanied by a week of radio and television programs promoting the preservation of the bird. A newspaper supplement was printed, and 300 children were taken on a walk through the rain forest. Since then, the parrot has been prominently featured on T-shirts, stamps and posters; 20,000 school children have been reached through information packets delivered to classes; and thousands more have been taken through the bird's habitat.

This St. Lucia Parrot preservation program has since been used as a model on several other islands to save threatened parrots. It is abundantly clear that conservation programs must include public education if they are to succeed. See Chapters 15 and 17 for descriptions of other "save the parrot" campaigns.

All in all, our day in St. Lucia's Edmond Forest produced twenty-five bird species. Besides those already mentioned, we also found the Ruddy Quail-Dove, Purple-throated Carib, Antillean Crested Hummingbird, Caribbean Elaenia, Lesser Antillean Flycatcher, Gray Kingbird, Scaly-breasted and Pearly-eyed Thrashers, Gray Trembler, Bananaquit, Black-whiskered Vireo, Adelaide's Warbler, Antillean Euphonia, and Lesser Antillean Bullfinch.

Our visit to St. Lucia had begun the night before with our arrival at Vigie Airport in the capital city of Castries and a two-hour after-dark drive on winding roads to Soufrière. It was almost midnight before we had acquired a room in the town center at the Home Hotel. Although the accommodations were inexpensive, the room was dirty and filled with mosquitoes, and the bathroom we shared with a dozen or so other guests was even worse. We decided to find other accommodations in the morning. As we explored the town and surroundings we discovered the Hummingbird Motel on the beach, where we had an excellent breakfast before relocating ourselves. We felt much more at home there for $45 each, a price which included one meal, than we had at the Home Hotel for one-third that cost.

DAY TWO

Our second morning was spent back within the Edmond Forest. Although we didn't find any additional bird species that second morning, we did get some wonderful observations of several unique species. Perhaps because we got an earlier start the second morning, we found many more parrots the second day and were actually able to watch five individuals feeding in trees on a nearby ridge. A St. Lucia Oriole put on a wonderful show for us in the early morning light, as well; its brown, orange, and black colors provided us with a contrasting perspective amid the green and gray foliage.

We also saw and heard several **Gray Tremblers** as we wandered along the path. Their songs seemed to me to be an odd mixture "between an oriole and thrush," I wrote in my field book. I had never before seen tremblers sing from high snags. All my other sightings of the two species had been limited to birds in the shadowy canopy. But on that morning on St. Lucia several were singing from the very top of high snags.

We left Soufrière at noon and drove back to Castries, where we acquired a room at the New Vigie Beach Hotel, adjacent to the airport. We soon found our way to Piton Flore, one of the high points at midisland. It is listed

Gray Trembler

at 1,871 feet elevation on the "Saint Lucia Tourist Map." Piton Flore was only 11 road miles distance from the hotel. The steep slopes contained some original forest habitat, although a small radio station building and tower had been built at the very summit; a trail runs from the end of the road to the station. Rob Norton, a friend from the Virgin Islands, had earlier suggested that we search this area for Semper's Warbler because of the relatively intact forest that still persists there. We spent almost three hours birding the very lush forest on the northwestern slope, but to no avail. In fact, we did not find any birds that we had not already recorded. Fred did discover a Ruddy Quail-

Dove nest in a notch of a small tree at eye level. I also was amazed at the presence of **Adelaide's Warblers** within the very moist undergrowth. The same species prefers arid landscapes on the western end of Puerto Rico and on Barbuda. I suspect that a study of this bird's habitat preferences throughout its range would make a valuable and fascinating thesis.

The trail to the summit of Piton Flore is only about 1 mile in length. It was well worth the time and effort. The views from the top, in spite of the presence of a tin shack and tower, were spectacular. To the south, the higher mountains of the nature reserve seemed close enough to touch. Mount Gimie, the island's highest point at 3,117 feet elevation, dominated the scene. Except for a few houses and other structures in the foreground, the mountains appeared very wild and remote. I gazed at the surrounding forest and imagined us finding the elusive Semper's Warbler there. Twenty percent of the island is in forest, and the majority of that is in the Edmond Forest Reserve. To the west, we could see the roadway between Castries and Soufrière now and then, winding like a serpent through the green valleys and over the slopes.

Many of the patches of greenery visible from the summit of Piton Flore, especially those on the lower and more gradual slopes, were composed of banana plantations, not native forest. Locally called "green gold," the banana crop makes up 80 percent of St. Lucia's annual economy, according to the June 1989 issue of *Tropical Traveler*, St. Lucia's complimentary vacation guide.

St. Lucia's nearest neighbor to the south, St. Vincent, only 26 miles beyond the island's southern tip, was blocked from view by Mount Gimie. Martinique, 21 miles north of St. Lucia, was only occasionally visible that day when the abundant clouds did not block the view.

The volcanic character of the summit provided good evidence of St. Lucia's geologic past. The southern half of the island is apparently younger than the northern half. Hot sulfurous streams and a large active fumarole near Soufrière attest to the active status of the region. The entire southern flank of the island is overlaid with an overflow of volcanic mud, ash, and boulders. This debris has produced extremely fertile soils where a large percentage of the island's agricultural activities take place. The older northern half of St. Lucia has been worn away, and only outlines of the old volcanoes still exist. The valleys there are much broader and flatter than the more recent ones to the south.

Marigot Bay was visible along the central coast. The narrative on the tourism map describes Marigot Bay as "one of the best known harbours—where the British hid their ships from the marauding French by disguising the masts as palm trees. It was here, too, that Hollywood filmed scenes for the movie 'Dr. Doolittle.'"

I had found St. Lucia to be a strange combination of English, French, and Spanish culture, and that perception was clarified when I learned that the island had changed hands fourteen times within a 150-year period between 1665 and 1814. St. Lucia was finally ceded to Great Britain and became a British crown colony under the Peace of Paris in 1814. On February 22, 1979, St. Lucia became an independent sovereign state within the British Commonwealth.

The north, especially the far end of the island, was not so green; it gave evidence of a much drier environment. Closer, the northeastern slopes of Piton Flore dip into a broad valley and then rise again into the La Sorcière uplands. All of that area seemed to be mature forest where a search for Semper's Warbler might prove fruitful.

THE EASTERN COAST

We didn't have to drive all the way back to Castries to get to the eastern side of the island, only back to Guesneau, from where we headed north and then east. We considered ourselves fortunate to have rented a jeep, as Paul Butler had advised. With few exceptions, our routes were seldom paved and often very rough and rocky.

By midafternoon we had found our way to the Louvet area, and we lunched along a ridge in the shade of a tree from where we could look down into a broad watershed known as Ravine la Chaloupe. It was there, along the ridge, that a pair of Gray Tremblers approached surprisingly close to us. One of them actually loafed on the open branches of our shade tree, so I was able to obtain several photographs. I couldn't help but notice the lighter overall color of these birds compared with those found on the other Windward Islands.

Although Bond and all the earlier Caribbean ornithologists list only one species of trembler, it was properly split into two separate species by the AOU in their 38th supplement (1991): the Gray Trembler (*Cinclocerthia gutturalis*) is resident only on St. Lucia and Martinique, and the Brown Trembler (*Cinclocerthia ruficauda*) resides "in the Lesser Antilles from Saba, St. Eustatius (where possibly extirpated), and St. Kitts south to Dominica; and on St. Vincent."

Our intention was to hike down into the Ravine la Chaloupe, which, according to what we had been told, was one of the last strongholds of the **White-breasted Thrasher** on St. Lucia. Although we started our hike into the canyon, we turned around in about a mile; Butler had given me directions on how to find the route, but we couldn't locate the trail even after walking back and forth along the upper roadway, searching for the trailhead. Since the afternoon was extremely hot and it was getting too late to properly explore the lower drainage, we decided to forgo the hike into the ravine and go on to our next stop, Grand Anse Beach. We later found that we both had acquired a good load of chiggers from beating our way through the grasses while trying to find the trailhead.

This same area formed the center of a rather extensive survey for White-breasted Thrashers by the St. Lucia Forest Department, April 22 through June 12, 1992. According to Forest Officer Lyndon John's report to the Society of Caribbean Ornithology, a "total of 81 birds were noted from this census." He added that the "species is restricted largely to the riverine vegetation and conservation measures are urgently needed to protect the remaining habitat."

Butler had also warned me about the potential danger of the poisonous fer-de-lance snake in the Ravine la Chaloupe. The area looked too hot and dry to possess a high population of fer-de-lance to me, but then I didn't expect to come away with chiggers either. The fer-de-lance (*Bothrus caribbaeus*) is one of five endemic reptiles known on St. Lucia and the only one that is poisonous. Another endemic snake, a small racer (*Liophis ornatus*), is also present. The other endemic reptiles are innocuous lizards: the anole or "house lizard" (*Anolis lucai*), a whiptail (*Cnemidophorus vanzoi*), and a gecko (*Sphaerodactylus microlepis*). See Chapter 12 for additional details about the fer-de-lance in the West Indies.

The much larger lizard on St. Lucia is the common iguana (*Iguana iguana*), which may be 4 feet in length. Its large head and mouth and scaly crest, which runs the entire length of its body, can make it look ferocious. But it is a vegetarian and not at all dangerous to humans, although it will bite when teased. Its tail is usually broadly banded with black and gray, and its general overall color ranges from green to brown to gray, depending on its background. It has the ability to change its color to match its surroundings.

Iguanas are tree dwellers, although they frequent the roofs of buildings and occasionally can be found along the roadsides, as well. Most zoologists believe that the species was introduced to the Windward Islands by the earliest settlers. Iguanas were eaten in their native lands of northern South America, from where the first St. Lucians originated. Others believe that iguanas were already present when the pre-Columbian peoples came to St. Lucia. The Carib Indians named the island Hewanorra, their name for the iguana; it apparently was already common when they arrived. It is likely that the earlier Arawaks had already introduced these large lizards as a convenient food supply.

Grande Anse is St. Lucia's longest beach. We were able to drive right up to the dunes, although the last 100 feet or so were barred by heavy-duty dump trucks. These vehicles were hauling sand from the beach to some inland destination, and their digging activities had created huge craters in the beach. Five truckloads left the site during the four hours we were present. Extensive sand mining has damaged reefs and beaches elsewhere in the Caribbean, and at Grande Anse sand mining also destroys nests of the leatherback turtle. These activities should not be condoned. Profits from such an industry will only benefit one or a few individuals, while the greater number of residents and visitors will eventually suffer the consequences. Sand mining was the only serious ongoing threat that we detected during our stay on the island.

South along the beach we found a pond that extended inland for several hundred feet where we found a lone Little Blue Heron and eight Common Moorhens. Looking out to sea, we could see a few terns fishing at the edge of the deeper water. We identified those pelagics as four Roseate and two Bridled Terns. A lone Brown Booby cruised north to south over the same general area.

Our principal reason for visiting the Grande Anse Beach area late in the day was to find the St. Lucia Nightjar, which, according to Butler, is reasonably common there. We birded along the beach and back into the scrubby riparian woodland as we waited for dusk, recording only expected species: several Zenaida Doves, Caribbean Elaenias, Scaly-breasted Thrashers, Adelaide's Warblers, Bananaquits, Brown-headed Cowbirds, and Black-faced Grassquits. There also were a few Mangrove Cuckoos, Lesser Antillean Pewees (with their very cinnamon bellies), and Yellow Warblers.

An American Kestrel flew overhead. I recorded three Caribbean Martins. Then out of nowhere came a **Bridled Quail-Dove,** hurtling directly at us and across the road and then disappearing into the hillside vegetation. We both had seen it extremely well and, being very familiar with the species on St. John and St. Croix (see Chapters 6 and 7), we were certain of its identity. But neither of us had seen that species in open flight before; it usually is found on the ground or in trees. It rarely flies much farther than the distance between the upper branches of trees. I half expected to see some predator right behind it, but none appeared.

As the sun crossed below the horizon, there was a considerable increase in bird song. Zenaida Doves became more vociferous. Caribbean Elaenia and Adelaide's Warbler songs increased. But the big surprise was the steady and loud chorus of Bare-eyed Robins. We had only seen a few of these birds near Soufrière, but suddenly the entire floodplain vibrated with their very distinct and loud songs. Bond described their song as "a clear 'ture-too-too,' repeated indefinitely and much like that of the American Robin." This is one of those South American species that somehow found their way into the Windward Islands to as far north as Martinique. I will never forget their evening chorus at Grande Anse.

Yellow-crowned Night-Herons, four of them, left their roosting sites and flew one by one out into the coming dusk. We stood on the roadway, positioned just above the floodplain in the drier woodland, waiting for our first nightjar songs. We were not disappointed. Suddenly it was nightjar time! Just as it was almost too dark to see well, the **St. Lucia Nightjar** calls began, first one, from reasonably close by, and then another farther back along the hillside. The calls were more like that of a Chuck-will's-widow than any other nightjar I had heard. Bond points out that the calls accent "the fourth syllable 'Jacques-pas-papa-ou,' repeated many times."

Within half an hour I counted what I believed to be eleven separate birds. We observed only two of these. The first one, probably the first one that called, suddenly appeared in the open branches of a small tree right along-side the road. We both got brief views through our binoculars, enough to see its shape and buffy appearance, and then it was gone. Another flew across the roadway and was visible for only a second or two. But thereafter, we were forced to be satisfied with only their songs. Within about forty-five minutes all the calling stopped, and we stood there in the dark waiting in silence.

We drove back to the hotel, watching all the way for nightjars on the roadway, but we did not see any. But that one experience at Grande Anse was enough. We had found another of the West Indian specialties. According to the 1983 AOU check-list, the St. Lucia Nightjar has a complicated distribution. It is found nowhere else in the West Indies, but it has been recorded in northern Venezuela from August to May. Those sightings may constitute two distinct populations, or the Venezuelan birds may simply be St. Lucia Nightjar transients.

St. Lucia, more than most of the West Indies, possesses numerous mysteries that we humans do not yet understand. The distribution of the St. Lucia Nightjar and the status of Semper's Warbler are but two of these. As more birders explore St. Lucia, some will undoubtedly be resolved, but new ones are likely to arise.

CHAPTER SEVENTEEN

St. Vincent POOR BUT WEALTHY

Whistling Warbler

We left our rental car at the end of the roadway at a little parking area at the start of the Vermont Forest Nature Trail. We followed the well-maintained trail across an open drainage and up a rather steep slope into the heart of the rain forest. Beyond this point the trail followed a narrow ridge for a quarter of a mile. It then crossed the head of a little canyon before it circled a forested area with rough-cut benches placed at viewing areas into the higher forest.

Our movement along the trail was purposefully slow and careful so that we would not miss any of the wildlife present within the forest. It had rained the previous afternoon and overnight, and water was still dripping from millions of leaves. The most obvious sound around us that early June morning was the almost monotonous songs, a double note repeated many times, of the Cocoa Thrush. The plaintive calls of this robin-size bird echoed throughout the forest. I spotted two individuals standing in the center of the trail in a typical thrushlike stance, but both immediately flew into the adjacent vegetation. One bird was finally located only a dozen feet away on a low branch inside the forest. It was a deep brown color, with a slightly orangish breast and whitish throat and undertail coverts. It was well camouflaged within the deep shadows.

The Cocoa Thrush is a South American species that ranges into the Lesser Antilles only as far north as St. Vincent. Some ornithologists lump it with the Hauxwell's Thrush of South America, but others think that the Cocoa Thrush of St. Vincent and Grenada is different even from the Cocoa Thrush of South America and should be a separate species. Whatever the final disposition of this bird might be, it was the dominant contributor to the Vermont Forest bird chorus that morning.

The loud whistle-songs of Black-whiskered Vireos were also common-place. The soulful notes of Ruddy Quail-Doves, like someone blowing across the mouth of a bottle, gradually fading in strength, were evident on several occasions. Then a weak "weet-weet-weet-witwitwitwit" song attracted our attention into the forest just ahead. The bird called again. We slowly moved closer to where we could see movement in the midlevel branches of a tall forest tree. Then, suddenly, a **Lesser Antillean Tanager** appeared in the open with a tiny purple berry held in its bill. Our binoculars immediately captured this lovely bird.

The Lesser Antillean Tanager is one of St. Vincent's most gorgeous birds. Although it is only 6 inches in length, its metallic golden back, distinctly greenish-blue wings and tail, and deep chestnut crown give it an imperial countenance. It is locally called prince bird, and older bird books refer to it as Hooded Tanager.

As we watched it foraging 30 feet away, a second bird, undoubtedly a female because of its duller appearance, suddenly appeared out of the forest. For several minutes we had both birds in sight, but then just as suddenly they took wing and disappeared into the tangle of vegetation beyond.

Fred Sladen and I had visited these same woods the previous day. We had found the Cocoa Thrush and Lesser Antillean Tanager in the forest, the St. Vincent Parrot, Purple-throated Carib, Caribbean and Yellow-bellied Elaenias, Grenada Flycatcher, Antillean Euphonia, and Lesser Antillean Bullfinch in the clearing, and Black and Lesser Antillean Swifts flying overhead. But we had missed the Whistling Warbler, which along with the

St. Vincent Parrot is one of St. Vincent's two endemic birds. We had decided to return to the Vermont Forest to spend whatever time was necessary to find the elusive Whistling Warbler. Paul Butler had earlier told me that these woods were our best hope for finding this endemic species.

We also had an excellent look at St. Vincent's version of the Common Black-Hawk. We found it perched on a rock in the center of the little stream, below the towering rain forest vegetation. Crouched in the streambed, it appeared wholly sooty-black, but as soon as it took flight its boldly marked, black-and-white banded tail was immediately apparent. We watched it for only a minute before it disappeared up the drainage.

The local name of this hawk is crab hawk, due to the fact that it feeds on yellow crabs that occur within the mountain streams. Herbert Friedmann, in his 1950 Smithsonian Institution monograph, *The Birds of North and Middle America, Part XI,* called it Antillean Crab Hawk. But the 1983 AOU check-list lumps it with the Common Black-Hawk of the southwestern United States, Mexico, Central and South America, and Cuba. I couldn't detect anything different about the birds we saw on St. Vincent. But the Cuban Black-Hawk is quite different; see Chapter 2 for further details.

We spent more than two hours along the upper ridge near the benches, listening and searching for the Whistling Warbler without success. We then decided to try the lower ridge again, a location where the day before we had detected warblerlike chips but had not been able to find the originator. The ridge slopes off steeply on both sides of the trail into deep green ravines. The vegetation was reminiscent of elfin woodland habitat with much moss and epiphytes and an abundance of lianas and vines. We searched the slopes for any movement.

A Scaly-breasted Thrasher squawked above us. We detected a circling pair of Broad-winged Hawks over the canopy. A pair of Scaly-naped Pigeons exploded from the dense vegetation almost at eye level in the ravine; perhaps a nesting pair. We discovered a lone **Gray Trembler** among the dense vines on the lower slope. It undoubtedly had found a source of food, and I watched it probe among the vegetation with its long, stout bill. Then suddenly, perhaps because it discovered itself to be under observation, it began to shake all over. Its wings drooped and its tail was held upright. Two unique species of tremblers occur only in the Lesser Antilles, from Saba south to St. Vincent; see Chapter 16 for details of their distribution. Tremblers command a genus name all their own, *Cinclocerthia. Cinclo* comes from the Greek word *kinkles,* meaning to bob up and down. *Certhia,* according to Edward Gruson, "is a Latinized form of the Greek *kerthios,* a name given by Aristotle to a tree-creeping bird."

Suddenly I detected movement near the ground about 40 feet down the slope. I could just barely make out a little black-and-white bird. "Fred, here, I think it's a warbler!" He had seen it, too, and we trained our binoculars on the spot, anxiously waiting for that shadowy creature to come out into the open. I spished ever so slightly, but there was no response. Then, less than 15 feet away, on an open moss-draped limb, a **Whistling Warbler** appeared. And what a bird it was! It was well worth the effort it had taken to find this incredible creature. For the next four to five minutes we had one to four birds in sight continuously.

The Whistling Warbler was very different from what I had expected from the little information available. True, it is a blackish bird with a white eye-ring and a broad black band across its whitish chest, but it also is an extremely charismatic creature that looks very different from its two closest relations. The AOU had placed it between Puerto Rico's Elfin Woods Warbler and the Black-and-white Warbler of North America. These two birds are very similar, but the Whistling Warbler—scientifically known as *Catharopeza bishopi*—is very different. We intently watched these birds, two adults and at least two immatures, until they moved away from view. I immediately jotted down notes on what I had just experienced: "Like Ovenbird; cocked tail; eye-ring white, large and distinct; breast band very broad; long legs. Long intervals between songs. Young are brown, faint eye-ring and buffy/rufous crissum." In a follow-up report I added: "I suspect it is more closely related to the genera *Vermivora*, *Seiurus*, or *Basileuterus*." Its song was described by James Bond, in *The Birds of the West Indies*, as "a series of short, rich notes, at first soft and low, then rising rapidly with crescendo effect, terminating with two or three emphatic notes." Father Raymond Devas, in his little book, *Birds of Grenada, St. Vincent and the Grenadines*, described the song simply as, "it warbles wonderfully."

St. Vincent's Vermont Forest contains what undoubtedly is the island's best remaining forest preserve. Allen Putney, in his 1980 *Survey of Conservation Priorities in the Lesser Antilles*, reported that only 9,750 acres of rain forest, 3,000 acres of moist forest, and 8,000 acres of cloud forest remain on the entire island.

Anyone wishing to see the unique **St. Vincent Parrot** in the wild should go to the Vermont Forest. From the parking area, one can at least hear some of these loud, obnoxious-sounding parrots. We found a total of fifteen individuals with very little effort. They were feeding in the tall trees at the edge of the clearings, and with binoculars we were able to watch them for as long as we wished. It was almost anticlimactic to find this endangered species with such little effort.

The status of St. Vincent's endangered parrot has improved considerably in recent years. This recovery is largely due to an energetic environmental education program undertaken by the Forestry Division with initial assistance from Paul Butler and financial support from RARE Center for Tropical Conservation and the St. Vincent Brewery. The brewery featured Vincie the St. Vincent Parrot on its logo and coined the slogan "One Love, One Bird, One Beer." Chris Wille, in a 1991 *American Birds* article on Butler and the parrot program, reported that the St. Vincent team "gave parrot programs to 18,000 schoolchildren, distributed 15,000 bumper stickers and 3,000 posters, placed four billboards, and sweetened the airwaves with 'Leave de National Bird in de Wild,' a jump-up calypso tune written by forest officer C. 'Fraggo' Wyllie."

The save-the-parrot program has been so successful on St. Vincent that the St. Vincent Parrot populations may be stabilizing. Wild populations increased from an estimated four hundred birds in 1985 to more than five hundred in 1990. Actual population numbers are difficult to assess because, as Joseph Forshaw pointed out in his book, *Parrots of the World,* the species prefers rain forest habitat in the moist valleys and does not frequent the shorter forests in the higher mountains. Undetected movement from one valley to another can result in unreliable estimates. Butler has since taken the popular save-the-parrot program format to St. Lucia, Dominica, and other West Indian islands. See Chapters 14 and 16 for additional details.

During the four days that Fred and I spent on St. Vincent, we found St. Vincent Parrots common within the Vermont Forest, a few birds in the Cumberland Valley area, and a number of caged birds within a captive breeding program at Kingstown's Botanical Gardens. Our best close-up looks at these marvelous birds were in their breeding cages. All these birds appeared to be in very good shape; their colors seemed as bright as those we found in the wild.

Of the world's approximately 340 parrot species, the St. Vincent's Parrot is probably the gaudiest. Bond described the species as a "large, beautifully coloured parrot. Head white, yellow and violet; breast mostly green; body plumage mostly golden brown, washed with green; wings variegated; tail green and violet-blue, broadly tipped with yellow."

THE BOTANICAL GARDENS

We spent several hours wandering through Kingstown's neat 20-acre Botanical Gardens, considered to be the oldest in the Western Hemisphere. Many native trees and shrubs are marked for easy identification.

One of these is a breadfruit tree that is said to be the direct descendant of one "brought from the South Seas by Captain Bligh of the *Bounty*." Another is one of the few surviving specimens of the Soufrière tree, St. Vincent's national flower. We also found a good variety of bird life on the grounds and surrounding area. Most interesting were the Short-tailed Swifts, strange-acting House Wrens, and black Bananaquits.

The Short-tailed Swift is a Chimney Swift look-alike but with a shorter tail that, through binoculars, shows bare feather-shafts at the tip of the tail and ashy-gray undertail coverts. The most interesting thing about this bird is its distribution. It is a South American bird that occurs regularly in the West Indies only on St. Vincent.

The St. Vincent's House Wrens were different from any House Wren I had ever seen. Those we found at the Botanical Gardens and elsewhere on St. Vincent looked more like small versions of the Carolina Wren in North America than the typical little House Wren. Even their call notes, as well as their behavior on the open branches of a large tropical tree, reminded me of Carolina Wrens. House Wrens are skulkers, not birds of the trees and open country. This group of birds needs much more study, and I predict sooner or later that the St. Vincent House Wren (locally called godbird) will become a separate species.

Then there were the Bananaquits, in both their normal yellow-and-black plumage as well as all coal-black. Although the melanistic birds still possess a spot of red on their lower mandible, they are otherwise fully black; they even lack the typical white patch on their primaries. Of an estimated seventy Bananaquits we saw at the Botanical Gardens, only two possessed yellow bellies. Devas wrote that these birds are locally called black see-sees, after their "zee-e-e-e-swees-te" songs. Devas also wrote that in 1954 "a male Black See-see mated with a female Yellow See-see. Three young birds were hatched, one of them black, two of them yellow."

OTHER ISLAND INTERESTS

On our second afternoon, after finding the Whistling Warbler, we drove north along the west coast, beyond the Buccament River Valley, the turnoff to the Vermont Forest, as far as Cumberland Bay. The western lowlands were considerably drier, and we added a few additional bird species to our growing list. Most important was the Eared Dove, another South American species that ranges north into the Lesser Antilles. Although it has been found on St. Lucia and Martinique, St. Vincent is the only one of the West Indies where it is reasonably common. This dove, earlier called

Violet-eared Dove, is somewhat smaller than the Zenaida Dove but with no white on its tail or wings. The male possesses a brown back, gray crown, and pinkish-cinnamon breast and face. Its name is derived from two small black stripes on each side of its head, like ears.

Kingstown is not only the country's capital city but it also contains a deep-water port and the adjacent E. T. Joshua Airport. We had arrived by air from St. Lucia, rented a car, and then driven into town to claim our reservations at the Heron Hotel. It provided comfortable accommodations and good food. The Heron Hotel is much nicer inside than it appears from the outside, and it became our base of operations throughout our stay.

The island's name comes from Christopher Columbus, who found the island on St. Vincent's Day, January 22, 1498. The Carib Indians controlled the island then and until the early 1700s. St. Vincent was a Carib strong-hold, and the first European settlers were required to make treaties with the Carib inhabitants. Carrol Fleming, in *Adventuring in the Caribbean*, summa-rized the island's subsequent history this way: "The British took the island from the French in 1762; the French recaptured it in 1779. A treaty restored it to Britain in 1783, and the British spent the rest of the century deporting the Caribs." St. Vincent and several of the Grenadines became a self-governing associated state of Great Britain in October 1979.

St. Vincent is entirely volcanic in origin, evident by the island's black-sand beaches and the high peaks that form the island's exceptionally steep backbone. The physical character of the island rivals Dominica as the most mountainous in the West Indies, but St. Vincent does not possess a cross-mountain roadway. The mountains reach their highest elevation at La Soufrière. A portion of the crater rim, resulting from an 1817 eruption, is 4,026 feet elevation and less than 2 miles from the sea. La Soufrière is only one of two active volcanoes in the West Indies. The other is Mount Pelée in Martinique; see Chapter 15. Both eruptions were explosive. The 1903 erup-tion of La Soufrière killed two thousand people and devastated the northern third of the island.

Sugar was once the economic mainstay of the island, but production de-clined here along with all the other sugar-producing islands. Arrowroot be-came an important economic crop soon afterward. Arrowroot was brought to the island by the Caribs and used for food and as a cure for wounds caused by poison arrows. When arrowroot starch, obtained from the rhi-zomes, became known as an easily digested food for invalids, St. Vincent had a monopoly on the world's market. Arrowroot demand also declined, as did the demand for cotton. Bananas remain the only stable market. Today, St. Vincent is considered one of the Caribbean's poorest countries.

Yet in spite of the tremendous changes in the island's economy, St. Vincent still has two bird, three reptile, and twelve plant species that are not found anywhere else in the entire world. These resources, along with the island's rugged character and raw beauty, are valuable ingredients on which to build a new industry. Ecotourism can become an important industry as long as the island's valuable natural and cultural resources are protected. If the people of St. Vincent put the same energy into protecting all of their resources and promoting ecotourism as they have in saving Vincie the St. Vincent Parrot, their economy will recover. The wealth of the island is all around them.

CHAPTER EIGHTEEN

Grenada THE ISLE OF SPICE

Grenada Dove

Until the island's 1983 "rescue" by U.S. and Caribbean troops, Grenada was best known only as the world's principal supplier of nutmeg. Its nutmeg spice industry earns more than 4.5 million U.S. dollars annually. Introduced from the East Indies in 1843, the evergreen nutmeg tree can grow to 70 feet. It possesses long, pointed leaves with well-marked veins, and its pale yellow flowers droop in clusters. The fresh fruit look like golden-yellow pears hanging among shiny, gray-green leaves. When the fruit ripens, it hardens and then splits open at the top, revealing a scarlet to yellow membrane that partly covers the kernels. These kernels are then grated or ground for nutmeg and the waxy membrane is used for mace, a slightly different spice. A mature nutmeg tree can produce 1,500 to 2,000 nuts annually. Nutmeg has so dominated Grenada that the national flag, a colorful red, green, and gold banner, depicts a nutmeg fruit.

Grenada and the southern Grenadines became independent in 1947, after 184 years of British domination. France settled the island in the 1600s, and Columbus named it Concepción in 1498. However, early Spanish sailors referred to the island as Granada, because of a province with similar green hills in Spain.

Grenada received little world attention until October 25, 1983, with the so-called invasion of Grenada. Grenadians refer to the arrival of 1,900 U.S. soldiers and a smaller number of Caribbean troops as a "rescue mission." Charles Cobb, Jr., in a 1984 *National Geographic* article, explained that on Bloody Wednesday (October 19), Prime Minister Maurice Bishop and about forty friends and relatives were shot down. Deputy Prime Minister Bernard Coard took power and immediately "imposed a 24-hour curfew and warned that violators would be shot on sight." Shortly afterward, members of the Organization of Eastern Caribbean States requested help from the United States, Barbados, and Jamaica to deal with the "unprecedented threat to the peace and security of the region created by the vacuum of authority in Grenada." The rescue began four days later. The small Grenadian army and eight hundred Cuban troops (present on Grenada to build an airport) put up token resistance but were suppressed within three days.

Fred Sladen and I arrived by air from St. Vincent on June 4, 1989, at the Point Salines International Airport, the airport started by the Cubans but completed by U.S. forces. It was one more stop on our island-hopping Liat excursion to visit all the Caribbean nature islands, experience the natural environment, and see all the single-island endemic birds.

Grenada has only one single-island endemic bird, the Grenada Dove, but it has several additional species that do not occur elsewhere in the Lesser or Greater Antilles. For instance, the same Hook-billed Kite that occurs from Texas to South America is found on Grenada. The Gray-rumped Swift and Rufous-breasted Hummingbird of Central and South America also occur on Grenada. The little Euler's Flycatcher of South America is known from Grenada. The Blue-black Grassquit of Mexico south through South America is found only on Grenada. In addition, Grenada has two species that it shares only with adjacent St. Vincent, the Grenada Flycatcher and Lesser Antillean Tanager.

Our first goal was to find a dry scrub woodland habitat in which Grenada Doves might occur. This bird is listed by the 1983 AOU check-list as an isolated population of the Gray-fronted Dove, but it once was a separate species, *Leptotila wellsi*, and several ornithologists believe it should be separated again. I wanted very much to see it for myself, but there is very little information on this bird. Guy Mountfort, in *Rare Birds of the World*, considered it a separate species and stated that it is "very rare in Grenada." He adds: "The last report was of five birds seen in the scrublands near Grand Anse in 1971, a region now being developed for housing." Timothy Johnson devoted almost half a page to it in his ICBP monograph, *Biodiversity and Conservation in the Caribbean*. He described the bird's typical habitat as a "relatively dry secondary forest of *Bursera* sp., *Acacia* sp., *Gliricidia* sp., *Pitecelobium* sp., *Tabebuia* sp. and *Tecoma* sp. disturbed by grazing, charcoal burning and vegetable production." Johnson also referred to a 1987 survey report by Blockstein, who estimated the entire Grenada Dove population at 105 individuals, "all located in 500 ha between Grand Anse village and the Lance aux Epines peninsula in the south-west. Most (80 percent) occurred in wooded hills of the Mount Hartman estate and government farm."

It didn't sound very promising, but we decided that our best bet might be the government farm, since that area sounded a little more isolated than the Grand Anse village and Mount Hartman estate. Our first stop was to check into our reserved room at the No Problem Motel (that name sounded appropriate to me and the price was right). It was a good decision. We soon discovered that it was only about ten minutes from the airport and a couple of miles from the government farm.

The government farm was a fairly large agricultural area situated between some low dry hills. The hillsides were covered with a dense thicket of small trees and shrubs, seemingly impossible to penetrate. We decided to walk a wide loop around the edge of the fields to see what we might find. The most obvious bird life consisted of Cattle Egrets, Eared Doves, Common Ground-Doves, and Carib Grackles. I also recorded a few Smooth-billed Anis, Gray Kingbirds, and Black-faced Grassquits.

We also discovered a pair of Blue-black Grassquits feeding on weedy plants along the farm road only a few yards away. Although I had seen this species numerous times in Mexico and Panama, it was my first Caribbean sighting. Males are entirely blue-black with a tiny white spot on the wing and a stout but sharp-pointed bill. Females have brown upperparts and streaked underparts. Father Raymund Devas, in his little book, *Birds of Grenada, St. Vincent and the Grenadines*, reported that this bird was present on Grenada only during the months of July and August. That would suggest that it was a postnesting visitor only, but our sightings of a pair in early June suggest it is a breeder, as well.

Mangrove Cuckoo calls rumbled out of the dense hillside; there were at least three separate birds. A Lesser Antillean Tanager sang its "weet-weet-weet-witwitwitwit" song. Then from somewhere along the slope I detected a mournful, descending "ooooo" call. Fred and I looked at each other, knowing that we had heard a Grenada Dove. It repeated its mournful song again. Farther down the ridge came a second call, then both birds began to call at intervals. James Bond, in *The Birds of the West Indies*, reported that these doves repeat their songs at eight-second intervals. Their timing was right on.

We backed away from the slope so that we might possibly see a bird perched in the open. No such luck. We scanned the vegetation in the direction of the calls but realized very soon that it was going to be necessary to get beneath the canopy. *Leptotila* doves, the genus of which the Grenada Dove is a member, spend most of their time on the ground. We had to somehow maneuver ourselves into a position to see the slope itself. We also realized that the calls we were hearing were extremely ventriloquistic; it was going to be difficult to track down a bird by its song alone.

We discovered a little cut in the dense vegetation and decided to see how far we could go. Suddenly, a pair of **Zenaida Doves** exploded almost at our feet, flying away with their white-trailing wings and tail. Although we weren't able to make any progress going straight up the hill, we located a secondary cut off to the left, leading in the opposite direction from the Grenada Dove calls. Then directly in front of us a **Grenada Flycatcher** appeared. I focused my binoculars on this bird just as it dropped from its perch and made a sweep of the adjacent twigs. I actually saw it grab a bright green anole off a small branch with its heavy bill. It immediately landed on an adjacent perch and proceeded to swallow its catch. It wasn't until then that I began to realize that this *Myiarchus* flycatcher was actually large enough to capture a lizard that I estimated to be at least 4 inches in length. It took only a few seconds to swallow the lizard completely. I not only admired the bird's very large and heavy bill but its rusty tail feathers as well.

We began to realize that at least two additional Grenada Doves were calling along the slope to our right. We recorded at least eight individuals. We had hit the **Grenada Dove** jackpot, but how were we going to see the birds? Fred was several yards ahead of me when he called out, "Here is a trail." Sure enough, the little opening exposed a narrow track that ran horizontally along the slope directly under the dense vegetation, approximately 100 feet above the lower flats. We moved very slowly, inching our way to the right. We were also careful not to disturb wasp nests such as those we had found at the base of the slope. I have never seen such strange, bell-shaped nests before. They were about 10 inches long, tan color, and partially covered with little black-brown wasps. If they are anything like the jack-Spaniards of the Virgin Islands, it was an insect we did not want to disturb within Grenada's thorny thicket.

It took us about half an hour to reach the area where we believed we had heard the first Grenada Dove calls. We got a fairly good look at a Mangrove Cuckoo en route. We recorded another Grenada Flycatcher, but this one, apparently concerned about our intrusion, immediately moved elsewhere. The bird of our quest was silent now, although we could still hear other birds farther on. Not knowing what to do, we decided to sit a spell and watch. The day was hot and the thicket was more humid than I had expected.

We sat perfectly still for at least half an hour, barely talking, just gazing up and down the trail and along the shadowed slope below us. We had found a way to get under the canopy, but so far it wasn't helping us find our bird. We waited another ten minutes, and then I decided to move back along the trail a few yards, thinking that we might have a greater opportunity to scope more area at separate locations. I very slowly got up and inched my way back along the trail. In about 30 feet I sat down and waited, searching the open slope below me.

There it was! Almost as if by magic, a very plump, light-colored dove walked across a little clearing approximately halfway down the slope. "Fred, here it is," I whispered, but my binoculars remained focused on the Grenada Dove. Fred was immediately by my side; how he covered 30 feet from a sitting position with such speed I'll never know. But the dove had frozen when it heard my call. As soon as Fred was still it continued to walk around its little open space. It seemed to be moving almost in circles, searching for seed or insects, I couldn't be sure. Every now and then it pecked at the ground. When it walked through a shaft of sunlight it was highlighted as if it were on a stage, and the bird's subtle beauty was obvious. Blues, greens, and purples were evident within its gray-brown exterior. It was lighter color underneath and on its forehead. Its feet were reddish, and there also was red around its eye. We watched this bird for about twenty minutes as it gradually worked its way down the slope and disappeared from view. Not until then did we shake hands to congratulate one another on one more wonderful wildlife experience.

There is something very special about finding and watching a wild animal in its native environment. To be part of that other world that so few humans understand or appreciate was very important to both of us that day. As we worked our way back out of the thicket, past the wasp nests, and across the fields to our vehicle, we felt deep satisfaction.

I was awakened by the loud song of a Carolina Wren, but I knew that was impossible. There are no Carolina Wrens on Grenada. There it was again, directly outside my window at the No Problem Motel. Then it dawned on me that this was the song of Grenada's House Wren, probably the same House Wren I had seen on St. Vincent. I was immediately at the window and gazing out at the plump Carolina Wren–like House Wren working its way along the porch beam. Then it was gone. A few minutes later I found it again in an adjacent patch of vegetation, where it was foraging along the trunk of an old, partially dead tree.

None of the available literature provided an adequate description of the House Wrens that we found on Grenada and St. Vincent until I saw Guy Tudor's painting in Robert Ridgely and Guy Tudor's 1989 book, *The Birds of South America: The Oscine Passerines.* Bird number two on plate 4 illustrates our bird very well, with the difference that our bird was more rusty brown.

Our plan for the day was to visit the highland forest habitat at Grand Etang, a lake within the forest preserve at about 2,000 feet elevation. But the day was overcast and rainy, so we took our time en route.

The capital city of St. George's is undoubtedly one of the most picturesque places in all the West Indies. It is built around a harbor, like so many other cities, but unlike those other places it has retained its Old World charm. St. George's appears to be free of the typical trash and squalor so common at most of the other port cities. The green mountain backdrop provides a magnificent setting to the blue bay waters and the abundant red-roofed buildings.

The Grand Etang Forest Preserve covers an area of about 3,800 acres. Hurricane Janet caused extensive damage in September 1955, and most of the area was replanted with blue mahoe trees. Oxford forester J. S. Beard studied the island's vegetation during the 1940s, and his 1949 paper, "The Natural Vegetation of the Windward and Leeward Islands," provides good information about the mountain forests. The high, steep slopes are mostly clad with a palm brake (mountain cabbage palm), while the mountain summits are dominated by elfin woodland habitat, with tree ferns and balisier. The lower, more sheltered slopes contained rain forest vegetation, often dominated by the huge gommier tree, chataignier, bois, marouba, and smaller bois gris. Unaltered mountain forest habitats are limited to 720 acres of rain forest and 400 acres of cloud forest in the central mountains of the preserve, according to Allen Putney's final report, *Survey of Conservation*

Priorities in the Lesser Antilles. The highest peak is Mount St. Catherine (2,757 feet), the youngest volcanic structure on the island. Grand Etang is the result of explosion craters created approximately 12,000 years ago and since filled with rainwater. The only evidence of volcanism still present on Grenada are the various hot springs on Mount St. Catherine and a few other sites.

Grand Etang is located at 1,740 feet elevation. A national park planning document describes the surrounding vegetation thus: "the trees are smaller at lower altitudes and are more thickly covered with epiphytes such as ferns and mosses. On exposed ridges and high peaks amidst the drifting clouds the densely growing trees are stunted and twisted into strange shapes, hence the name 'Elfin Woodland.'" That description very adequately portrayed the scene we encountered at Grand Etang, complete with clouds and blowing rain.

In spite of the bad weather, we proceeded to walk the trail that circles the lake. Black-whiskered Vireo songs echoed through the mist. We heard the wheezy "zee-e-e-e-swees-te" songs of Bananaquits, as well. A hummingbird zoomed by, creating excitement, until we realized it was the smaller Antillean Crested Hummingbird instead of the Rufous-breasted Hermit of our quest.

We searched the sky whenever the boiling clouds cleared enough to see any distance. This is where we expected to find the Gray-rumped Swift, but it was not to be. Bond described it as "a small, mostly black swift with ashy grey rump and underparts. The tail is longer than that of the Short-tailed Swift and is black, not grey." We also searched the forest for the very rare peweelike *Empidonax* flycatcher, known as Euler's Flycatcher, recognizable by its conspicuous buff-colored wing-bars. Bond points out that "the Grenada race has the upperparts dark olive, the crown dusky; underparts largely yellowish, with a greyish olive band across chest." Some ornithologists believe that this race may already be extinct.

We did get one brief look at a Rufous-breasted Hermit. A lone bird suddenly appeared out of the greenish mist, hovered in front of me for only a second, and then dashed off into the forest. Its large size, very brown underparts, and long, decurved bill were obvious. No other Caribbean hummingbirds possess all those characteristics. Both Caribs, of approximately the same size, are also present on Grenada, but they possess dark underparts with either a purple or green throat.

Father Devas refers to the Rufous-breasted Hermit as Hairy Hermit or Brown Hummingbird. He describes this bird as follows:

It may be said to be glossy green above and rich brown below, and it is very beautiful, its tail and some other of its feathers being tipped with white. It has a long curved bill, with which it probes flowers, even those on the altar in church! For though this hummer habitually lives in the hills, it will sometimes come down to the lowlands. Unlike our other hummingbirds, which build neat cup-shaped nests, this one makes an untidy affair hanging from a plantain or banana leaf.

Our day in the Grand Etang highlands progressed from bad to worse. By the time we had completed our loop walk around Grand Etang, rain was falling harder, and the trail was becoming very muddy and slick. We visited the little forest preserve visitor center, perched on a little hill covered with an array of flowering shrubs. We stood on the front porch for a while, out of the worst of the weather, and examined the few exhibits inside. But it was obvious that no one expected visitors on such a day.

Later I reviewed the national park planning document to see what is expected for the Grand Etang area but found little reference to on-site developments. The plan is more a guide to the development of the National Parks and Protected Areas System for Grenada and adjacent Carriacou. The executive summary includes this summary statement:

A total of 27 areas for Grenada and sixteen for Carriacou are recommended for inclusion within the National Park System. Of the total, three units are recommended as National Parks, eleven as Protected Seascapes, eleven as Natural Landmarks, twelve as Cultural Landmarks, and four as Multiple-use Areas. This represents approximately 11,008 acres of terrestrial area or about 13% of the total land surface of the country. In addition, several marine areas are proposed for inclusion within the System.

This is a far-sighted program and extremely important for the long-term stability of Grenada. Grenadians should be proud of this effort and give it their utmost support.

AFTERWORD

"*S*mall is beautiful" is a common West Indian saying, and as I gaze out on the island of Saint Lucia, I must agree. However, as everywhere else, the passage of years has brought profound changes to this tiny Eastern Caribbean island. I have had the privilege of working and living on Saint Lucia for almost two decades, and I have witnessed many of those changes. Where lush forests once were, land has been converted to agriculture. Where bird-filled swamps dotted the coastal area, now there are marinas, garbage dumps, and development zones. Twenty years ago traffic jams occurred only in the more developed nations. Today, I too sit in long lines as I hustle my way to work.

Saint Lucia is not alone. Neighboring Caribbean islands have undergone similar changes, some less pronounced, some even more pronounced. We have developed, but at a price. Some would argue the price has been too high with the decline of biodiversity and degradation of once pristine habitats, debts that we hand our children and for which they will hold the decision-makers of our islands responsible.

Today, the West Indies face difficult times. Agriculture, the backbone of many of our islands, is under threat from the possible withdrawal of preferential trade agreements and drying up of foreign aid. Burgeoning populations and a limited resource base have left land a scarce commodity. Periods of fallow have become progressively shorter, and now land is worked continuously, sustaining production only after the application of fertilizers. Increasingly, marginal areas are brought into production, and mountain forests, vital for soil and water conservation, are being cleared for cultivation.

The protection of West Indian forests is more than just an esoteric matter. Trees bind the soil, provide nutrients, and protect vital watersheds that sustain the island's entire population. Conserving the region's wildlife and wild places are too often taken for granted. The Caribbean's picturesque hillsides and coastlines, the iridescent shimmer of a fleeting hummingbird, and the delicate beauty of a native orchid are all at risk in our modern world of development.

Protecting reefs provides feeding grounds and nursery sites for many fish and other species of marine life, vital links in the food chain. The richness of the area's natural attractions and the perception that they remain as yet unspoiled serve as a lure that attracts literally millions of overseas visitors to our shores.

Our politicians and people are continuously told that conservation is not anti-development, and that sustainable growth must be built on the husbanding and wise use of the planet's natural resources. While this is true in the long run, it is often difficult to affirm in the short term. When one is eking out a living, it is only today that matters. These individual issues must be addressed. And the answer must be found within a conservation framework.

The past several decades have been a time when Caribbean men and women have risen to international prominence. Many have become household names in Europe and the USA. Musicians such as Bob Marley, The Mighty Sparrow, and Lord Kitchner carry the Caribbean word around the globe. Sports personalities such as Viv Richards, Brian Laura, and Clive Lloyd have mesmerized millions, while the literary words of Saint Lucia's Derek Walcott have brought him the Nobel Prize.

Rightly, all these individuals have been showered with praise and financial rewards. Their deeds are written about in the press, and they have become cherished heroes in the eyes of fellow West Indians, as well as those living beyond our shores.

Yet there is another group of West Indians whose work, dare I say it, is even more important, and whose contribution affects each of us who live in the Caribbean. These are the region's conservationists. They come from all walks of life; some are Forestry or Fisheries Officers, while others work for National Trusts or private conservation groups. In light of the multitude of problems they face, their task of protecting the region's natural patrimony seems unending, and the rewards they accrue are few—these are the unsung heroes of the Caribbean. Names like Gabriel Charles, David Smith, Patti Bedasse, Gerard Grey, Sarita Francis, Félix Grégoire, Arlington James, Ron Charles, Brian James, Chris Cox, Brian Johnson, Ruth Knights, and Alan Joseph, to name only a few, may mean nothing to the readers of this book, but without these individuals, and the many others that limited space precludes me mentioning, there would be no wildlife remaining in the islands that you have read about.

As Director for Conservation Education for the Philadelphia-based RARE Center for Tropical Conservation, I have had the honor and privilege of working hand in hand with these unsung heroes. Day in and day out these unselfish individuals work to preserve the Caribbean's natural environment. At RARE Center we are dedicated to assisting them. RARE Center believes that for conservation to become integrated into the lives of people living in less developed countries, their natural resources must pay tangible dividends in the form of income generation and employment. At the same time, people must understand the fragility of those resources and the need to preserve them to ensure that rural development is truly sustainable.

RARE Center believes that a holistic approach to conservation is required, since measures that address only a single part of this complex "equation" will have little effect if the remainder are not tackled simultaneously. Working with local people, we strive to change attitudes, promote economic linkages between the environment and local economies, and work toward resolving the problems caused by spiraling population growth.

The results of our joint activities have been spectacular: reserves have been established in the Bahamas (Abaco), the Cayman Islands (Cayman Brac), Grenada, and Dominica. Wildlife legislation was revised in Saint Vincent and Saint Lucia. Endangered populations are rebounding: the Saint Lucia parrot population has doubled over the past decade. Chapters 14, 16, and 17 of this book, on Dominica, Saint Lucia, and Saint Vincent, respectively, describe these parrot conservation programs.

In addition, Dominica's Syndicate Trail to view the endemic Imperial and Red-necked Parrots has been upgraded (permission must be obtained from the Forestry Division), and a recent observation platform has been constructed at Saint Vincent's Vermont Forest. On Anguilla and Grenada, the Zenaida Dove and Grenada Dove, respectively, were declared the islands' "National Birds." Also on Grenada, a Mount Hartment Reserve, which includes the upper slopes of Government Farm, a refuge for the endemic Grenada Dove, was established.

Saint Lucia's Central Rainforest Trail provides yet another example of a holistic conservation program. In 1991, Saint Lucia's Forestry Department requested assistance in rehabilitating the trail. The Canadian government agreed to contribute US$40,000 to the repair of access roads, while RARE Center donated US$25,000 for the trail itself. These funds were used to leverage more than US$40,000 in contributions from the Saint Lucian government.

Trail construction commenced in 1992 and was completed in late 1993. At the peak of construction, more than eighty laborers were employed, all from communities bordering the forest preserve. Those small villages experienced a major boost to their economy. In the first full year of operation the trail generated about US$40,000 for the Forestry Department. That figure equaled the total capital invested in the trail by the Saint Lucian government. Recurrent labor and material costs amounted to US$28,809, while depreciation (over five years) was estimated at US$40,680. This produced an annual profit of US$6,871, or about 17 percent of the total revenue for the Forestry Department. In fact, at the time, forest tours represented the largest share (56 percent) of the Department's total revenue.

During the same period, income derived from bus transportation, commissions, sale of lunches, and park entry fees raised by the trail increased the total revenue in excess of US$225,582. This represents a fairly sizable input into Saint Lucia's economy; more important, virtually all of the money remains in Saint Lucia, as the tour companies are locally owned, the bus drivers are native Saint Lucians, and the food provided on the tour is prepared by small local private enterprise.

The Central Rainforest Trail is also well used by Saint Lucians, for whom it serves as a place for quiet recreation and a site of learning. During the first year about a thousand local people (schoolchildren, youths, church and community groups) also visited the trail.

In projecting future trends, at the rate of two tours per weekday, each sold to capacity, and one on the weekend, visitation would increase to 14,300. This would generate revenues of US$133,395 for the Department and pump US$786,430 into the island's economy.

The key words are sustainable development. We can no longer afford development of our West Indian resources only for personal gains or if that development will destroy any remaining natural habitats on which the island ecosystem depends for its long-term survival. Our fragile resources, whether the rugged beauty of volcanic Saint Lucia or the pristine coral atolls that make up the Bahamas, are fragments of one of our earth's last remaining bits of paradise.

RARE Center's Conservation Education Campaign is a locally driven, one-counterpart, one-year outreach program that uses marketing techniques, colorful flagship species, and national pride to generate grassroots support for conservation. Now active in fourteen countries of the wider Caribbean and the South Pacific, this program has reached out to more than 1.25 million people through fact sheets, posters, billboards, bumper stickers, costumes, songs, school, community, and church visits. Campaigns strive to build pride and awareness for the target species—usually an endangered bird—thereby assisting with its conservation as well as providing a solid foundation for continuing outreach to promote a more comprehensive environmental consciousness.

Ro Wauer's book clearly describes many of the most significant and irreplaceable resources still remaining in these tiny Caribbean islands. He also describes some of the conservation programs underway. His writings will convince many others to visit the islands. This book will undoubtedly encourage ecotourism in the West Indies, and that activity is the most promising answer to the long-term perpetuation of our magnificent natural resources.

Paul Butler
RARE Center for Tropical Conservation
Saint Lucia, West Indies
August 1995

APPENDIX
Common and Scientific Plant Names

acacia. *Acacia* spp.

allamanda. *Allamanda cathartica*

algarrobo. *Bucida buceras*

algarrobo (Puerto Rico).
    Hymenaea courbaril

alemandro. *Andira inermis*

almond, tropical. *Terminalia latifolia*

almond, West Indian.
    Terminalia catappa

anthurium, heartleaf.
    Anthurium cordatum

arrayán. *Myrica cerifera*

arrowroot. *Maranta arundinacea*

ashwood. *Casearia sylvestris*

balate. *Oxytece pallida*

balisier. *Heliconia* spp.

bamboo. *Bambusa vulgaris*

banana. *Musa acuminata*

bay rum. *Amomis grisea*

bitterbush. *Rauvolfia viridis*

black torch. *Erithalis fruticosa*

black torch tree. *Amyris elemifera*

blackwattle. *Piper amalgo*

bois bandé. *Richeria grandis*

bois canon. *Didymorpanax attenuatum*

bois diable. *Lucania ternatensis*

bois doux, yellow. *Phoebe elongata*

bois doux, Isabelle. *Ocotea leucoxyion*

bois gris. *Lucania ternatensis*

bottle brush. *Callistemon citrinus*

bougainvillea. *Bougainvillea spectabilis*

breadfruit. *Artocarpus altilis*

bucero. *Bucida buceras*

bulletwood. *Manilkara bidentata*

butterfly tree. *Bauhinia monandra*

buttonbush. *Cephalanthus* spp.

buttonwood. *Conocarpus erectus*

cacao-motillo. *Sloanea berteriana*

caca-ravet, mountain.
    Rapanea guianensis

cactus, pipe-organ. *Cephalocereus royenii*

cactus, pricklypear. *Optunia* spp.

caimitollo. *Micropholis chrysophylloides*

calabash tree. *Crescentia cujete*

caper. *Cappatis* spp.

carapate or carapite. *Amanoq carbaea*

cattail. *Typha* spp.

cattle tongue. *Heliotropium indicum*

cedar, bitter. *Cedrela odorate*

cedar, white. *Tabebuia pentaphylla*

century plant. *Agave* spp.

chataignier petit coco.
    Sloanea berteriana

chataignier petit feuille.
    Sloanea caribaea

chestnut, white. *Dacryodes excelsa*

coco-plum. *Chrysobalanus icaco*

coffee. *Coffee arabica*

coffee, wild. *Casearia guianensis*

coral plant. *Russelia equisetiformis*

cordia. *Cordia* spp.

cotton. *Gossypium* spp.

custard apple. *Annona reticulata*

elephant-ear, giant. *Colocasia* spp.

eugenia. *Eugenia maleolens*

fern, strap. *Polypodium phyllitidis*

fern, swamp. *Acrostichum danaeifolium*

fern, tree. *Cyathea* spp.

fig. *Ficus* spp.

fire dart, giant. *Malvaviscus arboreus*

fishing rod. *Randia aculeata*

fish poison. *Piscida piscipula*

flamboyant. *Delonix regia*

frangipani. *Plumeria alba*

genip. *Meliococca bijugata*
ginger Thomas. *Tecoma stans*
gommier. *Dacryodes excelsa*
gri or gri-gri. *Bucida buceras*
guassatunga, true. *Casearis inaquilatera*
guava. *Psidium guajava*
guayabota. *Eugenia borinquensis*
gumbo limbo. *Bursera simaruba*
heliconia. *Heliconia* spp.
hibiscus. *Hibiscus* spp.
hogplum or hog plum. *Spondias nombin*
hurillo. *Calycogonium squamulosum*
ice cream bean. *Inga fagifolia*
immortelle, mountain.
    Erthrina poeppigiana
impatiens. *Impatiens* spp.
ixora. *Ixora* spp.
jasmine. *Jasminum* spp.
jacquinia. *Jacquinia* spp.
kaklin. *Clusia venosa*
kapok. *Ceiba pentandra*
lancepod or lance pod.
    Lonchocarpus longistylus
laurel. *Nectandra patens*
laurel, yellow. *Aniba bracteata*
laurier rose. *Podacarpus cinaceus*
mahoe, blue. *Hibiscus* spp.
mahogany, broadleaf.
    Swietenia macrophylla
mahogany, West Indian.
    Swietenia mahogani
mammee apple. *Mammea americana*
mammee, wild. *Clusia rosea*
mampoo. *Pisonia albida*
mampoo, water. *Pisonia subcordata*
manchineel. *Hippomane mancinella*
mangle, mountain. *Clusia venosa*
mango. *Mangifera indica*
mangrove, black. *Avicennia nitida*
mangrove, red. *Rhizophora mangle*
mangrove, white. *Laguncularia racemosa*

mangrove, yellow. *Symphonia globulifera*
manjack. *Cordia sulcata*
manjack, white. *Cordia alba*
marbri. *Richeria grandis*
marouba. *Simarouba amara*
matchwood. *Didymopanax attenuatum*
mauricif. *Byrsonima spicata*
mauricif (Guadeloupe).
    Byrsonima martinicensis
miconia. *Miconia laevigata*
nemoca. *Ocotea spathulata*
nutmeg. *Myristica fragans*
olive, mountain, *Cyrilla racemiflora*
orchid tree. *Bauhinia monandra*
painkiller. *Morinda citrifolia*
palicourea, red. *Palicouria riparia*
palm, coconut. *Cocos nucifera*
palm, date. *Phoenix* spp.
palm, mountain cabbage.
    Euterpe globosa
palm, royal. *Roystonea borinquena*
palm, sierra. *Prestoea montana*
palmiste montagne. *Euterpe globosa*
palmetto, mountain. *Euterpe globosa*
palo colorado. *Cyrilla racemiflora*
papaya. *Carica papaya*
peperomia, *Peperomia* spp.
pepper. *Piper* spp.
philodendron. *Philodendron* spp.
pineapple. *Ananas comosus*
pine, Australian. *Casuarina equisetifolia*
pine, Caribbean. *Pinus caribaea*
pine, West Indian. *Pinus occidentalis*
pitch apple. *Clusia rosea*
pitchpine sweetwood. *Ocotea leucoxylon*
pois doux blanc. *Inga laurina*
résolu. *Chymarrhis cymosa*
rubber tree. *Ficus elastica*
samán. *Pithecolobium saman*
savonette. *Lonchocarpus benthamianus*
sawgrass. *Cladium* spp.

sea grape. *Coccoloba uvifera*
soapberry. *Cupania triquetra*
Soufrière tree. *Spachea perforata*
soursop. *Annona muricata*
Spanish lime. *Melicoccus bijugatus*
Spanish-oak. *Inga laurina*
spindle tree. *Cassine xylocarpa*
sugarcane. *Saccharum officinarum*
sweet lime. *Triphasia trifolia*
tabonuco. *Dacryodes excelsa*
tallow, Chinese. *Sapium sebifera*

tamarind. *Tamarindus indica*
tan-tan. *Leucaena glauca*
tibet. *Albizzia lebbek*
trumpet-tree. *Cecropia peltata*
tulip tree, African.
　　Spathodea campanulata
Turk's cap. *Malvaviscus* spp.
white-cedar. *Tabebuia pentaphylla*
yuca. *Manihot esculenta*
yucca. *Yucca* spp.

REFERENCES

Abbot, R. Tucker. 1974. *American Seashells.* New York: Van Nostrand Reinhold Co.

American Ornithologists' Union (AOU). 1983. *Check-list of North American Birds,* 6th ed. American Ornithologists' Union, Washington, D.C.

———. 1985. Thirty-fifth Supplement to the American Ornithologists' Union *Check-list of North American Birds. Auk* 102: 680–686.

———. 1989. Thirty-seventh Supplement to the American Ornithologists' Union *Check-list of North American Birds. Auk* 106: 532–538.

———. 1991. Thirty-eighth Supplement to the American Ornithologists' Union *Check-list of North American Birds. Auk* 108: 750–754.

———. 1993. Thirty-ninth Supplement to the American Ornithologists' Union *Check-list of North American Birds. Auk* 110: 675–682.

Arendt, Wayne J. 1994. Effects of Hurricane Hugo on Montserrat's Forest Birds and Their Habitats. *El Pitirre* 7 (3): 5.

Arendt, Wayne J., and Angela I. Arendt. N.d. Distribution, Population Size, Status, and Reproductive Biology of the Montserrat Oriole (*Icterus oberi*). Xeroxed report to U.S. Forest Service.

Askins, Robert A., D. N. Ewert, and R. L. Norton. 1989. Effects of Habitat Fragmentation on Wintering Migrants in the U.S. Virgin Islands. Xeroxed report.

Baedeker's Caribbean Including Bermuda. 1988. Norwich: Prentice Hall Press.

Barlow, Jon C. 1978. Another Colony of the Guadeloupe House Wren. *Wilson Bulletin* 90 (4): 635–637.

Beard, J. S. 1944. Climax Vegetation in Tropical America. *Ecology* 25 (2): 127–158.

———. 1949. *The Natural Vegetation of the Windward and Leeward Islands.* Oxford Forestry Memoirs 21.

Bellamy, Frank. 1979. *Caribbean Island Hopping: A Handbook for the Independent Traveller.* London: Gentry Books.

———. 1987. *Cadogan Guides: The Caribbean.* Chester, Conn.: Globe Pequot Press.

Bond, James. 1957. The Resident Wood Warblers of the West Indies. In *The Warblers of North America,* ed. Ludlow Griscom and Alexander Sprunt, Jr. New York: Devin-Adair Co.

———. 1985. *The Birds of the West Indies,* 4th ed. Boston: Houghton Mifflin Co.

Bradley, Patricia. 1985. *Birds of the Cayman Islands.* George Town, Grand Cayman: P. E. Bradley.

Brown, Sandra, A. E. Lugo, S. Silander, and L. Liegel. 1983. *Research History and Opportunities in the Luquillo Experimental Forest.* Institute of Tropical Forestry, GTP, SO-44, USDA.

Burton, Maurice. 1962. *University Dictionary of Mammals of the World.* New York: Thomas Y. Crowell.

Butler, Paul. 1989. Saint Lucia. *Supplement to El Pitirre* 2 (1): 7–11. Society of Caribbean Ornithology.

Clarke, Nicholas, and Tighe Geoghegan. 1986. *North Sound, Virgin Gorda, BVI.* Tortola: National Parks Trust.

Cobb, Charles U., Jr. 1984. Marking Time in Grenada. *National Geographic* (November): 688–710.

Collar, N. J., and P. Andrew. 1988. *Birds to Watch: The ICBP World Checklist of Threatened Birds.* Cambridge: ICBP Technical Publication no. 8.

Colli, Claudia. 1983. *Welcome to Our British Virgin Islands.* Tortola: BVI Tourist Board.

Critchfield, William B., and Elbert L. Little, Jr. 1966. *Geographic Distribution of the Pines of the World*, USDA Miscellaneous Publication 991. Washington, D.C.: GPO.

Cruz, Alexander, James W. Wiley, Tammie K. Nakamura, and William Post. 1989. The Shiny Cowbird *Molothrus bonariensis* in the West Indian Region— Biogeographical and Ecological Implications. In *Biogeography of the West Indies, Past, Present, and Future*, ed. Charles A. Woods, pp. 519–540. Gainesville, Fla.: Sandhill Crane Press.

Curry-Lindahl, Kai. 1972. *Let Them Live.* New York: William Morrow & Co.

Devas, Father Raymund P. 1970. *Birds of Grenada, St. Vincent and the Grenadines.* St. George's, Grenada: Carenage Press.

Ditmars, Raymond L. 1933. *Reptiles of the World.* New York: Macmillan Co.

———. 1962. *Snakes of the World.* New York: Pyramid Books.

Dod, Annabell Stockton. 1987. *Aves de la República Dominicana.* Santo Domingo: Museo Nacional de Historia Natural.

Downer, Audrey. 1989. Anyone for Bird-watching? *Skywritings 66* (December): 53–55.

Downer, Audrey, and Robert Sutton. 1990. *Birds of Jamaica—A Photographic Guide.* Cambridge: Cambridge University Press.

Dyde, Brian. 1986. *Antigua and Barbuda: The Heart of the Caribbean.* London: Macmillan Caribbean.

Eastern Caribbean Natural Area Management Program. 1980. *Saba Preliminary Data Atlas.* St. Croix, Virgin Islands: Eastern Caribbean Natural Area Management Program.

Ehrlich, Paul R., David S. Dobkins, and Darryl Wheye. 1988. *The Birder's Handbook.* New York: Simon and Schuster.

Emmons, Louise H. 1990. *Neotropical Rainforest Mammals: A Field Guide.* Chicago: University of Chicago Press.

Evans, P. G. H. 1988. *The Conservation Status of the Imperial and Red-necked Parrots on the Island of Dominica, West Indies.* Cambridge: ICBP.

Ewel, J. J., and J. T. Whitmore. 1973. *The Ecological Life Zones of Puerto Rico and the U.S. Virgin Islands.* Forest Service Research Paper ITF-18, Inst. Trop. Forest. Río Piedras, Puerto Rico: USDA.

Faanes, Craig. 1990. Field Notes from Jamaica, May 29–June 4, 1990. Xeroxed report.

Fergus, Howard A. 1983. *Montserrat: Emerald Isle of the Caribbean.* London: Macmillan Caribbean.

Fleming, Carrol B. 1989. *Adventuring in the Caribbean.* San Francisco: Sierra Club Books.

Forshaw, Joseph M. 1977. *Parrots of the World.* Neptune, N.J.: T. F. H. Publishers.

Friedmann, Herbert. 1950. *The Birds of North and Middle America, Part XI.* U.S. National Museum, Bulletin 50. Washington, D.C.: Smithsonian Institution.

Frome, Michael. 1981. South Seas in the Caribbean. *Travel & Leisure* (December): 32, 37–39.

Gosse, P. H. 1847. *The Birds of Jamaica.* London.

Government of Grenada. 1988. *Plan and Policy for a System of National Parks and Protected Areas.* Organization of American States.

Griscom, Ludlow, and Alexander Sprunt, Jr., eds. 1957. *The Warblers of America.* New York: Davis-Adair Co.

Gruson, Edward S. 1972. *Words for Birds: A Lexicon on North American Birds with Biographical Notes.* New York: Quadrangle Books.

Hall, E. Raymond. 1981. *The Mammals of North America.* New York: John Wiley and Sons.

Hargreaves, Dorothy and Bob. 1960. *Tropical Blossoms of the Caribbean.* Kailua, Hawaii: Hargeaves Co.

Harrison, Peter. 1985. *Seabirds: An Identification Guide.* Boston: Houghton Mifflin Co.

Hayman, Peter, John Marchant, and Tony Prater. 1986. *Shorebirds: An Identification Guide.* Boston: Houghton Mifflin Co.

Haynes-Sutton, Ann. 1988. Hurricane Gilbert Strikes Jamaica's Unique Birdlife. *World Birdwatch* 10 (3–4): 1, 11.

Henderson, Robert W., and Brian I. Crother. 1989. Biographic Patterns of Predation in West Indian Colubrid Snakes. In *Biogeography of the West Indies, Past, Present, and Future,* ed. Charles E. Woods, pp. 479–518. Gainesville, Fla.: Sandhill Crane Press.

Highfield, Arnold. 1972. *The Beautiful British Virgin Islands.* Road Town, Tortola: Spectra Graphics.

Hillinger, Charles A. 1990. Storm Revives Rare Trees, Plants. *Victoria Advocate,* Sunday, July 8, p. 6.

Hoagland, Donald B., G. Roy Horst, and C. William Kilpatrick. 1989. Biogeography and Population Biology of the Mongoose in the West Indies. In *Biogeography of the West Indies, Past, Present, and Future*, ed. Charles A. Woods, pp. 611–634. Gainesville, Fla.: Sandhill Crane Press.

Honychurch, Penelope N. 1990. *Caribbean Wild Plants and Their Uses*. London: Macmillan Caribbean.

Imsand, Shirley, and Richard Philibosian. 1987. *Exploring St. Croix*. Pasadena, Calif.: Travelers Information Press.

Jadan, Doris. 1985. *A Guide to the Natural History of St. John*. Environmental Studies Program, Inc. St. Thomas Graphics.

Jane, Cecil, ed. 1988. *The Four Voyages of Columbus*. New York: Dover Publications.

John, Lyndon. 1994. Critical Status of the White-breasted Thrasher. *El Pitirre* 5 (3): 13.

Johnson, Timothy H. 1988a. *Biodiversity and Conservation in the Caribbean: Profiles of Selected Islands*. ICBP Monograph 1. Cambridge: ICBP.

———. 1988b. Caribbean Island Paradises Threatened. *World Birdwatch* (July–December): 6–7.

Jones, J. Knox, Jr. 1989. Distribution and Systematics of Bats in the Lesser Antilles. In *Biogeography of the West Indies, Past, Present, and Future*, ed. Charles A. Woods, pp. 645–660. Gainesville, Fla.: Sandhill Crane Press.

Lack, David. 1976. *Island Biology Illustrated by the Land Birds of Jamaica*. Berkeley: University of California Press.

Lanyon, Wesley E. 1967. Revision and Probable Evaluation of the *Myiarchus* Flycatchers of the West Indies. *Bulletin of the American Museum of Natural History* 136 (6): 329–372.

Lawrence, George N. 1880. Description of a New Species of *Icterus* from the West Indies. *Proceedings of the U.S. National Museum* 3: 351.

Lawrence, Miles. 1989. Preliminary Report Hurricane Hugo 10–22 September 1989. Xeroxed report.

Lee, Alfonso Silva. 1984. *Chipojos, bayoyas y camaleones*. Ciudad de la Havana, Cuba: Editorial Científico-Técnica.

Leland, Elizabeth. 1988. French Guadeloupe Is a Caribbean Island of Contrasts. *Salt Lake Tribune*, Sunday, November 13, p. T5.

Low, Rosemary. 1987. Endangered Amazon Parrots. *Bird Talk* (March): 70–74.

MacArthur, Robert H. 1972. *Geographical Ecology*. New York: Harper and Row.

MacLean, William P. 1982. *Reptiles and Amphibians of the Virgin Islands*. London: Macmillan Caribbean.

Mattheissen, Peter. 1967. *The Shorebirds of North America*. New York: Viking Press.

Menninger, Edwin A. 1962. *Flowering Trees of the World for Tropical and Warm Climates*. New York: Hearthside Press.

Morris, Percy P. 1982. *A Field Guide to Shells of the Atlantic.* Boston: Houghton Mifflin Co.

Mountfort, Guy. 1988. *Rare Birds of the World: A Collins/ICBP Handbook.* Lexington, Ky.: Stephen Greene Press.

National Geographic Society. 1987. *Field Guide to the Birds of North America.* Washington, D.C.

Natural Park of Guadeloupe. N.d. Guadeloupe Natural Parks. Photocopy.

Palmer, Ralph S. 1962. *Handbook of North American Birds, Volume 1: Loons through Flamingos.* New Haven: Yale University Press.

Perry, Frances, and Roy Hart. 1982. *A Field Guide to Tropical and Subtropical Plants.* New York: Van Nostrand Reinhold.

Peterson, Roger Tory, and Edward L. Chalif. 1973. *A Field Guide to Mexican Birds.* Boston: Houghton Mifflin Co.

Peterson, Wayne R. 1983. Northern Waterthrush. In *The Audubon Society Master Guide to Birding,* ed. John Farrand, Jr. New York: Alfred A. Knopf.

Pfanstiehl, Natalie and Paul. 1985. *Saba: The First Guidebook.* Newport, R.I.: Van Steel Press.

Philibosian, Richard, and John A. Yntema. 1981. Endangered and Extinct Vertebrate Fauna of the Virgin Islands. Xeroxed report.

Putney, Allen D. 1980. *Survey of Conservation Priorities in the Lesser Antilles: Preliminary Data Atlas: Guadeloupe.* St. Croix, Virgin Islands: Eastern Caribbean Natural Area Management Program.

———. 1982. *Survey of Conservation Priorities in the Lesser Antilles, Final Report.* St. Croix, Virgin Islands: Eastern Caribbean Natural Area Management Program.

Raffaele, Herbert A. 1989a. *A Guide to the Birds of Puerto Rico and the Virgin Islands.* Princeton, N.J.: Princeton University Press.

———. 1989b. The Ecology of Native and Introduced Granivorous Birds in Puerto Rico. In *Biogeography of the West Indies, Past, Present, and Future,* ed. Charles A. Woods, pp. 541–566. Gainesville, Fla.: Sandhill Crane Press.

Recher, Harry F. and Judy T. 1966. A Contribution to the Knowledge of the Avifauna of the Sierra de Luquillo, Puerto Rico. *Caribbean Journal of Science* 6 (304): 151–186.

Reynard, George B. 1962. The Rediscovery of the Puerto Rican Whip-poor-will. *Living Bird* 1: 51–60.

Ridgely, Robert S., and Guy Tudor. 1989. *The Birds of South America, Volume 1: The Oscine Passerines.* Austin: University of Texas Press.

Robbins, C. S., and W. T. Van Velzen. 1966. *The Breeding Bird Survey, 1966.* Bureau of Sport Fishing and Wildlife, Special Science Report—Wildlife 102.

Robertson, William B. 1962. Observations on the Birds of St. John, Virgin Islands. *Auk* 79: 44–76.

Robins, C. Richard, and G. Carleton Ray. 1986. *A Field Guide to Atlantic Coast Fishes of North America*. Boston: Houghton Mifflin Co.

Rouse, Irving. 1989. Peopling and Repeopling of the West Indies. In *Biogeography of the West Indies, Past, Present, and Future*, ed. Charles A. Woods, pp. 119–136. Gainesville, Fla.: Sandhill Crane Press.

Saint Lucia Tourist Map. 1982. Castries: St. Lucia Tourist Office.

Schubert, Thomas H. 1979. *Trees for Urban Use in Puerto Rico and the Virgin Islands*. Río Piedras, Puerto Rico: Southern Forest Experiment Station, Institute of Tropical Forestry, USDA.

Schwartz, Albert, and Robert W. Henderson. 1975. *Amphibians and Reptiles of the West Indies: Descriptions, Distributions, and Natural History*. Gainesville, Fla.: University of Florida.

Seaman, George A. 1989. *Ay Ay: An Island Almanac*. London: Macmillan Caribbean.

———. 1993. *Every Shadow Is a Man: A Journey Back into Birds and Time*. St. Croix: Antilles Graphic Arts.

Serle, W., G. J. Morel, and W. Hartwig. 1977. *A Field Guide to the Birds of West Africa*. London: William Collins Sons and Co.

Short, Lester L. 1982. *Woodpeckers of the World*. Greenville: Delaware Museum of Natural History.

Siegel, Allan. 1983. *Birds of Montserrat*. Montserrat National Trust.

Stokes, F. Joseph. 1980. *Handbook to the Coral Reef Fishes of the Caribbean*. New York: Lippincott and Crowell, Publishers.

Strong, Kathy. 1985. *The Caribbean Bed and Breakfast Book*. Charlotte, N.C.: East Woods Press.

Szulc, Tad. 1987. *Fidel: A Critical Portrait*. New York: Avon Books.

Temple, Stanley C. 1985. Why Endemic Island Birds Are So Vulnerable to Extinction. In *Bird Conservation 2*, ed. Stanley C. Temple. ICBP. Madison: University of Wisconsin Press.

Terres, John K. 1987. *The Audubon Society Encyclopedia of North American Birds*. New York: Alfred A. Knopf.

Thorsell, J. W., and George Wood. 1976. Dominica's Morne Trois Pitons National Park. *Nature Canada* (October/November): 1–5.

Udvardy, Miklos D. F. 1969. *Dynamic Zoogeography*. New York: Van Nostrand Reinhold Co.

Van Halewyn, Rudd, and Robert L. Norton. 1984. The Status and Conservation of Seabirds in the Caribbean. In *Status and Conservation of the World's Seabirds*, ed. J. P. Croxall, P. G. H. Evans, and R. W. Schreiber. ICBP Publication no. 2. Cambridge: ICBP.

Voous, K. H. 1983. *Birds of the Netherlands Antilles*. Curaçao: De Walburg Press.

Voss, Gilbert L. 1976. *Seashore Life of Florida and the Caribbean.* Miami: Banyon Books.

Wadsworth, F. H. 1951. Forest Management in the Luquillo Mts. I. The Setting. *Caribbean Forestry* 12: 93–114.

Wallace, George E. 1991. Bird Surveys in Cuban Forests: A New Phase in Cuban/Canadian Cooperative Research. *Long Point Bird Observatory Newsletter* 23 (1): 24–25.

Wauer, Roland H. 1987a. Report on the April 27 to May 2, 1987, Bird Bonanzas Trip to Puerto Rico. Xeroxed report.

———. 1987b. Notes on a Birding Trip to Dominican Republic. Xeroxed report.

———. 1988a. Report on a Second Birding Trip to Dominican Republic. Xeroxed report.

———. 1988b. *Virgin Islands Birdlife.* Cooperative Extension Service. St. Croix: University of the Virgin Islands.

———. 1989a. Virgin Islands Wildlife Resources. Xeroxed report to National Park Service.

———. 1989b. Report on a 1989 Virgin Islands Audubon Society Trip to Puerto Rico. Xeroxed report.

———. 1989c. Notes on Birding, St. Lucia, St. Vincent and Grenada. Xeroxed report.

———. 1989d. Notes on a Birding Trip to Jamaica, June 6–12, 1989. Xeroxed report.

———. 1990. The Greater and Lesser Antilles. *Birding* (February): 42–45; (August): 186–189.

———. 1991. Report on a Trip to Cuba—March 23–30, 1991. Xeroxed report.

Wauer, Roland H., and Joseph M. Wunderle, Jr. 1992. The Effect of Hurricane Hugo on Bird Populations on St. Croix, U.S. Virgin Islands. *Wilson Bulletin* 104 (4): 656–673.

Wetmore, Alexander. 1927. *Scientific Survey of Puerto Rico and the Virgin Islands. Volume IX, Part 4. The Birds of Puerto Rico and the Virgin Islands, Psittaciformes to Passeriformes.* New York: New York Academy of Sciences.

———. 1965. *Water, Prey, and Game Birds of North America.* Washington, D.C.: National Geographic Society.

Wetmore, Alexander, and Bradshaw H. Swales. 1931. *The Birds of Haiti and the Dominican Republic.* U.S. National Museum Bulletin 155. Washington, D.C.: Smithsonian Institution.

Wilcox, Bill. 1985. *A Hiker's Guide to the Blue Mountains.* Jamaican Camping and Hiking Association and Ministry of Tourism. Kingston, Jamaica: Department of Forestry.

Wiley, James W. 1985. Bird Conservation in the United States Caribbean. In *Bird Conservation 2*, ed. Stanley A. Temple. ICBP. Madison: University of Wisconsin Press.

Wiley, James W., and Gerald P. Bauer. 1985. Caribbean National Forest, Puerto Rico. *American Birds* (spring): 12–18.

Wille, Chris. 1991. Paul Butler: Parrot Man of the Caribbean. *American Birds* (spring): 26–35.

Williams, Ernest E. 1989. Old Problems and New Opportunities in West Indian Biogeography. In *Biogeography of the West Indies, Past, Present, and Future*, ed. Charles A. Woods, pp. 1–46. Gainesville, Fla.: Sandhill Crane Press.

Woodbury, Roy O., and Peter L. Weaver. N.d. The Vegetation of St. John and Hassel Island, U.S. Virgin Islands. Xeroxed report.

Woods, Charles A. 1989a. Introduction to West Indian Biogeography. In *Biogeography of the West Indies Past, Present, and Future*, ed. Charles A. Woods, pp. ix–xviii. Gainesville, Fla.: Sandhill Crane Press.

———. 1989b. The Biogeography of West Indian Rodents. In *Biogeography of the West Indies, Past, Present, and Future*, ed. Charles A. Woods, pp. 741–798. Gainesville, Fla.: Sandhill Crane Press.

INDEX

Boldface page numbers indicate illustrations.

Area Management Program), 108
Ecotourism, x, xii, 30, 76–77, 100,
129, 149, 170, 201, 209, 215
Egret: Cattle, 97, 99, 103, 118, 124,
204; Great, 43, 45, 99, 102, 103,
135; Reddish, 45; Snowy, 43, 57,
102, 119
Ehrlich, Paul, et al. (*The Birder's
Handbook*), 119
Elaenia: Caribbean, 8, 92, 95, 99, 102,
103, 104, 108, 118, 121, 132, 169,
177, 178, 180, 187, 192, 195; Greater
Antillean, 8, 26; Jamaican, 8, 26;
Yellow-bellied, 195
Emerald: Antillean, 174; Cuban, 7, 42;
Hispaniolan, 7, 60, 63; Puerto Rican,
7, 70, 75
Esbrada, Alberto, 40
Euphonia: Antillean, 10, 26, 60, 63, 73,
75, 132–133, 148–149, 167, 187,
195; Blue-hooded, 60, 167;
Jamaican, 10, 26
Evans, P. G. H., 161, 164
Ewel, J. J., and J. T. Whitmore (*The
Ecological Life Zones of Puerto Rico and
the U.S. Virgin Islands*), 67

Faanes, Craig, xiii, 21
Fergus, Howard (*Montserrat: Emerald
Isle of the Caribbean*), 143, 144
Fish, 40, 121
Flamingo, Greater, 45, 57
Flatbill, Eye-ringed, 61
Fleming, Carrol (*Adventuring in the
Caribbean*): Dominica, 168; Saba,
112–113; St. Lucia, 200
Flicker: Fernandino's, 8, 37; Northern,
37
Flycatcher: Ash-throated, 56, 74;
Brown-crested, 56, 74; Euler's, 203,
208; Grenada, 8, 195, 205, 206; La

Sagra's, 8, 54, 154; Lesser Antillean,
8, 54, 153, 154, 177, 188; Puerto
Rican, 8, 54, 73, 74, 92–93, 95, 154;
Rufous-tailed, 8, 25, 26; Sad, 8, 25–
26; Stolid, 8, 26, 53–54, 56, 92, 154
Forshaw, Joseph M. (*Parrots of the
World*), 198
Francis, Sarita, 212
Friedmann, Herbert (*The Birds of North
and Middle America*): Broad-winged
Hawk, 133; Common Black-Hawk,
44, 196; Red-tailed Hawk, 82
Frigatebird, Magnificent, 45, 74, 84,
85, 114, 122, 136, 169
Fus, 94

Gallinule, Purple, 43, 47
Gannet, Northern, 85
García, Nelson, 35, 42
García, Rogelio, 35, 37
Geoghegan, Tighe, xiii
Glass-eye, 23
Gnatcatcher, Cuban, 9
Godbird, 199
Goose, P. H. (*Birds of Jamaica*), 28, 29
Grackle: Carib, 169, 180, 204; Greater
Antillean, 11, 59, 73
Grassquit: Black-faced, 10, 43, 92, 99,
104, 113, 114, 118, 127–128,
136–137, 147, 148, 153, 156, 157,
169, 173, 185, 192, 204; Blue-black,
203; Cuban, 10, 43; Yellow-
shouldered, 10, 12, 26
Grebe, Pied-billed, 43
Grégoire, Félix, 170, 212
Grey, Gerard, 212
Griscom, Ludlow, and Alexander
Sprunt, Jr. (*The Warblers of North
America*): Plumbeous Warbler, 153;
Yellow Warbler, 118
Gros-bec, 178

Ground-Dove, Common, 29, 56, 60, 99, 103, 118, 128, 137, 169, 204
Grupo Jaragua of Dominican Republic, xi
Gruson, Edward (*Words for Birds*), 196
Gull, Laughing, 41, 45, 84, 104, 122, 124, 128

Hall, E. Raymond (*The Mammals of North America*): agouti, 46; prehensile-tailed hutia, 163
Harrier, Northern, 45, 93
Harrison, Peter (*Seabirds: An Identification Guide*), 85
Hassell, Carmen, 106, 107, 114
Hawk: Antillean Crab, 196; Broad-winged, 70, 132, 133, 164, 169, 186, 196; crab, 196; Cuban Crab, 44; Gundlach's, 6, 45, 46; Red-tailed, 26, 81, 82, 92, 99, 111–112, 125, 132, 133; Ridgway's, 6, 57; Sharp-shinned, 46, 70
Haynes-Sutton, Ann, 30
Hermit: Hairy, 208; Rufous-breasted, 208
Heron: Great Blue, 45, 57, 95, 102, 128, 135; Green, 43, 95, 97, 119, 169; Little Blue, 43, 95, 97, 103, 119, 128, 192; Tricolored, 41, 45, 57, 102, 135
Highfield, Arnold (*The Beautiful British Virgin Islands*), 79
Hillis, Beth, xiii
Holder, Houston, xiii, 53, 57, 59, 61
Honychurch, Penelope (*Caribbean Wild Plants and Their Uses*): guava, 81; hogplum, 90; piper, 94; savonette, 168; sea grape, 121
Hopping Dick, 23
Hummingbird, Antillean Crested, 7, 12, 84, 92, 95, 99, **100**, 118, 138,

147, 169, 170, 187, 208; Bee, 7, 12, 42, 60; Black-chinned, 56; Blue-headed, 7, 12, 174; Brown, 208; Costa's, 56; Rufous-breasted, 203; Vervain, 7, 12, 60
Hurricane, 12; David (1979), 164, 170; Gilbert (1988), 27, 29; Hugo (1989), 65, 66, 82, 96, 97, 98, 99, 100, 101, 149; Janet (1955), 207

Ibis: Glossy, 45, White, 45
ICBP (International Council for Bird Protection), 11, 22, 204
Institute of Tropical Forestry, 66, 68, 89
Isherwood, Jay, xiii
Isherwood, Sandy, xiii, 169

Jabbering crow, 28
Jacana, Northern, 43
Jacquot, 164, 166
Jadan, Doris (*A Guide to the Natural History of St. John*): Pearly-eyed Thrasher, 95; tan-tan, 90–91; wild mammee, 94
Jamaican Conservation and Development Trust, xi
James, Arlington, 212
James, Brian, 212
Jay, Blue, 83
Jilguero, 62
John, Lyndon, 191
John Phillips, 83
Johnson, Brian, 212
Johnson, Timothy (*Biodiversity and Conservation in the Caribbean: Profiles of Selected Islands*): bromeliad crab, 22; Dominica, 161; Grenada Dove, 204; Montserrat, 146; St. Lucia House Wren, 184–185
Jones, J. Knox, 178

Joseph, Alan, 212
Julian chi-vi, 73

Kepler, Cameron and Kay, 69, 72, 73
Kestrel, American, 26, 56, 81, 92, 97,
99, 114, 118, 128, 132, 147, 148, 192
Killdeer, 43, 45, 57, 124, 135
Killy-hawk, 81, 147
Killy-killy, 81
Kingbird: Cassin's, 56; Giant, 8; Gray,
8, 26, 36, 54, 56, 92, 95, 97, 99, 103,
104, 107, 113, 118, 127, 132, 169,
180, 187, 204; Loggerhead, 8, 26,
59, 73, 75
Kirkconnell, Arturo, xiii, 34, 41, 43,
44, 45, 46
Kite: Hook-billed, 203; Snail, 45
Knausenberger, Walter, xiii
Knights, Ruth, 212

Lack, David (*Island Biology Illustrated
by the Land Birds of Jamaica*), 20, 27;
Cuban Bullfinch, 40; Jamaican
Crow, 28; Jamaican Lizard-Cuckoo,
27; Puerto Rican Lizard-Cuckoo,
70; Rufous-sided Solitaire, 23, 173,
185
Lanyon, Wesley, 92–93, 154
Lawrence, George N., 141
Limpkin, 46
Lizard-Cuckoo: Great, 11, 42;
Hispaniolan, 6, 11, 60; Jamaican,
6, 11, 27, 28; Puerto Rican, 6, 11,
70–72, **71**
Long Point Bird Observatory, 34, 46
Low, Rosemary, 186
Lugo, Ariel, 66, 72

McCrea, Doug, xiii, 34, 39, 40, 41, 43,
46
Mallard, 10

Mammals: agouti, 163; dog, 124; house
cat, 124; hutia, 46; mongoose, 73,
89, 162, 179; rat, 73, 89, 124, 162,
179; Schwartz's myotis bat, 178
Mango: Antillean, 7, 54, 56, 73; Green,
7, 70; Jamaican, 7, 25
Mannikin, Bronze, 176
Man-'o-war bird, 85, 136
Martin: Caribbean, 8, 70, 81, 92, 118,
153, 169, 192; Cuban, 8, 44; Purple,
44, 81
Martínez, Chino, xiii, 32, 33
Meadowlark, Eastern, 45
Merlin, 45, 93
Mistletoe bird, 133
Mockingbird: Bahama, 9; Northern,
23, 53, 56, 92, 99, 104, 132, 158–
159; Tropical, 158–159, 169, 180
Montserrat National Trust, 141, 147,
148
Moorhead, Bruce, xiii
Moorhen, Common, 43, 128, 135, 147,
192
Morris, Percy (*A Field Guide to Shells of
the Atlantic*), 120
Mountford, Guy (*Rare Birds of the
World*): Grenada Dove, 204;
Gundlach's Hawk, 46; Martinique
Oriole, 175; West Indian Whistling-
Duck, 43; White-breasted Thrasher,
179; Zapata Wren, 33–34

National Geographic Society (*Field
Guide to Birds of North America*):
Black-whiskered Vireo, 113
National Hurricane Center, 96
National Park Service, 94, 100, 101
National Park Trust (BVIs), 79, 84
Nature Conservancy, The, ix, xi
Nighthawk: Antillean, 7, 74, 104;
Common, 74

Night-Heron: Black-crowned, 102;
Yellow-crowned, 119, 193
Nightjar: Greater Antillean, 7; Puerto
Rican, xiv, 7, 72–73; St. Lucia, 7,
183, 192, 193
Noddy, Brown: 85, 129, 159, 176
Northrup, Bradford C., xii, xiii
Norton, Rob, xiii, 173, 175, 177, 178,
179, 188

Ober, Fred A., 141
Old man bird, 26
Old woman bird, 27
Orangequit, 10, 12, 25, 26
Oriole: Black-cowled, 57, 75, 139, 175,
185; Jamaican, 11, 22; Martinique,
11, 173, 175, 176; Montserrat,
11, **139**–142, 145, 148, 149, 175;
St. Lucia, 11, 183, 185, 187; Scott's,
74
Osprey, 45, 102
Ovenbird, 93, 102, 146, 183
Owl: Ashy-faced, 7; Bare-legged, 7,
42–43; Burrowing, 42, 59;
Flammulated, 42; Jamaican, 7, 11,
18; Long-eared, 41; Spotted, 42;
Stygian, 41, 49
Oystercatcher, American, 95, 120

Pájaro bobo mayor, 70
Palmchat, 9, 11, 58–59, 61
Palmer, Ralph (*Handbook of North
American Birds*), 57
Palm-tanager: Black-crowned, 10, 12,
54, 59, 61; Gray-crowned, 10, 12
Parakeet: Cuban, 6, 43–44; Hispani-
olan, 6, 60; Olive-throated, 28, 29
Parrot: Black-billed, 6, 28, 29; Cuban,
6, 41; Hispaniolan, 6, 60; Imperial,
6, 162, 163–**165**, 166, 213; Puerto
Rican, 6, 66, 67; Red-necked, 6, 162,

164, 166, 213; St. Lucia, 6, 183, 186–
187, 213; St. Vincent, 6, 195, 197,
198, 201; Yellow-billed, 6, 28–29
Parula, Northern, 92, 102, 146, 147
Pee-whistler, 108, 121
Pelican, Brown, 41, 84, 99, 102, 103,
122, 128, 129, 136, 159
Peregrine Falcon, 102, 103
Peterson, Wayne, 92
Pewee, Greater Antillean, 8, 26, 32, 60,
61; Lesser Antillean, 8, 73, 184, 192
Pfanstiehl, Natalie and Paul (*Saba: The
First Guidebook*), 106
Phalarope, Wilson's, 103
Piculet, Antillean, 8
Pigeon: Plain, 6, 28, 29, 60; red-
necked, 138; Ring-tailed, 6, 26, 29;
Scaly-naped, 6, 60, 70, 83, 92, 95,
98, 99, 103, 104, 107, 125, 138, 147,
148, 153, 162, 163, 185, 196; White-
crowned, 6, 29, 33, 92, 98, 99, 102,
103, 125, **137**–138
Pintail: Northern, 119, 120, 135–136;
White-cheeked, 102, 103, 119–120,
135–136
Plover: Black-bellied, 45, 103, 124;
Piping, 102; Semipalmated, 124–
125; Snowy, 102; Wilson's, 45
Poorwill, Least, 7
Prince bird, 195
Puerto Rico Department of Natural
Resources, 89
Putney, Allan, xiii; (*Survey of
Conservation Priorities in the Lesser
Antilles*), Antigua, 132; Dominica,
161; Grenada, 207–208;
Guadeloupe, 154; St. Vincent, 197
Pygmy-Owl: Cuban, 7, 36, 41;
Ferruginous, 36

Quail-Dove: Blue-headed, 6, 11, 39;

van Halewyn, Rudd, and Rob Norton: Guadeloupe, 159; St. Martin, 128–129; Virgin Islands, 84–85

Vilella, Francisco "Tito," xiv, 73

Vireo: Black-whiskered, 9, 22, 32, 61, 83, 92, 95, 99, 102, 103, 104, 113, 118, 157, 158, 163, 169, 187, 195, 208; Blue Mountain, 9, 22, 26; Cuban, 9, 32; Flat-billed, 9, 61; Gray, 22; Jamaican, 9, 22; Puerto Rican, 9, 73; Red-eyed, 113, 157; Solitary, 22; Thick-billed, 9; White-eyed, 22, 61, 73; Yellow-throated, 93, 102

Voous, K. H. (*Birds of the Netherland Antilles*): Purple-throated Carib, 109; Saba, 112; St. Martin, 125, 127

Vulture, Turkey, 26, 33

Wadsworth, Frank, 67

Walcott, Derek, 212

Walsh, Mike, xiv, 169

Warbler: Adelaide's, 9, 73, 74, 187, 189, 192; Arrow-headed, 10, 23–24, 26; Black-and-white, 22, 62, 63, 69, 92, 93, 102, 146, 197; Blackpoll, 93, 102, 103; Black-throated Blue, 62, 63, 69, 93, 146; Black-throated Green, 93, 146; Blue-winged, 93, 102; Cape May, 62, 93, 102; Elfin Woods, 10, 23, 68–69, 75, 197; Fan-tailed, 74; Golden-winged, 26; Grace's, 74; Green-tailed Ground, 10, 12, 62, 63; Hooded, 74, 92, 93, 102, 146, 183; Kentucky, 146; Lucy's, 74; Magnolia, 93, 102, 146; Olive-capped, 9, 49; Oriente, 10, 12, 183; Pine, 49, 61; Plumbeous, 10, 153, 154, 156, 157, 166–167, 169, 170; Prairie, 62, 93, 102, 146; Prothonotary, 146; Semper's, 10, 12,

183, 188, 189, 190, 193; Vitelline, 10; Whistling, 10, 12, 183, **194**, 195, 196, 197, 199; White-winged, 10, 12, 62, 63; Wilson's, 62; Worm-eating, 92, 93, 102; Yellow, 45, 74, 92, 93, 95, 99, 102, 103, 104, 118, 127, 132, 146, 147, 169, 177, 192; Yellow-headed, 10, 12; Yellow-rumped, 102, 146; Yellow-throated, 146

Waterthrush: Louisiana, 32, 146; Northern, 91–92, 93, 103, 146, 147

Wauer, Betty, xiv, 59, 106, 117, 120, 126, 131, 133, 140, 142, 152, 173, 174, 179, 180, 181

Weaver, Village, 177

Wedrego, 112

Wetmore, Alexander, and Bradshaw Swales (*The Birds of Haiti and the Dominican Republic*): Antillean Euphonia, 60; Black-crowned Palm-Tanager, 54; Bridled Quail-Dove, 88; Green-tailed Ground Warbler, 62; Palmchat, 58, 59

Wheeler, Bert, 148

Whelk-crackers, 120

Whimbrel, 45, 180

Whistling-Duck, West Indian, 6, 43, 102

Wilcox, Bill (*A Hiker's Guide to the Blue Mountains*), 19

Wild pine sergeant, 21

Wiley, James, 66, 92

Wille, Chris, 164, 198

Willet, 57, 102, 119

Williams, Dave, 170

Wilson, Edward O., xii

Wilson, Liz, xiv

Woodbury, Roy, and Peter Weaver, 89, 90

Woodpecker: Acorn, 152; Cuban